TODAY'S
CHOICES
FOR
TOMORROW'S
MISSION

TODAY'S
CHOICES
FOR
TOMORROW'S
MISSION

TODAY'S CHOICES FOR TOMORROW'S MISSION

An Evangelical Perspective
on Trends and Issues in Missions

David J. Hesselgrave

Academie
Books Grand Rapids,
Michigan
Zondervan Publishing House

TODAY'S CHOICES FOR TOMORROW'S MISSION

Copyright © 1988 by David J. Hesselgrave

ACADEMIE BOOKS
is an imprint of
Zondervan Publishing House
1415 Lake Drive, S.E.
Grand Rapids, Michigan 49506

Library of Congress Cataloging in Publication Data
Hesselgrave, David J.
    Today's choices for tomorrow's mission: an evangelical
perspective on trends and issues / David J. Hesselgrave.
        p.
    Bibliography: p.
    Includes index.
    ISBN 0-310-36821-9
    1. Missions—Theory.   2. Evangelicalism.   I. Title.
BV2063.H44 1988
266'.009'048—dc 19   87-30274
                                                                              CIP

Bar graphs are courtesy of D. Bruce Graham, Associate Director, U.S. Center for World Mission.

Edited by Gerard Terpstra

Designed by Louise Bauer

Printed in the United States of America

88 89 90 91 92 93 94 95 / CH / 10 9 8 7 6 5 4 3 2 1

To

Mr. and Mrs. Merton Sheldon

representatives of
the kind of lay Christians
who gladden the hearts
and stimulate the minds
of missionaries and missiologists alike

CONTENTS

ABBREVIATIONS

ACMC	Association of Church Mission Committees
ACMI	Association of Christian Ministries to Internationals
AEPM	Association of Evangelical Professors of Missions
APM	Association of Professors of Missions
ASM	American Society of Missiology
BGEA	Billy Graham Evangelistic Association
CPC	Contingency Preparation Consultants
CWME	Commission on World Mission and Evangelism
DAWN	Discipling a Whole Nation
DFM	Division of Foreign Missions
DOM	Division of Overseas Missions of the National Council of Churches
DWME	Division of World Mission and Evangelism
ECFA	Evangelical Council for Financial Accountability
EFMA	Evangelical Foreign Missions Association
EMIS	Evangelical Missions Information Service
EMQ	*Evangelical Missions Quarterly*
FMC	Foreign Mission Conference
FOM	Fellowship of Missions
IFMA	Interdenominational Foreign Mission Association
IMC	International Missionary Council
IRM	*International Review of Missions*
LCWE	Lausanne Committee for World Evangelization
MARC	Missions Advanced Research (and Communications) Center
NAE	National Association of Evangelicals
NCCUSA	National Council of Churches of Christ in the United States of America
TAM	The Associated Missions of the International Council of Christian Churches
TEAM	The Evangelical Alliance Mission

TEE	Theological Education by Extension
TEF	Theological Education Fund
WCC	World Council of Churches
WEF	World Evangelical Fellowship
YWAM	Youth With a Mission

FOREWORD

This book could not have appeared at a more opportune time. Politically, economically, socially, and spiritually, the world is in a state of unprecedented change. The balance of world power in the nineteenth century was located in Europe. In this century it has moved to the United States. In the twenty-first century it is likely to move to the western rim of the Pacific Ocean. If China ever realizes her potential and links up with Japan, Korea, and Taiwan, that coalition may well mark the demise of Western supremacy.

Political, economic, social, and spiritual changes in the world will have a profound effect on the church and therefore also on world missions. The next twenty-five years are going to see unprecedented change in the world mission of the Christian church. That is the subject of this book.

Overseas, we are facing difficulties, dangers, and problems never before encountered. There are some who tell us that we are coming to the end of the missionary era as we have known it. Maybe yes, maybe no. In this book Hesselgrave comes to grips with ten major problem areas in world missions—all of them extremely important.

At the outset, Hesselgrave informs us that he is more interested in trends than issues for the latter grow out of, and are determined by, the former. He is also at pains to warn us that in dealing with trends we had better take seriously what the Scriptures have to say; otherwise we will be no wiser than the children of the world who must depend solely on their own understanding and experience.

The author is no armchair strategist. He is eminently qualified to deal with the future of world missions. He spearheaded the work on the Evangelical Free Church in Japan (a notoriously unresponsive people) during the American occupation; so he has been a practitioner as well as a professor of missions. His three excellent books dealing with various aspects of crosscultural missions established his reputation as a first-rate scholar with something positive and pertinent to say. He has edited other books coming out of the Trinity seminars on mission and theology.

Many of the issues in this book are controversial and have good and wise scholars supporting varying positions. Hesselgrave is always the Christian gentleman, treating his detractors and opponents with sensitivity and finesse. He is an avowed Evangelical and so points out what he perceives to be the weaknesses of the Conciliar and Charismatic movements. At the same time, he is not afraid to scold his fellow Evangelicals. They, too, are in danger of superficial thinking, erroneous assumptions, and false conclusions. They, too, may inadvertently take their agenda from the world.

I like Hesselgrave's style. He is progressive without being avant-garde, comprehensive without being diffuse, scholarly without being pedantic, and irenic without being wishy-washy. Above all, he has a delightful sense of humor that adds spice and sparkle to his literary style.

Altogether, Hesselgrave has produced a remarkable book—wide-ranging, hard-hitting, and straight-shooting—a book that will be read and reread many times, each time with pleasure and profit. If this book does not become a best seller, it will certainly be at the top of the list as far as missiologists, mission executives, and students of missions are concerned. In a word, the book is a superb piece of research and writing. For what it is worth, I give it my enthusiastic unqualified endorsement.

J. Herbert Kane
Oxford, Ohio

PREFACE

The Christian mission is the grandest enterprise on earth. That is because it was conceived in heaven. Missionary annals are replete with evidences of this. We ask even unbelievers to look at the record objectively. They will find that, although not all instances of missionizing are as outstanding as that of John Williams' work on Samoa, similar cases abound.

John Williams went to Samoa in 1830. He seems to have been preceded by a Samoan who had heard the gospel in Tonga. In any event, Williams proceeded with his usual strategy of winning and training some local leaders. When he left after a short time, eight Tahitian teachers were carrying on the work. The church grew rapidly to a total of two thousand by the time the first European missionaries arrived on the scene, and it continued to grow to the point where a majority of the populace was Christian.

About one hundred years later, H. P. Van Dusen surveyed what had happened and wrote:

> It is doubtful if there is another people on the face of the earth who, in proportion to their numbers, have given so many missionaries to the Church, or have paid so great a price in sacrifice and martyrdom. At home not only do they build and maintain their own churches, schools, and other institutions, but they sustain their missionary guests as well. They regularly support the worldwide work of their Churches.[1]

To the critics of Christian missions—of which there are many—I ask, Is it too much to ask for the kind of objectivity that acknowledges literally thousands of remade societies and multiplied millions of reborn individuals down through history and around the world? I think not. But at the same time, we must honestly admit that the Christian mission is not without its weaknesses and even its failures. That is because God in his infinite wisdom and grace has elected to give his twice-born but still often erring children an integral part in it.

All of this being true, it is of incalculable importance that all of us who have to do with mission not only "do mission" but also measure as best we can exactly what we are doing by what God has said we *should be doing.* The Christian mission is worthy of sacrificial participation. It is needful of objective evaluation. And that is what we are about here.

MISSIONS AND BANDWAGONS

No small amount of missions appeal is based on the bandwagon effect: missions is where the action is; millions are waiting for us to come; thousands are responding to the message; the church is growing as never before.

Some years ago a major Evangelical magazine ran a cartoon in which two missionaries sat side by side in the front pew of a local church. As one prepared to ascend to the podium, he turned to the other and whispered, "Should we tell them the truth or should we keep them happy?"

The cartoon is funny until one thinks about it. Then it is not funny at all. And that, of course, is just the effect that the cartoonist was after. He wanted us to laugh; but more than that he wanted us to think.

The appeals above do have a considerable amount of truth in them. But they do not contain the whole truth. They are one-sided. Missions are experiencing successes, but they are also encountering problems. Of course, it is possible to dwell only on the problems and obstacles in missions. Not long ago a senior missionary to Muslims in North Africa attempted to "encourage" a new recruit by telling him that he could expect about one convert for every twenty years of service! About the most that can be said for that missionary is that he is quite likely Evangelical in his faith. Many non-Evangelicals have totally given up on missions that aim to convert people of other faiths—especially Muslims!

Perhaps one of the greatest obstacles to preparing for tomorrow's mission is an inability or unwillingness to face all of today's facts squarely and openly. An Evangelical publishing house has just released the prospectus of a new series of mission books to potential authors. One of the stated purposes of publishing the series is to emphasize trends in missions today—"especially those that are positive." But objectivity and balance are what we need.

An older and wiser colleague of mine, J. Herbert Kane, talks about pessimists who see problems without solutions and optimists who see solutions without problems. When it comes to missions, both can do irreparable damage—the inveterate pessimist by convincing Christians to give up on the task, and the unflinching optimist by inviting disillusionment when the whole truth becomes known.

Actually, the better part of wisdom might be to preserve the labels for cases instead of for people. Then we can listen more carefully and analyze more objectively. For example, in his book *How Democracies Perish*,[2] the French journalist-philosopher Jean-François Revel predicts the demise of democracy by the end of this century. Aware that his critics will immediately charge that he is a pessimist, he gets the jump on them by arguing that it is the case that is pessimistic, not the person making the case. That is a good line. It helps us focus on the case itself rather than attempting a psychological analysis of the person making it.

To take an example from missions, over a period of years the leaders of a certain mission in Africa annually reported a large number of baptisms and church additions in their work. What they did not report was the number of people who were dropped from the church rolls each year (about two-thirds of the number of additions). Of course, since total membership was also reported, if supporters had simply subtracted the total membership of the previous year from any given year's total, they would have come up with the actual growth figure. Few did that because they were not encouraged to do so and, in any case, to do so would have required that they go back to the reports of previous years in order to perform the necessary calculations. No deceit was intended. Nor were the reported statistics in error. In fact, the leaders had nothing but the overall good of the mission in view when they simply omitted statistics on dismissals from the church. But the results were that some knowledgeable supporters were disillusioned and, just as important, helpful analyses of the reasons for reversion were discouraged for many years.

In his bestselling *Megatrends*[3] John Naisbitt says that the book signals "the end of denial"—a reversal of the inability of Americans to admit the erosion of their industrial base even though it has been happening before their eyes. To the extent that we have arrived at the end of denial it has been good for us—bad for our egos, perhaps, but good for our future. It has enabled us to become learners (especially from the Japanese) and not just teachers. And it has helped us to think in terms of the kind of adjustments we will have to make to be competitive in to norrow's world.

Thus Harold L. Bussell, Dean of Chapel at Gordon College, actually does the churc a service when he exposes the fiction that says Evangelical youth are immune to the cults. He says that, in fact, a number of them are drawn to them. Among the reasons he gives for this are two that are especially germane to an analysis of contemporary missions: (1) Evangelicals evaluate leaders on their ability to sway them emotionally and (2) Evangelicals have not encouraged their young people to think critically.[4]

Both the church and its missions need this kind of objectivity. There is good news and bad news in Christian missions today. But I have profound faith in the kind of Christian believers who do today, and will in the future, form the backbone of the missionary enterprise. Armed with as much information as possible and as much accurate information as procurable, they will pray and participate more intelligently and more fervently.

THE NEAR SIDE—THE FAR SIDE

If after what has been written above, and after surveying the material that has gone into this book, someone insists that I divulge whether I am pessimistic or optimistic about the future of missions, I will take refuge in the position of still another colleague who is older and wiser than I, Kenneth Kantzer. Writing with characteristic lucidity, Kantzer comments on the success and failure of Orwell's predictive effort in his novel *1984*.[5] He says that Orwell's inability to see the great Evangelical advance in Africa, South America, Korea, and China—an advance he terms an "astounding revival of supernatural Christianity"—resulted in the failure of his prophecy. At the same time, Kantzer says that he is well aware that the "alien forces" recognized by Orwell still conspire to reverse these great advances. He therefore speaks of a "near-side pessimism" and a "far-side optimism" and says that with George Orwell he is a pessimist on the near side, though he is an optimist concerning the final goal of history. Finally, he observes that he is not an absolute pessimist even on the near side because he knows that God sovereignly controls the present as well as the future.

That is not just safe and sensible. It is profoundly spiritual, not only as it relates to the larger world scene, but especially as it relates to the missions scene.

There is a fundamental tension in missions. It is revealed by the contrast between two kinds of biblical statements. On the one hand are these: "This gospel of the kingdom shall be preached in the whole world as a witness to all the nations" (Matt. 24:14) and "Thou wast slain, and didst purchase for God with Thy blood men from every tribe and tongue and people and nation. And Thou hast made them to be a kingdom and priests to our God; and they will reign upon the earth" (Rev. 5:9–10). And on the other hand are these statements: "In the world you have tribulation" (John 16:33) and "When the Son of Man comes, will He find faith on the earth?" (Luke 18:8). Look at *all* the data, and you will discover the tension. But know that it is neither unspiritual nor unmissionary to recognize it, to pray about it, to think about it, to communicate it, and to deal with it. As Stephen Neill[6] and others have reminded us, tension can be creative. *Can* be? *Will* be! For out of tension, indeed out of conflict, will come God's victory.

There is good news and bad news in Christian missions today. Personally, I think that right now the good news outweighs the bad news, and by a fairly wide margin. If we must be optimists or pessimists, I am a near-side optimist and a far-side optimist. But I must admit that I am a more convinced far-side optimist than I am a near-side optimist! In any event, this book has to do with God's plan and our performance. Both merit a careful, prayerful look as we move toward Christ's appearing. And I am convinced that there is a large number of Christian young people in our colleges, universities, and seminaries, and a large number of dedicated believers and leaders in our churches who want to think and pray and work and witness with the larger picture in view.

THINGS THAT DIFFER—TRENDS, ISSUES, PREDICTIONS, PROPHECIES, AND MISSIONS

Question: When is a trend not necessarily a trend?

Answer: When it is an issue, a prediction, or a prophecy.

In the differences between these concepts a fundamental ambiguity in missionary (and other) literature is discoverable because these words are often used with little regard for the distinctions between them. For example, one entire series of books on mission trends actually deals with mission issues that may or may not correlate with mission trends.[7] The series would more aptly be called mission issues because no serious attempt is made to establish the general directions being taken by missions today. Obviously, it is important to identify issues, but they should not be confused with trends.

Or, to take another illustration, the future of the Christian mission has been a favorite topic of discussion in recent years. These discussions have often featured predictions as to how population, production, economic, and political trends will affect missions in the years ahead. Like the consideration of mission issues, this is an extremely important exercise. It helps us to plan for various contingencies. But while population and other trends certainly affect missions, they do not necessarily establish them. And predictions based on these trends do not enjoy the status of biblical prophecy.

To avoid confusion, it will be well to define these terms as they are used in this book even though we do not attach unusual meanings to them.

Trends and Megatrends

Quite often a trend is thought of as a statistically detectable change over a period of time. But in a more general sense a trend can be thought of as a prevailing inclination or tendency. When speaking of contemporary mission trends, I have reference to the general directions or tendencies of missions at this point in history. These can best be understood by examining the course that missions have taken over a period of time. Therefore, we will be examining the course of Christian missions in the twentieth century and particularly during the post–World War II period—a period that includes what Ralph Winter has so aptly termed the "unbelievable years."[8]

Unquestionably, the past generation has been one of the most significant and eventful generations in the entire history of Christian missions. More than that, although missions will very likely change quite radically in the next generation should God yet grant us more time, the *tendency* will be that missions will continue as they have during the recent past. Thus, as the post–World War II generation of missionaries now gradually exits from the world scene, it should prove exciting and helpful to the next generation of missionaries (and, indeed, to the entire church) to see what precedents have been established for missions in the future.

What about megatrends? Concerning his bestselling *Megatrends*, John Naisbitt writes:

> This book focuses on the megatrends or broad outlines that will define the new society. No one can predict the shape of that new world. Attempts to describe it in detail are the stuff of science fiction and futuristic guessing games that often prove inaccurate and annoying. *The most reliable way to anticipate the future is by understanding the present.*[9]

In Naisbitt's view, then, megatrends are the broad outlines of the present that will define the way things will be in the future. Megatrends are trends that are broad enough and deep enough to possess explanatory and predictive potential. For Naisbitt, they constitute the most reliable indicators of the future. Of course, as Christians, we have a "sure word of prophecy," much of which does indeed tell us the shape of the future. We know where the world and the church are headed. But we do not know all the twists and turns that will propel us there. So we need to know the broad outlines of the past and, especially, the present. *They help us anticipate the future.*

Although we will not use his terminology here, one important dimension of this book has to do with the attempt to discover and analyze the *broad outlines* of Christian mission—with what Naisbitt would call megatrends. Such things as the newly awakened interest in missions to Muslims, the emphasis on Theological Education by Extension (TEE), and the upswing in the number of short-term missionaries seem to qualify as trends rather than fads.

Indeed, they may prove to be megatrends. But for the present they possess somewhat limited explanatory and predictive potential. In fact, at present they seem to require explanation themselves. Of trends such as these we constantly inquire as to why they have come about and whether or not they will prove important in the long term. *In answering those questions we probably come closer to identifying broad outlines or megatrends in contemporary missions.*

Issues in Missions

Mission issues have to do with the major points of debate that occupy the attention of missiologists and mission leaders at any given time. As such they may alert us to trends and megatrends because they act as signposts indicating the various roads that are open to our missions. They are important to all of us who are serious about our mission in the world because they identify areas where choices must be made. But considered in isolation, they do not tell us which choice has been made or by how many. So they must be differentiated from trends.

For example, some years ago John Gatu proposed that missions declare a moratorium and withdraw from the mission fields for five years in order to give national churches an opportunity to establish their separate identities and programs. Subsequently, moratorium became an important issue. But though the proposal was widely debated, few missions—and no Evangelical ones—opted for a moratorium. Gatu had raised an important issue, however. There was potential for the establishment of a trend. But a trend did not materialize.

Trends (and especially major trends or megatrends), on the other hand, almost invariably give rise to issues. To resort to another example, it seems incontrovertible that we are in the midst of a shift in the balance of church membership and mission participation from the Northern to the Southern hemisphere and from the Western to the Eastern world. If so, this shift gives rise to a number of issues such as the viability of supporting Third-World missionaries from the West, the advisability of international teams, and so forth.

Predictions and Prophecies

What about predictions and prophecies? In general parlance these terms are more or less synonymous. In this book, however, I will distinguish between them by using the former to refer to any attempt to forecast the future on the basis of purely human calculations, and the latter to refer to the Holy Spirit–inspired foretelling of Scripture. There is, after all, a gigantic difference between the two even though in ordinary usage the words may not always indicate this.

When it comes to missions, most predictions of mission trends are based on either the considered judgments of the experts or on statistically established directions of missions in the past. However, as we will see, the experts often disagree. The best we can do on the basis of the opinions of the experts is to try to arrive at some kind of consensus. Also, statistics can be deceiving. Categories and definitions are often arbitrary and misleading. And statistical forecasting is a complex science that is replete with pitfalls for the uninitiated. It is far more complicated than just extending lines on a graph.

In the final analysis, human predictions do not enjoy the status of prophecy. In the first place, our reading of what is actually happening may be faulty. Second, that which is unlikely may well occur. History is full of surprises! Third, the options we choose today will mightily affect what will happen tomorrow. There will be an intimate connection between today's choices and tomorrow's mission!

Despite the difficulties connected with biblical interpretation, for the Christian nothing—absolutely nothing—is as important as the prophetic Word of God when it comes to understanding whence we have come, where we are now, where we are going, and the best way of getting to our destination. To neglect that Word is to neglect our only sure guide. Human predictions that are "out of sync" with Bible prophecy are automatically disqualified.

We have arrived at a day of great confusion as to the nature and future of the Christian mission. Some say that the day of missions is past. Others say its finest hour is just before us. Some spend large amounts of energy and time in discussions designed to determine exactly what the church's mission is or should be. Others proceed on the assumption that the nature of that mission is abundantly clear and time spent talking about it would be better spent doing it. Mention the Christian mission, and some exude excitement. Others simply shrug their shoulders.

This book is about the Christian world mission. It is written from an Evangelical perspective. As concerns the interpretation of the Christian mission, this means that our conclusions will be based on Evangelical presuppositions and commitment to a fully authoritative Scripture. After all, nothing can be weighed or evaluated apart from some standard. And both honesty and good sense require that the standard be known.

As concerns methodology, this perspective will be reflected in two ways. First, we will largely confine our considerations to the materials of Protestant churches and missions, though not exclusively so. Second, our primary focus will be on the North American churches and missions. This is not to denigrate the missionary contribution of Christians in other parts of the world, much of which is thoroughly Evangelical and all of which is of unquestioned importance. But it recognizes that during the postwar generation North Americans have been in the vanguard of missionary thinking and activity. Admittedly, that may change in the future, as we shall see. But for now, statistics will show that our perspective is justified.

It is my fervent hope that the Evangelical posture represented here will not make this book less valuable to readers of various persuasions. I have had numerous opportunities to interact with, and even minister among, those of other ecclesiastical connections and theological convictions. Almost invariably these relationships have been most amicable and rewarding. I greatly benefit from knowing what others are thinking and entertain hopes that in some small way they benefit from my thinking. What I find most difficult to countenance is a situation in which everyone is expected to act as though there were no such differences or as though, if differences there be, they must necessarily be inconsequential. It is that ambiguity that I have learned to avoid, both in my associations and in my writings. Perhaps it is not too much to hope that many others share my feelings in this regard.

I use the word *mission* in this book to refer to the missionary task of the church. *Missions* will ordinarily be used to signify either the mission agencies or the missionary enterprise. I trust that this clarification and the contexts in which these words are used will make the usage clear in most instances. Also, I have tried to be uniform in capitalizing such designations as Protestant, Catholic, Conciliar, Ecumenical, Fundamentalist, Pentecostal, Charismatic, and Evangelical when the primary reference is to a movement or grouping, or when it is to a position held by the movement or grouping in view. I do this for the sake of consistency (if Protestant, why not Evangelical instead of evangelical?) and to highlight the importance of these distinctions.

The various missions and associated activities and institutions are often identified by acronyms. An attempt will be made to connect the two on the first occasion of their use. Thereafter the acronym will usually be used. A list of abbreviations is provided on page 7.

As for the generic use of the words *man* and *mankind*— an English-language usage that has become suspect in modern times—I have tried to be sensitive without resorting to contrivances like "he/she" or using "he" and "she" alternately. Quite often words like *person* and *people* are preferable, but when on occasion phrases such as "man's sin" and "the blessings of mankind" appear in the text, in all likelihood women are included in the meaning.

My sincere appreciation goes to my long-time colleague, Professor Emeritus J. Herbert Kane, who has written the foreword and provided many helpful suggestions; to my colleagues on the faculty of Trinity Evangelical Divinity School who have lent encouragement; to professors Donald McGavran, John Gration, Carl F. H. Henry, C. Peter Wagner, and Ralph Winter and to mission administrators Wade Coggins and Jack Frizen, Jr.—all of whom have reflected on all portions of the manuscript; to Mrs. Barbara McIntosh and Margaret Hayman; to John Siewart and his colleagues at MARC; to my doctor-of-missiology students at Trinity; to Bruce Graham of the U.S. Center for World Mission; and to the representatives of Zondervan Publishing House. Finally, my wife Gertrude and my children and their family members come in for special mention—the former for sacrificing many hours that by rights belonged to her, and the latter for being the kind of family and extended family that occasion so little cause for concern and so much cause for joy and gratitude.

This book, then, is about the Christian mission, the

direction it has taken during the recent past, the choices it faces now, and the direction it may take in the future. To me, that mission is the greatest and most important enterprise on earth. It has its human dimension, since we who are engaged in it are human and all too subject to human weaknesses. But it also has its Divine dimension because God the Father conceived it, God the Son commanded it, and God the Holy Spirit directs it. It is therefore my prayer that this book may contribute to the progress of that mission, for long ago I became married to it, for richer, for poorer, in sickness and in health, till death do us part.

Part One:

Ten Major Trends
and Issues in Missions Today

1

MULTIPLE OPTIONS—
ENTREPRENEURSHIP IN
CHRISTIAN MISSIONS

Every Christian should have the opportunity of attending at least one of the great Urbana missionary conventions sponsored by Inter-Varsity Christian Fellowship. The first impression will almost certainly be one of amazement at the sight of thousands of committed youth gathered in one arena and giving undivided attention to one concern: the world mission of the church.

Stay at Urbana for even a day and Impression #1 will be supplemented by Impression #2: the seemingly endless number of possibilities for missionary preparation, affiliation, and service. The sports arena, the armory, and other buildings are literally jam-packed with scores of brilliantly appointed displays, hundreds of enthusiastic personnel, and tens of thousands of pieces of attractive literature representing an arresting array of schools, missions, and ministries.

Depart Urbana and reflect on the experience. In a day when the youth culture is identified with hard rock, rampant drug use, and free sex, Urbana attracts more than sixteen thousand young people devoted to Christ and his cause. Moreover, there are thousands—tens of thousands—of young people who do not make it to Urbana but are committed to Christ and his mission.

Again, in a day when some have prematurely relegated missions to the archives of church history, hundreds of organizations bent on completing the Great Commission have their representatives in Urbana. And hundreds more—some with gigantic missionary conventions of their own—are not represented.

Without doubt, today's mission is more variegated, more complex, and, in quantitative terms at least, more vitally active than at any time in history.

DECISIONS, DECISIONS, DECISIONS

Perhaps one best senses the pulse of contemporary missions by assuming the perspective of the Urbana participant who has made the really big decision. He or she is convinced that God wants him or her in missions. That question has been settled. For such a person Urbana represents an opportunity to get further direction. If we can put ourselves in the position of that missionary candidate, we can get an existential feel for the diversity that has come to characterize the missionary enterprise. Putting aside the numerous questions that may still surface in regard to the meaning and significance of the "missionary call," our imagined candidate still has an impressive list of important questions to be answered—each of which can (and probably will) evoke a wide variety of responses:

Where shall I go?

What kind of ministry should I prepare for?

To what people will I be going?

What strategy should I employ?

Should I serve on a professional or a nonprofessional basis?

Will I be a long-term or short-term missionary?

Is it best for me to be single or married?

Shall I go as a member of a team or separately?

With what kind of mission shall I serve?

When shall I go?

What preparation do I need?

How will I be supported?

This list is by no means all-inclusive. Nor is there a simple answer to any of these questions, as the candidate will soon discover. Different advisers not only offer differing slants on these matters, they also represent differing opportunities for missionary preparation and involvement—opportunities that will become available upon filling out an appropriate form.

There was a time when the average missionary candidate had fewer questions and far fewer options. That time is long gone. Barring catastrophic change, it will never return—particularly in the United States. John Naisbitt writes that "America is exploding into a free-wheeling, multiple-option society."[1] According to *Insight* magazine:

> The United States leads the world in business specialization and business bonhomie—or at least it seems that way from the constantly growing number of trade and professional associations, councils, unions, fraternities, societies, institutions, federations and guilds. At last count there were more than a half-million of them, of which about 19,000 have national memberships.[2]

For good or for ill—or for good *and* for ill—options in missions more than keep pace with the rest of North American society.

THE "MULTIPLE OPTION PRINCIPLE" IN PROTESTANT MISSIONS

The Rise of Protestant Missions

Mission historians are quick to point out various reasons for the delay in getting Protestant mission "on track" following the Reformation: the Reformers were fighting for their lives; the Reformers were fighting one another; the Reformers generally thought that the Great Commission had been given to, and had been fulfilled by, the original apostles; and so forth. All of these reasons for the delay are important. But none is more significant than still another that is sometimes overlooked; namely, when the Reformers left their Roman Catholic moorings behind them, they also left the Catholic missionary orders behind them. An authoritative Bible, some Reformed congregations, support by important princes and other powerful individuals, a missionary vision—all of these they possessed to various degrees. But they did not possess anything comparable to the Franciscan, Benedictine, and other orders that had carried the Catholic faith far and wide. And they did not develop comparable mission vehicles for a long time.

Gradually, the Pietistic movement nourished a renewal that resulted in the formation of new Protestant structures for world mission. Ordinary believers, church leaders, and heads of Protestant states—often for different reasons—were involved in the formation of certain mission societies in England and on the continent in the seventeenth and eighteenth centuries.

It remained for William Carey at the end of the eighteenth century, however, to provide a primary impetus to the mission movement as we know it today. Carey proposed "the use of *means* for the conversion of the heathen." In Carey's terminology, *means* had a different meaning than we attach to it today. Carey was calling for Christians with missionary vision to band together so as to facilitate world mission. In this he was certainly successful. In addition to his own Baptist Missionary Society (1792), before the end of the century England had spawned other societies such as the London Missionary Society (1795) and the Church Missionary Society (1799).

Before many more years had passed, Americans added foreign mission societies to the Indian and frontier missions that had absorbed their men and money for the better part of a generation. They organized the American Board of Commissioners for Foreign Missions (1810). A Baptist society was hastily formed in 1814 when Adoniram Judson was converted to Baptist convictions by Carey. Three years later the United Foreign Missionary Society came into being.

During the nineteenth century, the so-called Great Century of Christian Missions, numerous mission organizations came into being—some representing church communions and others operating more or less independently of the churches as such—until at the turn of the twentieth century some three hundred such societies existed in England and North America alone.

Forces and Efforts That Have Tended to Limit Mission Options

Almost from the beginning of this modern era of missions inaugurated by William Carey there were forces and efforts that have had the effect of bringing Protestant missions together: the Evangelical Alliance in England (1846); and in America the Foreign Mission Conference of North America (1911), the Interdenominational Foreign Missions

Association (1917), the Evangelical Foreign Missions Association (1945), and the Associated Missions of the International Council of the Christian Churches (1948). Great mission conferences brought mission and church leaders together from time to time. The most notable early ones were held in New York and London in 1854, in London in 1888, in New York in 1900, and the first official World Missionary Conference met in Edinburgh in 1910. Comity agreements in many countries—sometimes insisted on by governmental authorities—diminished friction by marking out geographical areas in which the various missions would concentrate their efforts and by establishing arbitration committees and cooperative enterprises.

There were other factors that served to limit options and in that sense uncomplicate mission as well. Travel was slow (Carey was almost six months en route to India), and therefore missionary service was thought of in career terms. Missionaries engaged in all sorts of evangelistic and relief efforts, but after the middle of the nineteenth century especially, the indigenous-church strategy of Henry Venn in England and Rufus Anderson in the United States tended to form the mold for most mission operations.

By the middle of the twentieth century the world mission had resulted in a world church. To some it seemed that the time had finally arrived when the missions could be gradually dismantled and their tasks assigned to the churches in the various countries. Aid in the forms of personnel and monies could pass between churches without going through mission structures as such. In any case, the idea of missions from the West to the rest of the world seemed out of keeping with the times.

Fueled by conference discussions at Whitby (Canada) in 1947, Willingen (Germany) in 1952, and Ghana in 1958, ecumenically oriented mission leaders reflected the emphasis on "one gospel and one church" by changing their focus from the work of the various missions to the one mission that God had enjoined upon the churches everywhere. "From missions to mission" became a common slogan. Consequently, when the International Missionary Council became a division of the World Council of Churches in 1961, it was identified as the Commission on World Mission and Evangelism. Similarly, shortly after the meeting of the WCC in Uppsala in 1968, the *International Review of Missions* became the *International Review of Mission*. Unity and uniformity seemed to be the trend.

Forces of Diversity and Multiformity

From one perspective the distinction between *missions* (the agencies) and *mission* (the task) was and is a useful one. And simplicity, comity, unity, and uniformity were and are preferable to their opposites. But one can make a case for saying that throughout the history of modern Protestant missions and in spite of the forces and efforts referred to above, the deeper trends have been toward complexity, diversity, and pluriformity. It is as though the missionary enterprise has been impatiently waiting for ships to sprout wings and fly. Its entrepreneurial thinkers have been waiting for input from new sources of information and the output of new centers of communication before giving birth to new approaches. In one way or another its associations and organizations have shut out some missions while inviting others in. Its comity agreements were opposed by a significant number of missions. And within five or six years of Uppsala at least one prominent scholar in the ecumenical camp concluded that it had been a mistake to discard the "s" and move from *missions* to *mission* so precipitously:

> When the *missio Dei* concept is tested by trinitarian thinking, the question arises: Is not the term *missiones Dei* the more genuine starting point? Already the many *missiones* by God—through the prophets, through his Son, through the Holy Spirit, through the apostles— suggest the need for a pluriform approach. And the same thing is indicated when we consider the present *missiones* of God, the manifold ways in which God makes himself present in the Holy Spirit in our period of history.[3]

We conclude that the development of multiformity and multiple options constitute a major trend in modern missions that is at the same time new and not new. In terms of the possibilities opened up by Protestant emphases on believer priesthood, Bible authority, and ecclesiastical autonomy on the one hand, and scientific developments on the other, multiformity has been a gradual development over the past two hundred years. But in terms of the sheer number of mission agencies and approaches—and the choices they offer for missionary service—multiformity and multiple options have fully flowered in postwar years and have become the order of the day.

MULTIFORMITY IN MODERN MISSIONS— THE EVIDENCE

The multiform (or pluriform) character of modern missions, particularly those from North America, is perhaps best demonstrated by looking at hard data in four areas: the increase in the number of missions organizations, the variety of mission structures, the diversity of strategies and operations, and the choices today's candidates are making.

Growth in the Number of Mission Agencies

World statistics on the growth of Christian missionary and service agencies of all kinds are indeed impressive. David Barrett indicates that there were over thirteen times as many Christian service agencies (including foreign missions) in 1986 than there were in 1900 (19,700 as compared to 1,500), and he predicts that there will be sixteen times as many (24,000) such agencies by the year 2000. As for strictly foreign mission agencies as such, the number increased sixfold from 600 in 1900 to 3,600 in 1986. Barrett projects that their number will increase eightfold to 4,800 by the year 2000!

Chart 1.1[4]

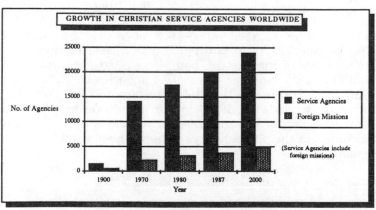

If Protestantism was largely bereft of mission agencies

for almost two hundred years following the Reformation, the same cannot be said for the better part of the past two hundred years—especially during the present generation. While the agencies connected with the Conciliar churches have tended to stagnate or decline, the number and variety of agencies have constantly increased. Since 1940 the number of new mission agencies being formed per decade in North America alone has tripled and even quadrupled the number formed in previous decades.

Chart 1.2[5]

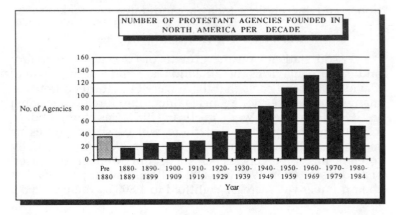

Patrick Johnstone concludes that there are approximately 81,000 missionaries world-wide serving in about 1,800 Protestant mission agencies—650 of which are based in North America, 500 in Europe, and an increasing number in other parts of the world.[6] The *Mission Handbook,* however, indicates that there are at least 764 agencies based in North America.[7] This means that there are close to 2,000 Protestant agencies world-wide. If one were to include the churches that are acting as their own foreign mission agencies (and not included in the above figures), the number would be even greater.

The Variety of Mission Types

Of course, the number of agencies per se tells only part of the multiple-options story. When missiologists get around to differentiating among various types of missions, the layperson can be forgiven for responding with a look of bewilderment. Missiologists themselves are hard pressed to know how best to categorize them. Perhaps one of the best ways to get a handle on the situation is to subsume some of the usual distinctions under four major considerations as follows:

1. The relation of the mission to the organized church at home and abroad—denominational/interdenominational; denominational/"faith"; church planting/parachurch and service.
2. The internal structure of the mission—international/national; board-governed/member-governed; centrally administered/decentralized administration.
3. The relation of the mission to inter-mission associations: Division of Overseas Ministries (National Council of Churches of Christ—USA); Evangelical Foreign Missions Association (National Association of Evangelicals); Interdenominational Foreign Mission Association; Fellowship of Missions; The Associated Missions, International Council of Christian Churches; and the unaffiliated missions.
4. The function or ministry of the mission—home/foreign; evangelistic and church planting/ service, relief, development; sending/nonsending; crosscultural/intracultural.

The listing is not all-inclusive nor are the categories necessarily mutually exclusive, but it serves to point up the variegated nature of the missions today.

The Diversity of Strategies and Functions

Western culture—particularly of the North American stripe—has been especially characterized by individualism, volunteerism, and entrepreneurship since the frontier days. Its missionary effort reflects these characteristics not only in the increase and variety of organizations but also in the diversity of their operations. Bibles for the World, Inc., does not send missionaries, but Bibles. World Literature Crusade, Inc., conscripts individuals to personally deliver Christian literature to every home in a given area or country. Wycliffe Bible Translators, Inc., specializes in reducing languages to writing and in translating Scripture. The Pacific Broadcasting Association came into existence in order to produce and air programs for Japanese-speaking people. DAWN (Discipling a Whole Nation) has recently been organized in order to coordinate nationwide evangelistic and church-planting efforts. The U.S. Center for World Mission in Pasadena houses about one hundred different departments and organizations dedicated to carrying forth Christian mission in every conceivable way from the use of the arts in mission to the production of television programs designed to appeal to nonreligious stations the world over.

A survey designed to collect data for the current *Mission Handbook* (North America only) listed some fifty-three functions that agencies could identify as being performed by their missionaries. Ten functions (see below) were indicated by just under 50 percent of the missions. *Over 50 percent of the responses were distributed among another forty-three functions!*

Chart 1.3[8]

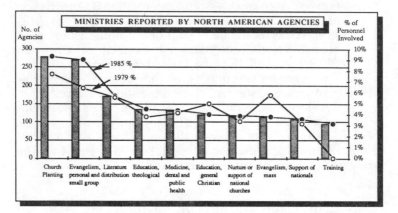

Note: The actual number of missionaries involved in training was not reported in 1979.

The Choices Being Made in Missionary Service Today

More and more North American Protestant Christians are responding to the call for overseas service than ever before. As of 1985, approximately 67,200 North Americans were serving overseas. This is more than double the number serving in 1960.

Overall, these figures are encouraging. But in what direction are today's candidates moving?

Chart 1.4[9]

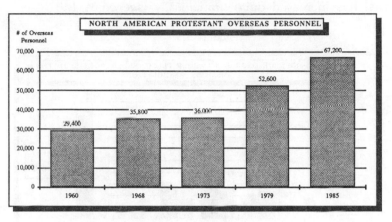

First, they are moving from Conciliar missions to Evangelical missions. Over the past decade mission agencies connected with the Division of Overseas Missions of the National Council of Churchs (DOM) have continued to show the steady decline in missionary numbers that began about 1960. EFMA and IFMA and unaffiliated missions (most of which are Evangelical) have grown significantly (see chart 1.5).

Second, candidates are moving from affiliated to unaffiliated missions. This becomes apparent by comparing the number of missionaries in the affiliated and unaffiliated categories above (see chart 1.6).

Third, they are moving from ministries designed to assist existing churches to other ministries such as planting new churches and, especially, service ministries (see chart 1.7).

Fourth, candidates are opting for short-term service in greater numbers than for career service. This is perhaps one of the most striking features of contemporary missions. Although the number of mission agencies reporting short-term personnel has decreased somewhat in recent years, there is a continued and accelerated upswing in short-term service. *Some 42 percent of the 67,200 North American missionaries are short-term personnel!*[10] *(See chart 1.8.)*

Fifth, while the percentage of missions with short-term

programs has declined somewhat over the last sixteen years, the number of missions relying largely on short-term personnel has increased quite dramatically (see chart 1.9).

Chart 1.5[11]

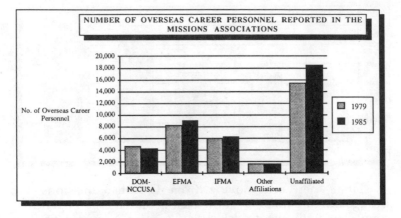

When we also take the numerous possibilities there are in other countries for "tentmaking," nonprofessional missionary service, into account, it is safe to conclude that although tens of thousands of missionary candidates are seriously considering service opportunities in Christian missions, they must face serious questions about where to serve, what type of service to prepare for, and under whose auspices to serve. It can safely be conjectured that no one individual, no matter how well informed, is able to identify all the acronyms, explain all of the intricate strategies, or enumerate all of the services available within the context of North American missions operations today.

To sum up, thousands of the church's best minds and most committed hearts are dedicated to this central task of reaching the world for Christ. But more must be said.

THE MORE, THE BETTER?

We may grant that the more, the merrier. But is it true that the more, the *better*? When, if ever, can it be said that we have enough mission organizations? At what point should we conclude that there needs to be more unity of a practical kind? that we need more consolidation and less proliferation in missions? that a more uniform strategy would be preferable to more multiformity?

Chart 1.6[12]

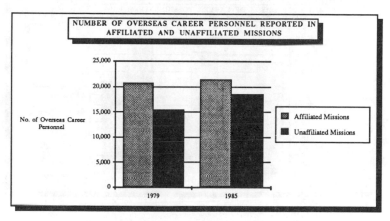

Chart 1.7[13]

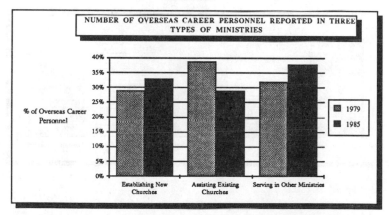

These questions are, of course, often posed and strenuously debated. Some analysts—both Catholic and Protestant—have argued that the church does not *have* missions, it *is* mission. Others—Evangelicals for the most part—have argued that the church not only *has* missions, it *needs* missions.

Chart 1.8[14]

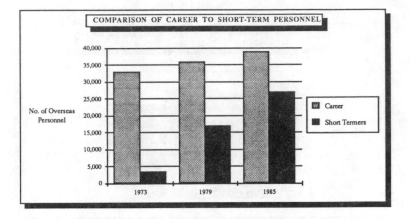

Chart 1.9[15]

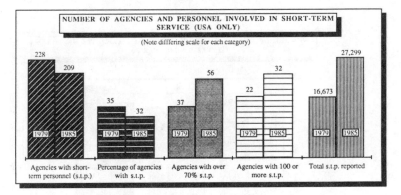

"The Church Is Mission"

The Second General Conference of the Bishops of Latin America held in Medellin in 1968 made a case for "basic ecclesial communities" (in the parish churches) as being "the initial cell of the Church structure and the source of evangelization. . . ."[16] Hope was held out for a maximum of vitality with a minimum of structures.

Some Protestants also have insisted that the "church is mission" and that the churches themselves should be the agencies of witness, not only at home but also around the world. Some have complained that agencies of the parachurch variety siphon off the very commitment and vitality that are needed in local congregations. They say that mission organizations often expect the churches to support them while they themselves give but little support to the churches. Some say that the leaders of organizations only loosely connected to the church are a law unto themselves and lack the discipline that is a part of church life. Still others call attention to the waste that accrues to so many missions maintaining separate offices, staffs, and promotional and recruitment programs at home, to say nothing of duplicating the efforts of others on the foreign fields.

"The Church Needs Missions"

Ralph Winter, for one, has argued quite convincingly for historical precedents and the contemporary validity of "independent" and specialized missions.[17] He finds cultural parallels between the Jewish synagogues with their evangelistic patterns and the Christian congregations who commissioned Paul's missionary band. He sees parallels also between Roman magisterial territories with their Roman military structures and Christian dioceses (with their parishes) and the monasteries (with their missionary outreach). Winter argues that there is a parallel between Catholic dioceses and the monastic movements on the one hand, and Protestant denominations (including local congregations) and Protestant missionary organizations on the other. Using terminology growing out of Catholicism, he calls the former *modalities* (structured fellowships without age or sex distinctions) and the latter *sodalities* (structured fellowships involving an adult decision beyond modality membership and with age, sex, and marital status conditions). Perhaps this can be better understood from the following diagram:

It is important to note that Winter is not arguing that there is a historical or formal relationship between Protestant denominations and missions and the earlier precedents. He is saying that there is a *functional* relationship. He maintains that modalities and sodalities are complementary. God has used both down through history and he uses both today. Winter's primary point is that we need to understand that God has used a structure other than the church modality to effect his mission in the world. In fact, the church modalities *need* the mission sodalities with their commitment, mobility, expertise, and entrepreneurship if the church is to extend itself and complete the Great Commission.

MODALITIES AND SODALITIES

Modalities	Sodalities
Jewish synagogue	Jewish evangelistic patterns
Early Christian congregations	Paul's missionary band
Roman magisterial territories	Roman military structures
Catholic dioceses and parishes	Catholic monastic movements
Protestant denominational structures	Protestant missionary organizations

Using a less complex but similar argument, C. Peter Wagner maintains that missions are the "legs" of the church: "The church can survive without missions (as the churches of the Reformation did), but they can't do a good job of proclaiming Christ's name throughout the world."[18] When missionary-minded sons and daughters of the church such as William Carey, Fredrik Franson, Mary Slessor, and Amy Carmichael launch out in Holy Spirit-directed faith and daring, then the mission becomes unleashed and effective.

"IT ALL COMES DOWN TO THIS . . ."

Peter Gets It Straight

One wonders what went through Peter's mind that day on the temple site. Herod's temple was one of the wonders of the world at the time. And the finely robed priests who attended its sacrifices were no doubt impressive. Gazing on the scene, Peter could hardly believe his ears when Jesus said, "Do you not see all these things? Truly I say to you, not one stone here shall be left upon another, which will not be torn down" (Matt. 24:2).

Did Peter recall the Lord's earlier words: "Blessed are

you Simon Barjona. . . . And I also say unto you that you are
Peter, and upon this rock I will build My church; and the
gates of Hades shall not overpower it" (Matt. 16:17–18)? We
have no way of knowing. But if he could not put all the
pieces together there on the temple site or on the Mount of
Olives and therefore did not fully comprehend Christ's plan
for this age at that time, he obviously understood later, for
he wrote, "You . . . as living stones, are being built up as a
spiritual house for a holy priesthood, to offer up spiritual
sacrifices acceptable to God through Jesus Christ" (1 Peter
2:5).

At the heart of Christ's program for this age is the
evangelizing of the world and the building of Christ's
church.

It is clear by now that choices must be made in today's
mission. The arguments are complex. The options are
numerous. In the kind of pressurized world described by our
Lord in the Olivet Discourse, in the face of a society that is so
decidedly individualistic and entrepreneurial, and in the
context of churches and missions characterized by so much
diversity, the right choices may not come easily. Rarely does
a week pass but that several bright, dedicated young people
(and sometimes older folk as well) come to my office seeking
counsel as to the nature of the missionary call, or the "right"
mission, or the greatest needs, or the amount of time
required for adequate missionary preparation—all of this in
the context of an extensive catalogue of opportunities and a
cacophony of conflicting counsel.

Multiple Options and "World Christians"

What "world Christians" must not lose sight of in the
plethora of words, the proliferation of organizations, and the
profusion of approaches is the fact that our Lord promised to
build but one entity—his church. They must always keep in
mind that he promised that the powers of Hades itself would
never overpower that one entity—his church (Matt. 16:18).

Multiple Options and Christian Pastors

What pastors in our churches must keep in mind today
is that missions do not exist to enhance the programs of local
churches, they exist to effect world evangelization. To
highlight the bizarre or tear-wrenching aspects of missions in

order to appeal to people at home without considering field priorities is indefensible.

Pastors and local church leaders should also be cautious about bypassing the expertise of the historic missions and functioning as their own sending agency. To assume the responsibility to recruit, select, train, and send out missionaries—and to make those missionaries responsible to the local church at home but not to church or mission bodies on the field—is questionable strategy. This is not to argue against the advisability of holding missionaries accountable to their sending church(es).

Multiple Options and Missionary Entrepreneurs

What missionary entrepreneurs must remember is that Paul, the leader of the greatest missionary band ever assembled, earned acceptance and received direction in the fellowship of believers of the church at Antioch. Moreover, he was willing to submit to the test of the validity of his gospel and mission by scheduling an audience with apostolic leaders of the church in Jerusalem. He did this in spite of the uniqueness of his call and authority as an apostle personally appointed by Christ. More than that, as a missionary par excellence and leader of a most significant band, Paul laid claim to nothing more than being a co-laborer in the church Christ himself was building (1 Cor. 3:9).

The church needs its missions. It may be that between 1979 and 1985 the world missionary enterprise needed three times as many new missionary organizations as mergers of existing organizations in North America (forty-eight new organizations as compared with sixteen mergers).[19] But it may also be that leadership in both new and existing missions needs to give more attention to the larger body of Christ.

Multiple Options and Field Missionaries

What field missionaries must keep in mind is that the establishment of priorities is one of their most important tasks. Some years ago when Theological Education by Extension (TEE) was all the rage in missions, I happened to be in a country in the Far East when a highly esteemed missiologist friend was also there. Our conversation centered on the number of schools (there were over fifty missions-related Bible institutes and colleges in that country at the time) that were inaugurating TEE and the number of personnel devoting themselves to programming textbooks, often with little expertise and considerable overlap of effort. I remarked that as we traveled about, it might be well to call attention to this state of affairs and encourage more communication and cooperation.

His response to my suggestion constituted a most insightful commentary on contemporary missions. He replied, "Don't say anything. Enthusiastic involvement on the part of as many as possible is the best way to go, even at the price of some inefficiency and duplication."

I cannot say that I was entirely convinced at the time. Nor am I today. No doubt much can be said for the idea that efficiency is costly, but in the case of missions, it may be well worth the price in the long run.

Multiple Options and Missionary Candidates

The system employed by the majority of Protestant missions places the responsibility for making highly critical choices on the shoulders of those who may be least qualified to make them. Think of the upswing in short-term missions. Consider the apparent ability of relatively new and untried agencies to attract candidates while many historic agencies go begging. Think of the ministry choices that might be made on the basis of their appeal to potential recruits instead of on the basis of field knowledge and need.

Missionary candidates should not forget the corporate as well as the individual aspects of the missionary call. As Michael Griffiths has reminded us:

> Not even one missionary call recorded by the Holy Spirit in the Acts of the Apostles was subjective or the result of individual initiative alone. In most cases, the subjective sense of call is not the aspect of the call which is brought to our attention by the Holy Spirit. In every case either the church or another missionary had a considerable part to play in the call. God's call is based primarily on objective external events rather than on subjective, internal experience.[20]

Let each be persuaded in his or her own mind. But in seeking the mind of Christ let those interested in serving also seek the ministry of the Spirit in the Word of God and the mind of trusted fellow believers who know them best!

An esteemed missionary colleague of mine, Arthur Johnston, spent a term in Paris winning students to Christ and molding them into an exciting organization. After a furlough he went back to pick up where he had left off. To his great disappointment most of these people could not be located. He was devastated. It was at that point that the Lord seemed to say to him, "I love the young. But please remember that I did not promise to build a youth group as such. I only promised to build my church." At that point he gained a new perspective on the Christian mission. An even more exciting—and lasting—work of God is to be found on the outskirts of Paris today, partly as a result of his subsequent ministry.

2

TARGETING AND STRATEGIZING— A VISION FOR WORLD EVANGELIZATION

What do missiologists mean by the following words and phrases:

"evangelized" and "unevangelized"?

"reached" and "unreached"?

"people group"?

"hidden people"?

It depends on which missiologist you ask. There is—or at least there has been—a great deal of confusion as definitions have been proposed, analyzed, and modified for at least two decades. But there has been something very positive about all of this because world evangelization is no longer just a slogan, nor is it just a dream. Places and people are being identified and targeted. Strategies are being debated and determined.

We have come a long way since William Carey pored over his maps and plotted the paths of the explorers. We have made considerable progress since Samuel Zwemer outlined the world's Muslim areas and prayed for Muhammad's followers. We have taken giant steps since John Mott and others challenged the church to evangelize the world in a generation.

"WHERE THERE IS NO VISION . . ."

When it comes to fulfilling the Great Commission and taking the gospel to the whole world, there has been a not-so-obvious problem. The world to be evangelized has been growing through the centuries! If Paul realized his ambition to get to Spain, he barely made it to the end of the Mediterranean world. If the apostle Thomas went as far as India, he still got no farther than the gateway to the Orient. Think of the vastness of the lands and the concentrations of people to the west of Spain and to the east of India. Think of the centuries that were required to "discover" and explore them.

By the time of Carey's departure for India at the end of the eighteenth century, of course, the extent of the world to be evangelized had become clear. He estimated that two-thirds of the world still needed to be touched by the gospel. The nineteenth century became, in Latourette's phraseology, the "great century of Christian missions" as missionaries from Europe and America set out to reach people in the world's remotest corners. That concern came to be summed up by a few in the word "evangelism" and by many others in the word "evangelization."

The words "evangelize" and "evangelization"—and phrases that included them—gradually came to the fore in the Protestant and Anglican worlds of the nineteenth century. By the time of the 1858 Great Awakening, G. S. Faber, Alexander Duff, and Joseph Parker had written or spoken of the Christian duty to "evangelize the world." Then a series of world missionary conferences (Liverpool in 1860, London in 1888, New York in 1900, and Edinburgh in 1910) promoted the idea.

In 1885 the Bible teacher and editor of the *Missionary Review* (USA), A. T. Pierson, included an article in the publication entitled "A plan to evangelize the world." He called for an international meeting to make plans for world evangelization by the year 1900. The following year in July 251 students from 87 colleges answered Dwight L. Moody's summons to Mt. Hermon, Massachusetts. There they heard Pierson's challenge that if the world is to be evangelized and Christ's coming hastened, "all should go, and go to all." Before the conference was over, one hundred students had responded to that challenge, and the Student Volunteer Movement for Foreign Missions had been conceived.

Pierson is usually credited with coining the watchword "the evangelization of the world in this generation," and John R. Mott, Robert Wilder, Robert Speer, and others are credited with popularizing it. However, there is evidence to indicate that the initial concern was to evangelize the world by the year 1900 and that the phrase "in this generation" was added sometime in the decade of the 1890s when it became apparent that world evangelization by 1900 was impossible. In 1897 the Church Missionary Society published a paper that had been read at a conference of clergy in Stockport sometime earlier; it had the title "The Evangelization of the World in This Generation." At any rate, the watchword became the focus of attention not only at student missionary conferences but in thousands of churches as well. Thus as hundreds and then thousands of recruits presented themselves for foreign service, they gradually received more and more enthusiastic support.[1]

The slogan was not without its critics, especially in Europe. None other than the "father of the science of mission," Gustav Warneck at Halle, opposed it. He charged that it led to superficiality—that it encouraged proclamation of the gospel but not the founding of local and national churches so basic to a right understanding of mission. He also was critical of the notion that mission work would hasten the *parousia* or coming of Christ for his church. (Pierson, among many who espoused the slogan, linked the concept with premillennialism and a plan for world evangelization in order to hasten "the day of the Lord.")

But Mott rejected Warneck's criticism. He said that the slogan was not a prophecy and did not support one particular eschatology. He also insisted that it was a means to the objectives of enthroning Christ in all spheres of life and of planting and developing self-propagating churches.

World evangelization was usually defined in terms of providing all people with the opportunity to hear the gospel. Whether the watchword encouraged sound mission *planning* is debatable, though attention was given to the means that could be used to evangelize the world. But there is no debate about its role in inspiring believers to become involved in world evangelization. It served as the watchword of the Student Volunteer Movement for a generation. And although that movement had largely run its course by the 1930s, and the watchword itself had fallen into disuse by the time of World War I, subsequently it has demonstrated its resilience. By the 1960s the Inter-Varsity Christian Fellowship and other Evangelical groups began to revive it. Sponsored by the EFMA and IFMA, the Wheaton Congress (1966) employed it in the Wheaton Declaration:

We . . . do covenant together . . .
To seek . . .
The Mobilization of the Church
For the Evangelization of the World in This Generation.[2]

The original proponents of the slogan felt that the world could be evangelized by the turn of the century. One hundred years later we still espouse the concept, and many believe that world evangelization can be accomplished by the year 2000. Is this nothing more than a case of history repeating itself? No. We are much closer to achieving that goal today. And, just as important, the watchword—or at least the concept—has been used by God to encourage a *plan* for world evangelization as well as to evoke the *vision* for it!

A MARRIAGE MADE IN HEAVEN

World evangelization has two essential types of ingredients: evangelistic impetus and intellectual input, motivation and information, or vision and strategy. The way in which God the Holy Spirit has brought these ingredients together since World War II is one of the most remarkable stories of contemporary missions. It is much too long to relate in detail here, but it must be told in outline form at least.

Ideas, Ideas, Ideas

No doubt about it. Some of the greatest "idea people" of modern missions have come to the fore in this generation. And some of the most important of their ideas have come through the crucible of criticism and have become important elements for carrying through with world evangelization.

1. *Church growth.* The idea that missionary activity should result in the growth of the church is as old as mission itself. Warneck was right in being concerned about it and in strategizing to accomplish it. But in our generation *both the vision and the strategy* have been given tremendous impetus by one man especially—Donald A. McGavran. What was

new in McGavran's approach to church growth as it evolved in the 1950s and 1960s was the weaving together of biblical mission and socio-anthropological understandings in such a way as to make the growth of the church analyzable and popular (in the good sense of that word). By the time church planting and church-growth strategy came together in the decade of the 1970s, most Evangelical missions were beginning to place a high priority on this aspect of mission once again.

2. *People groups.* Important to church growth theory early on was the idea of "homogeneous units" of people who, because of their basic identity with each other, tend to think alike and act together. As McGavran, anthropologist Alan Tippett, systems analyst Edward Dayton, and others thought this through, they realized that there must be a better way to think of world evangelization than to think of it in terms of continents and nations and individuals. The idea of the "people group" was born.

As originally proposed by McGavran, the idea of targeting homogeneous groups of people for evangelization rather than concentrating on individuals only made good missiological sense. Two problems emerged, however. First, his ethnolinguistic definition of a "people group" as people who share a common ancestry and language and who marry within the group seemed too restrictive. Second, his interpretation of *panta ta ethnē* ("all nations" in Matt. 28:19 KJV) as "people groups" appeared to some to be a case of reading contemporary understandings into the biblical text.

In 1977 the Lausanne Committee for World Evangelism sponsored the Strategy Working Group. Under the direction of its chairman, C. Peter Wagner, this group redefined a "people" as a "significantly large sociological grouping of individuals who perceive themselves to have a common affinity for one another."[3] The new definition had the potential of applying to groups that were distinguishable from their original culture or the larger culture in which they were included but that still possessed their own distinctives—for example, Indians on Malaysian rubber plantations and divorced American yuppies. But to some this definition appeared to be too broad and elastic, and therefore of limited utility.

As for *ethnē* in the Great Commission, its definition also awaited resolution. Some missiologists have insisted that it refers to people groups and that "this is the way God sees the world," though they have been at a loss to say which of the definitions of "people group" is divinely sanctioned! On exegetical grounds other missiologists have remained unconvinced, believing that *ethnē* is a more general reference to Gentile peoples (but not necessarily excluding Jews).

In any case, although problems still remain, almost all agree that whether the Great Commission *requires* it or not, the best way to plan for world evangelization is to divide its population up into some kind of identifiable and homogeneous groupings for which sound strategy can be devised and implemented. For those who are informed in missions theory, it is unlikely that "people" will ever again mean just a conglomerate of individuals. It will mean an "affinity group" of one kind or another.

3. *Hidden peoples.* Three years after the Lausanne Congress, Ralph Winter founded the U.S. Center for World Mission with a vision of bringing many mission agencies together in one place that would serve as a nerve center for world evangelization. A primary focus was unreached people groups of a certain kind. Building on his Lausanne challenge, Winter emphasized the fact that among the unreached people of the world are to be found thousands of groups that not only have had no gospel offered and no viable church, but also are not yet identified or recognized by churches near or far. They are somehow isolated or sealed off from Christian view. They are "hidden" from the conventional outreach of existing churches and mission agencies. It is the duty of missions today to undertake whatever research is necessary to identify them and to bend every effort to push back the mission frontiers so as to reach them. Along with Don Richardson and others, Winter has made the phrases "hidden peoples" and "frontier missions" into household words for tens of thousands of Christians.

4. *Reached and unreached peoples.* "Unreached people" might appear to be synonymous with "unevangelized people." But those who prepared for the International Congress on World Evangelization at Lausanne in 1974 suggested that a distinction may be made. It may be argued, for instance, that Europe was evangelized years ago but that millions of Europeans are still unreached with the gospel today. By the time of the Congress, the Missions Advanced Research and Communications Center (MARC) had produced an *Unreached*

Peoples Directory listing 424 specific unreached people groups. At the Congress, Ralph Winter eloquently challenged delegates with the fact that at that time over two billion or about 80 percent of the non-Christians of the world were separated from the gospel by significant barriers—cultural, social, linguistic, religious, and so forth. Not only were they "unreached," but they would never become "reached" until someone crossed these barriers to take the gospel to them.

Obviously, unreached people had no Christian churches or missionaries among them. But early on, mission thinkers asked themselves how large the church among any given people group would have to become before those people could really be considered "reached." Enter sociological diffusion of innovation theory, which indicated that if between 10 and 20 percent of a population accept a new idea, it will have gained enough momentum to ensure wider acceptance. A "reached people" became a people with a church comprising 20 percent of the population.[4]

Predictably, such a definition was destined for criticism. On such a basis, how many places and peoples could be considered reached? Even South Korea, one of the places where missions had been most successful, could barely have been considered reached at that time! Furthermore, the definition said nothing about the readiness of the existing churches to actually propagate the gospel.

The *World Christian Encyclopedia* settled for simplified and more or less synonymous meanings for both "evangelized" and "reached." It defined both in terms of the state of having had the gospel made available or offered to a person or people. Specifically, evangelized non-Christians are "persons who are not Christians in any recognized sense but who have become aware of Christianity, Christ, and the gospel, and yet have not, or not yet, responded positively by accepting them."[5] Neither this more classical definition nor the sociologically sophisticated definition have satisfied many, however.

Recently, Ralph Winter has clarified the definitional process involving key terms related to world evangelization in a way that makes it possible to discuss and plan for world evangelization in a meaningful way. He writes as follows:

> . . . in February of 1982, the newly created Frontier Peoples Committee of the Interdenominational Foreign

Mission Association voted to suggest to all of its 90 or so member mission agencies that they each begin to employ synonymously the three commonly used goal phrases, *Unreached Peoples, Hidden Peoples,* and *Frontier Peoples,* and that the definition for these be the E-80 [Consultation on Frontier Missions, Edinburgh, 1980] wording.

Then, in March of 1982, the Lausanne Committee for World Evangelization's Strategy Working Group decided to adopt essentially the same (E-80) definition. In so doing, they replaced their own earlier working definition of *Unreached Peoples,* which had been based on a 20 percent-Christian measurement. Their slight modification was no doubt for the better. It now read:

> *An Unreached People is a people group among which there is no indigenous community of believing Christians with adequate numbers and resources to evangelize this people group.*

This valuable definition, however, builds in turn upon a key term which itself deserves attention: what is a *people?* The March 1982 meeting convened by the Lausanne Committee also dealt decisively with this question. Their definition:

> *For evangelization purposes, a people group is the largest group within which the Gospel can spread as a church planting movement without encountering barriers of understanding or acceptance.*

It is important to note that the wording here defines a group which normally would be capable of having with it a *church movement.*

By contrast, I have recently suggested the term "bridge peoples" for those often smaller, highly specialized groups like Osaka barbers, or Taipei taxi drivers, or Manila prostitutes, within whose more restricted fellowship evangelism can often be startlingly effective but which might not result in a church movement as such.

Once such individuals become Christians, they will seek to help their families, which likely will not fit in the restricted fellowship where the first one was reached. As a result, the entire family might best find church membership in some larger, more diverse sphere. Yet the existence of such evangelistic "bridge peoples" explains why the word *largest* is crucial in the definition of the kind of people groups that are candidates for a church movement.

As I see it, the careful consensus of March 1982 on the definitions of *peoples* and *unreached peoples* produced a marvelously wise pair of formulations. These two definitions can help us avoid many pitfalls and protect us from misunderstanding the key goal of "A Church for Every People by the Year 2000."[6]

Both of these latter definitions have their strengths. From a practical (and perhaps from a biblical) point of view, it would seem that any person or people group that has had an understandable hearing of the gospel should be considered evangelized even when they have not accepted the gospel and believed in Christ. Still, if there is no viable, evangelizing church established, there will be no continuing agency for evangelization indigenous to the people group. In any society, a local church is the best means of evangelizing both present and future generations.

And so, over the years since World War II both the vision and the plan—the impetus and the strategy—for world evangelization have slowly emerged. The slogan "the evangelization of the world in this generation" has taken on new meaning. People groups must be identified, described, and targeted. Then the gospel must be proclaimed with a view to establishing viable churches among them. From a theoretical point of view at least it is a marriage made in heaven.

AN EXPANDING DATA BASE AND A SHRINKING WORLD

When the Evangelical theologian Carl F. H. Henry told a gathering in Nairobi several years ago that our evangelistic impetus has outrun our intellectual resources, he was challenging missionaries and nationals to more theological depth. That is something to think about—and to think about seriously. But as far as sheer information about the world and its peoples is concerned, the church and its missions have never been richer. Never before in history have so many Christians so devoted themselves to "lifting up their eyes and looking on the fields." Consider the evidence.

Literature

In addition to standard references such as *Mission Handbook, UK Christian Handbook,* and the *World Christian Encyclopedia,* the research of MARC, LCWE, the U. S. Center, and others has resulted in the *Status of Christianity Profiles* on scores of countries and major states of the world; the *Unreached Peoples* series; the periodical *Mission Frontiers;* books such as *Operation World, Planning Strategies for World Evangelization,* and *That Everyone May Hear* (the 1985–86 book list of the Global Church Growth Book Club included thirty-seven titles under "mission strategy"); and maps, audio-visuals, and much, much more. *(See Appendix 1 for an explanation of the thematic content analyses that form the basis for many of the statistics provided kin this and subsequent chapters.)*

As far as 444 book reviews in *Missiology* are concerned, 21 focus on church planting and church growth, 6 on urban and industrial mission, and another 6 on evangelism and witness for a total of 33, or 7.4 percent (see Appendix 3). That is a significant percentage, but not nearly so significant as the number of articles devoted to evangelization strategies that have appeared in mission journals in recent years. Although the emphasis on unreached and hidden peoples as such has been rather minimal even in the *EMQ* (until recently), themes related to world evangelization have been given increased attention in both the *IRM* and the *EMQ,* especially the *EMQ.* (See below and Appendix 2 for comparisons. The unreached/hidden peoples category is separated from the evangelism category in the tables below. Other categories may relate to evangelization.)

Missionary Deployment

A comparison of the types of ministries in which North American missionaries were deployed in 1985 as compared with 1979 reveals an upswing in every category of ministry closely related to world evangelization except one. Deployment increased in the ministries of literature distribution, nurture and support of national churches, church planting, and (especially) involvement in personal and small-group evangelism. Involvement in mass evangelism declined somewhat.[7]

Conferences and Consultations

I have already mentioned the International Congress on World Evangelization at Lausanne in 1974. Out of that congress came the Lausanne Committee for World Evangelization (LCWE), which has sponsored consultations on the Homogeneous Unit Principle in 1977, on Gospel and Culture and on Muslim Evangelization in 1978, on World Evangelization in 1980 (an international gathering), on the Relationship Between Evangelism and Social Responsibility (with the World Evangelical Fellowship) in 1982, and the National Convocation for Evangelizing Ethnic America in 1985.

Number of Articles (out of 949) in the IRM
Focusing on World Evangelization Strategies

Strategy	Number of Articles in Five-Year Periods				Totals	
	1966–70	1971–75	1976–80	1980–85	(Inc. '65 & '86)	
Evangelism	3	30	28	19	86	9.1%
Church planting/ growth	10	2	0	2	17	1.9%
Unreached/ hidden peoples	2	2	1	1	6	.6%
Urban mission	10	3	5	3	26	2.8%
Totals	25	37	34	25	135	14.4%

Initiated by Ralph Winter and the U.S. Center for World Mission, a World Consultation on Frontier Missions was held in Edinburgh in 1980. It is reported that more mission agencies sent delegates to that meeting than to any such gathering up to that time.

Simultaneous to, and overlapping with, the Edinburgh meeting, a consultation of younger leaders was convened. Out of that gathering came the Theological Students for Frontier Missions, the *International Journal of Frontier Missions*, and the commitment statement currently used by Caleb Project, a group that travels to many campuses and challenges students to be involved in fulfilling the Great Commission.

Recognizing the part that national evangelists play in completing the Great Commission, the Billy Graham Evangelistic Association has sponsored conferences for itinerant evangelists, the most recent being held in Amsterdam in 1986.

Number of Major Articles (out of 604) in the IRM
Focusing on World Evangelization Strategies

Strategy	Number of Articles in Five-Year Periods				Totals	
	1966–70	1971–75	1976–80	1980–85	(Inc. '65 & '86)	
Evangelism	4	10	13	11	39	6.5%
Church planting/ growth	4	9	12	14	42	7.0%
Unreached/ hidden peoples	0	0	1	3	4	.7%
Urban mission	2	0	0	5	7	1.2%
Totals	10	19	26	33	92	15.4%

Student movements such as the Student Missions Fellowship, the Summer Institutes of International Studies, and Inter-Varsity Christian Fellowship have highlighted the unreached peoples. Similar conferences sponsored by Christians in Asia, Europe, and other parts of the world have attracted thousands.

As for the future, the *Lausanne Communique* reports that a stream of conferences and consultations have been planned, leading up to a second international congress to be sponsored by the LCWE in 1989.[9]

Special Strategy Groups

In spite of the elastic understanding of people groups that prevailed by the time of the Congress on World Evangelization (Pattaya, Thailand, 1980), it was manifestly impossible for such a gathering to consider strategies for reaching more than a few of the thousands of groupings that qualified as people groups. Pattaya participants focused on adherents of the major religions, nominal Christians, urban dwellers, and refugees. The outcome was a series of strategy papers for reaching these groups, and these papers have been made widely available. Thus the Congress furnished additional impetus to a trend that had already begun. Sharpening the focus on certain peoples, special strategy groups have been doing research on China, Japan, Muslims, tribal peoples, diaspora peoples (student, refugee, and immigrant populations), urbanites, and others in recent years. Perhaps most visible is the work being done on world-class cities (cities of over one million) by LCWE appointee Raymond Bakke and also by Harvie Conn and Roger Greenway of Westminster's Urban Missions Program.

Prayer

It is widely recognized that prayer has always played a major role in evangelization. Accordingly, a great deal of attention has been given to the encouragement and facilitation of private and corporate intercessory prayer for world evangelization. As LCWE's Senior Associate for Prayer, David Bryant has traveled and spoken widely in order to call Christians to encourage emerging prayer movements. Patrick Johnstone's *Operation World: A Handbook for World Intercession* is arranged in such a way as to facilitate intelligent daily prayer for the countries of the world. The *Global Prayer Digest* enables multiplied thousands of Christians to pray intelligently for some people groups every single day. And, most recently, Wesley Duewel has given us his book *Touch the World through Prayer*, in which he encourages and instructs us as to how we should pray for our world.[10]

If the above seems somewhat overwhelming, please note that even so it is no more than a sampling. There can be no question about it. The Lord of the Harvest has so ordered affairs that at this time of burgeoning population growth and shrinking geography, the church will not lose sight of what it would mean to evangelize the world in this generation.

THE LAST AGE OF MISSIONS?

Larry Keyes writes about this age as being "the last age of missions."[11] Ralph Winter implies as much when he divides modern missions history into three overlapping eras.[12] In the first era (1792–1910) the coastal lands of the non-Western world were reached. The second era (1865–1980) witnessed a concentration on the inland areas that had largely been overlooked in the first era. Now in the third era (1934–2000?) we are searching out "hidden peoples" and targeting them for gospel penetration.

As much as we might cogitate and attempt "to see the world as God sees it," we must admit that our understandings are limited. We do not really know more for certain than what he has chosen to reveal about the "times and seasons" and the Divine criteria for an "evangelized world." Other than that, the best information at our disposal contains both good and bad news.

The "Bad News" in World Evangelization

Keeping in mind the fact that differing sources espouse different definitions, statistics on world evangelization are not altogether encouraging.

First, although an update of *World Christian Encyclopedia* statistics indicates that the percentage of Christians in the world is relatively unchanged since 1900 (gradually decreasing from 34.4 percent in 1900 to 32.9 percent in 1987 and projected to rebound to 34 percent by the year 2000),[13] many analysts would say that these statistics are far too optimistic. Some estimates of the percentage in 2000 reach as low as 20–22 percent.

Second, although hard data is very difficult to come by and much depends on one's definition, it is estimated that there are as many as 16,750 unreached *and* hidden people groups in the world. Of course, if one adopts a definition that emphasizes no more than an understandable hearing of the gospel, that number is reduced significantly. Nevertheless, the number would run into the thousands. That this many linguistically and culturally different groupings of people still remain to be reached after two thousand years of Christian missions does seem to be a discouraging sign.

Third, the farther we press forward with our research, the more barriers we discover and the higher some of them seem to be. Many will remember the time when, in their attempt to get some portion of the Word of God into the language of the roughly 2 percent of the world's population that had none, Wycliffe Bible Translators announced that there were "two thousand tongues to go" and that 1985 would be the target date for the completion of the task. Subsequently it became clear that a more accurate count of remaining languages would be closer to three thousand. And, of course, 1985 has come and gone, and all the while between three and four thousand Wycliffe translators have faithfully labored on.

Fourth, while Christian missions strategy focuses on the cities, it is reliably reported that the church is losing people in the cities at the rate of one per second, or 86,400 new non-Christian urban dwellers every single day. The percentage of urban dwellers who are Christian has fallen from 68.8 percent in 1900 to 45.5 percent today.[14]

Fifth, at the very time when we are devoting unprecedented efforts to reach Muslims with the gospel, statistics reveal that Islam is growing at a faster pace than Christianity. In fact since 1970, Islam has been the world's fastest-growing major religion, followed by Hinduism and then Christianity and Buddhism. The percentages of increase between 1970 and 1987 are as follows: Islam–55 percent; Hinduism–41 percent; Christianity and Buddhism–35 percent. Assuredly, most of the growth in these other religions has been biological (i.e., by natural reproduction). Nevertheless, when we realize that as recently as two or three generations ago many experts predicted the gradual demise of non-Christian faiths such as these, their current vitality is indeed disconcerting from a missionary point of view.[15]

It is very questionable whether the church of Christ is well served when we close our eyes to information such as the foregoing. Rather, we should be grateful to those who bring it to our attention.

The "Good News" in World Evangelization

In terms of what the Scriptures prophesy, to many of us it seems that the good news in world evangelization outweighs the bad news by a significant margin.

First, the update of *World Christian Encyclopedia* referred to previously provides statistics indicating that the percentage of the world's population that is unevangelized (the gospel unoffered to it) is declining significantly (see chart 2.1).

Second, an article in *Missions Frontiers* exemplifies a widely shared upbeat attitude by posing a hypothetical scenario for the year 1991—a scenario that will portend a world-wide celebration in the year 2000 that will include all nations, tribes, and tongues. The 1991 scenario is as follows:

Chart 2.1[16]

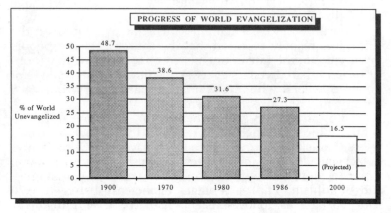

More information is available:

1. Global Mapping Project computerizes the data of all peoples.

2. World-wide network of Centers for World Mission expands from five to forty.

More missionaries are available:

1. The "Perspectives" course (a missions course offered through the Center) enrolls ten thousand new students per year in thirty-five countries.

2. Ten percent of "Perspectives" course enrollees become new missionaries.

More support has been forthcoming:

1. Every hidden people group is now "sponsored/adopted."

2. *Global Prayer Digest* sends out 750,000 copies monthly.

3. One million people are involved in Frontier Fellowships.[17]

Third, *Missionary News Service* reports:

> While some portion of the scriptures are available in almost 1,700 languages [now over 1,800], and some of these . . . languages also have Christian radio and TV, at least another 4,000 language groups have access to the gospel . . . through the spoken voice of a live person or a gospel recording. Gospel Recordings reports that . . . the gospel is now available on phonograph or cassette for missionary distribution in 4,386 languages.[18]

Fourth, students are sharing the vision for an evangelized world. Groups such as Theological Students for Frontier Missions and efforts such as the Caleb Project and the Joshua Project are making their mark on students by means of itinerant representatives, periodic conferences, and newsletters.

Fifth, the Christian and Missionary Alliance, the Evangelical Free Church, the Presbyterian Church of America, the Lutheran Church–Missouri Synod, the Southern Baptists, the Assemblies of God, and many other societies are committing large sums of money and numerous personnel to the planting of churches in world-class cities. Some of these programs have already paid off in terms of viable, gospel-propagating churches.

Finally, as we will see later, Third World churches are now getting involved in crosscultural mission in a most significant way.

"THIS GENERATION SHALL NOT PASS"

Our Lord said that the gospel would be preached in the whole world as a witness to all the *ethnē* and then the end would come (Matt. 24:14). He also said that there would be a generation that would not pass away until all that he had just prophesied had actually taken place (v. 34). We have already

considered some of the questions relating to these utter-
ances. But I have said nothing about the "generation [that]
shall not pass." Did he mean the same thing by it as Pierson,
Mott, and others meant when they talked about the "evangelization of the world in this generation"?

Some say that Jesus was referring to the time period
during which parents are succeeded by their children—
usually taken to be about thirty-three years. On this meaning
Jesus could have been referring to the generation of which he
and his disciples were a part, thus signifying that the
prophecies of the Olivet Discourse would all be fulfilled
within a few years. Of course, Evangelicals would not opt for
such an interpretation because, unless one strains the text
considerably, it would be tantamount to saying that Jesus
was mistaken. Many Evangelicals, however, interpret Jesus'
words to mean that toward the end of the age, events
(including world-wide proclamation of the gospel) will be so
accelerated that the generation that witnesses the beginning
of the final act of the age will also witness the final curtain.
This interpretation has problems, but it is a viable one.

A glance at the margin of many Bibles will reveal that
the Greek word usually translated "generation" (genea) in
Matthew 24:34 might also be translated "race." On that
reading, our Lord might well have been indicating that the
Jewish race would not be lost to history (despite the
diaspora) until all his prophecies for this age had been
fulfilled. On the basis of Romans 9–11 this seems to be the
most likely interpretation. If this is correct, the reemergence
of Israel as a nation-state and the world-wide attention being
focused on the Jewish people have profound significance for
world missions as we indicated previously.

Let each be persuaded in his or her own mind. Pierson
and Mott, of course, thought of generation as a time period,
and Mott, at least, recognized that a generation would be
somewhat different for every person depending on the time
of that person's birth. The point was that no believer can
reach either the preceding or succeeding generation, but that
every believer must take a share of the responsibility for
evangelizing his or her own generation. That cannot be
contested. It is a truism.

But Warneck's warning against superficiality must be
taken seriously. Our Lord's use of the words "preached" and
"witness" in Matthew 24 must be balanced with his use of

the words "disciple," "baptize," and "teach" in Matthew 28. Think for a moment of the implications for mission in the command to teach all that Christ has commanded. Paul not only proclaimed the gospel and witnessed to the lordship of Christ, he also established strategically located, viable churches that became the bases for extending the gospel in both space and time. And he continued to support those churches by prayer, instruction, and encouragement.

The fact is that though we know which generation is ours, we do not know which generation will be the last. The Scriptures teach us, and the Jewish presence in Israel may well remind us, that God's program for world evangelization cannot fail. With all that God has placed at our disposal, the generation that now lives could be evangelized and see the kingdom come in its fullness. Still we must admit that our understanding of all that is involved in world evangelization may not square entirely with God's understanding. Therefore we must continue to look to him for guidance in the task even as we look to him for grace to complete it.

It may seem odd to close this chapter with a reflection on a quotation from Naisbitt and Aburdene, but it seems wise to do so. These men wrote:

> Belief in vision is a radically new precept in business philosophy. It comes out of intuitive knowing; it says that logic is not everything, that it is not all in the numbers. The idea is simply that by envisioning the future you want, you can more easily achieve the goal. *Vision is the link between dream and action.*[19]

What should we see today when we envision the evangelized world of tomorrow? We should see gospel preaching of the kind that communicates so that men and women of the various people groups can make an intelligent decision for or against Christ.

What should we see? Churches among all people groups; churches composed of "living stones"; churches that will be the means of continued witness; churches that, imperfect now, will be a part of the perfected bride of Christ at his appearing—in this generation or one to follow.

One of the most exciting aspects of missions today, then, is that many of us clearly envision an evangelized world as composed of people groups that have received a meaningful hearing of the gospel of Christ and are accessible to a Bible-believing, Christ-exalting, evangelizing church. Therein lies the possibility and necessity of an all-important choice. First, we must choose to become involved at whatever level and in whatever way the Lord directs. Second, those who are directed to go to the missionary frontiers of our generation should choose to get preparation commensurate with a task as demanding as this. Willingness and dedication are necessary, but they are not enough. Faith and trust are essential, but still more is required: understanding, skill, and perseverence will be called for. *What we need is the kind of vision that links what we see with the right kind of action. Without that kind of vision, world evangelization by the year 2000 or even in a generation may remain little more than a dream.*

3

THE REACTIVE TREND—
THE CALL OF GOD AND
THE CRY OF THE WORLD

Missions are the eyes of the church focused on the wider world and the ears of the church attuned to its cries. Without its missions the church tends to become myopic and imbalanced, almost totally engrossed with what is near at hand.

There are exceptions but, generally speaking, it is the people of missions and their leadership who are aware of world concerns, world issues, and world trends *and are extremely responsive to them.* And, thanks to the media and our information society, missions people get the larger picture sooner and in greater depth than ever before.

Therein lies both a strength and a weakness of Christian missions today. Why? Because by their very nature missions react to what they see and hear in the world. And that is good, lest the church, like the priest and Levite, do no more than cast a glance at the wounded travelers of the world and pass by on the other side. But, on the negative side, it is possible for missions to become so sensitive to the world's problems—*and the world's solutions*—that they become little more than "world re-actors"! Why? Because men and women of mission are not back numbers as is often thought. They are front runners. In fact, they sometimes run too far in front! Marching into the world, they run the risk of losing cadence with the drumbeat of heaven and becoming removed from biblical mission. Unconsciously, or perhaps consciously, they risk picking up on the seductive rhythms of worldly tunes bewitchingly played by thousands of the world's self-appointed pied pipers. That, of course, is bad.

MISSIONS AS REACTIVE FORCES—THE DATA

Missions, as my colleague J. Herbert Kane often reminds his classes, constitute the single most magnanimous and altruistic enterprise the world has ever known. Inspired by the Great Physician, missionaries down through the centuries have gone into the world, have experienced its suffering in a new way, and have responded with a tremendous outpouring of selfless service. The approach of some missionaries may serve to reinforce the stereotype of the missionary as someone who preaches to souls with ears. But they are the exceptions. By and large, missionaries are more like Titus Johnson, the intrepid missionary to the Ubangi, who was so moved by pain and suffering that when he returned home, he went through medical school in order to return to the Ubangi as a physician of the body as well as a physician of the soul.

Now if we can imagine our way into Johnson's mind and heart when he first reached the Ubangi, it may be that we will better appreciate the dilemma that faces modern missionaries. Johnson first went to Africa in 1920 in response to Christ's command to take the gospel to the whole world. Once there, he was also moved by the cry of Africa for healing, health, and wholeness. He responded to that cry, as we all must if we are to be truly Christian.

How much tension these varied needs might have occasioned in Johnson's case we cannot be sure. But we can be sure that they have occasioned terrific tensions in contemporary missions: *the tension awakened by the call of God on the one hand and the cry of the world on the other.* Would to God these were always and everywhere the same. But they are not. We could also wish that there were one right way to respond. But since we all have differing gifts and opportunities, there is not.

The Foci of the Literature

Our analysis of strategy themes in 444 books reviewed in *Missiology* over the thirteen years of its publication (through 1986) highlights this tension (see Appendix 3).

Missionary Strategy Patterns
in 444 Missiology Book Reviews

Strategy Theme	Number of Books	Percentage
Socio-political Action		
1. Justice, liberation	70	15.8%
2. Relief from human suffering	6	1.4%
3. Urban, industrial missions	6	1.4%
Totals	82	18.6%
Evangelism and Church Growth		
1. Church planting, church growth	21	4.7%
2. Evangelism, witness	6	1.4%
Totals	27	6.1%

It must be remembered that *Missiology* is representative of the broad theological spectrum and therefore no more can be inferred from this than that, in regard to strategy and insofar as these book reviews might be representative, contemporary missiology is more taken up with the need for a more equitable world than for the evangelization strategies of traditional missions.

An analysis of major themes in the articles appearing in the *International Review of Missions* and the *Evangelical Missions Quarterly* over a twenty-one-year period also highlights the tension we have in mind (see below and Appendix 3).

These data require the following items of elaboration and interpretation.

First, it is obvious that both the Conciliar-oriented *IRM* and the Evangelical-oriented *EMQ* give considerable attention to the nature and objectives of missions.

Second, the former devotes over four times as much

attention to sociopolitical action than does the latter, and within that larger category it devotes far and away the greatest emphasis to political concerns (a growing emphasis over the years).

Missionary Strategy Patterns
in 949 Articles in the IRM *and 604 Articles in the* EMQ

Strategy Theme	Number of Articles and Percentages			
	IRM		EMQ	
Sociopolitical Action				
1. Justice, liberation	157	16.5%	6	1.0%
2. Urban, industrial missions	27	2.8%	7	1.2%
3. Development	25	2.8%	4	.7%
4. Relief, incl. medical	18	1.9%	8	1.3%
Totals	227	24.0%	25	4.2%
Evangelism and Church Growth				
1. Evangelism, witness	86	9.1%	42	7.0%
2. Church planting, church growth	17	1.9%	42	7.0%
Totals	103	11.0%	84	14.0%

Third, as concerns evangelism and church growth, the overall attention devoted to this area is about the same, but we should note that church extension as such receives but scant attention in the *IRM*. Also, in the *EMQ* articles witness is not always understood in the more traditional terms of preaching the gospel and aiming for conversion.

Fourth, there can be little doubt that relief (medicine, famine, crisis) occupies a much larger share of the missionary effort around the world than either the *IRM* or the *EMQ* figures (which tend to deal more with theory of mission) might indicate.

Fifth, it seems quite obvious that, insofar as the *IRM* and *EMQ* are representative, what we have termed the tension between the call of God and the cry of the world is very evident, and the ways in which this tension is resolved in modern missions are quite divergent.

The Involvements of Missionary Personnel

Data made available in the latest edition of the *Mission Handbook* generally corroborate the results of these content analysis studies, though with some interesting nuances that merit further reflection. When placed in four large categories, the distribution of missionary personnel by virtue of their involvement shows significant differences. As compared to the more Evangelical missions of the EFMA and IFMA (and nonassociated missions) the Conciliar missions of the DOM give considerably more attention to ministries other than church development. Moreover, in the DOM those involved in church development give much less attention to church planting—a task that is intimately associated with world evangelization.

Chart 3.1[1]

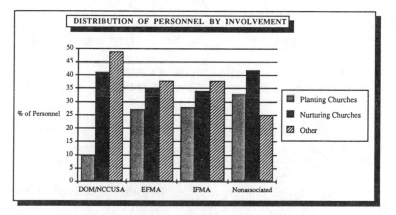

Movement Among Evangelicals?

Efiong S. Utuk, a Nigerian Presbyterian scholar, speaks of both Conciliarists and Evangelicals as coming to terms with our revolutionary age. Writing as a Conciliarist, he says:

> It must also be mentioned that the evangelical movement, consciously or unconsciously, has also come to terms with our revolutionary age. . . . The summoning of evangelical

congresses with representatives from different countries and from different sociopolitical contexts brought about a remarkable "revolution" in evangelical thought. We can see therefore, that the same nontheological factors that have affected the conciliar movement have, similarly, affected the evangelicals. Moreover, it cannot be denied that directly or indirectly the conciliar movement itself has had a determinative effect on the modification path the evangelical movement itself has taken since 1966. Conversely, the conciliar movement has had to recognize the presence of the evangelical movement since that same year.[2]

Notice that Utuk's conclusion is threefold. First, Conciliar *and* Evangelical change is significant enough to constitute a trend. Second, change has occurred as a reaction to nontheological factors in the world. Third, in the case of Evangelicals at least, the change may have come about *unconsciously*. (Notice also that he believes that Evangelicals have changed as a reaction to change in the Conciliar movement and that he does not say that the Conciliar movement has changed its position but only that it has had to "recognize the presence" of the Evangelical movement.) Using Utuk's understandings as a springboard, let's explore the reactive trend further.

THE REACTIVE TREND:
THE CONSCIOUS AND THOUGHT-OUT AGENDA
OF MISSIONS

"Missio Dei" Mission as a Part of the Reactive Trend

Due to the influence of the Bible institutes and the Student Volunteer Movement, the most common motivation for mission at the beginning of this century had to do with the conversion of pagan peoples. Before we arrived at the middle of the century, however, that motivation had been augmented (and in some cases superceded) by a concern for church development in foreign lands. Then at the Willingen Conference of the International Missionary Council in 1952 a change came about that some have called a "Copernican revolution in missions." An ancient term that was used in connection with the old Trinitarian discussions was revived and related to mission. That term was *missio Dei* and the intent was to turn from a conception of mission that centered in people and church (e.g., "our mission" and "the church's mission") to the triune God himself (therefore, "God's mission" and "the mission of Father, Son, and Holy Spirit"). Obviously, something was to be gained in this shift of emphasis. *But as conceived at Willingen* missio Dei *mission greatly expanded the task.* Perhaps Karl Hartenstein best summed up that understanding when he said:

> Mission is not only the conversion of individuals, it is not only obedience to a word of the Lord, it is not only the obligation to gather the congregation; it is participation in the sending of the Son, the *mission Dei,* with the all-embracing aim of establishing the Lordship of Christ over the whole redeemed creation.[3]

It took time for the full import of such an all-embracing interpretation of mission to take shape and gain acceptance in World Council circles. However, thanks to the writings of J. C. Hoekendijk (e.g., *The Church Inside Out*)[4] and others, this *missio Dei* understanding came to prevail. By 1968 when the WCC met in Uppsala, Sweden, for its Fourth Assembly, the theme was "Behold I make all things new"—a theme that reflected the new understanding. There—and subsequently—the cry of the world had an increasingly profound effect on the WCC interpretation of mission, an interpretation that is perhaps best understood in terms of several succinct statements.

1. *"The world sets the agenda."* For the "front runners" gathered in Uppsala, *missio Dei* involved a Trinitarian approach to mission, not solely a christological one. It is the essence of God the Father throughout history always to act in his Son and through his Spirit. Everywhere and always—in the church and outside the church—he is working out his purpose. Creation and redemption cannot be divided. God creates even saving faith outside the church and without the intervention of the church. The church is no more and nothing less than a community that understands God's purpose in history, reads the signs of his working, and then witnesses to those signs by word and deed participation. A part of that participation will be the preaching of the gospel. But the context of God's working is always history, and therefore it is essential that the believing community read contemporary signs correctly in order to participate meaningfully. As for the missions themselves (i.e., the agencies), they are transitory forms of obedience to the *missio Dei.*

No wonder Donald McGavran's plea "What about the two billion?" (a reference to the two billion unreached people then estimated to be in the world) largely fell on deaf ears at Uppsala. When God is always and everywhere at work even in the creation of saving faith, McGavran's question is not a primary one. A much more important consideration is revealed in one of the slogans that was widely used with reference to Uppsala—"the world's agenda, our business." Since two billion unreached people were not high on the world's agenda, they were not high on the WCC Uppsala agenda either!

Almost twenty years later, in 1986, two seemingly unconnected events furnished two more in a long line of illustrations of the world's concerns overriding other considerations in the determination of the church's agenda. First, his concern for peace prompted Pope John Paul to gather representatives of twelve major religions of the world on October 27, 1986, in Assisi, Italy (highly symbolic from a missionary point of view), to pray for world peace. Second, the former General Secretary of the WCC, Philip Potter, accepted the 1986 Peace Prize (twenty million yen or over $100,000) from the Rissho Koseikai, an aggressively propagating Buddhist organization in Japan. As patently desirable as world peace certainly is, difficult questions remain to be answered in cases such as these. Foremost among them is the missionary question.

2. *"The world provides the definitions."* The theme of a subsequent CWME meeting in Bangkok in 1973 was "Salvation Today." A cassette recording that was circulated as part of the preparation for that meeting contained definitions of the word *salvation* as it would be understood by people of different cultures and religions when translated into their respective languages. The idea was to discover the point at which a meaning common to the various cultures could be found.

Just before the meeting, one entire issue of the *International Review of Mission* was devoted to the "Salvation Today" theme in order to emphasize "the widest possible variety of expression in terms of contemporary experience." In that issue George Johnston asked, "Should the Church still talk about salvation?" and concluded that the word *salvation* is expendable, but what is not expendable is "the belief in God's . . . justice, mercy and love; and the implications of such beliefs . . . for the assurance that a meaningful life is possible provided people become truly human, truly men as God intends."[5] Masao Takenaka wrote, "We recognize increasingly today the immense value of grasping the meaning of salvation in connection with the process of humanization."[6]

This time it was the German missiologist Peter Beyerhaus who pleaded for a Bible-based approach to the subject of salvation, but to no avail.

3. *"The world constitutes the context for doing theology."* This can best be understood with reference to liberation theology. In his book *Liberation Theology* the Roman Catholic Gustavo Gutierrez, for example, proposes that the starting point for "doing theology" today is not so much to be found in the study of the Bible or the creeds of the church, but in participation in the struggle for justice on the part of the masses in the marketplace.[7] This does not mean that attention is not to be given to the Bible. Gutierrez, in fact, has over four hundred Scripture references in his book. What it means is that the Bible is valued for the way in which it reinforces the liberation and humanization theme. The Exodus is important because it is a kind of prototype of liberation. The Old Testament prophets are often referred to because they received and delivered their message (on justice, of course) in the marketplace. Jesus' ministry of liberation to the poor, downtrodden, and forgotten is highlighted, while his ministry of redeeming man from sin and reconciling man to God is downplayed. The Bible indeed is important in this view, *but its significance must be discovered in the context of contemporary concerns.* And the tendency is to interpret that context in the light of a Marxist analysis of the human predicament rather than in the light of a biblical analysis. As for the quoting of Scripture, we must not forget that the naturalist philosopher Thomas Hobbes also quoted the Bible extensively.

4. *"The world mediates God's Word."* Some years ago I attended a conference of mission leaders in which the speakers repeatedly urged their hearers to discover what God is saying and doing in the world and to join him in the saying and doing. During the final forum Emilio Castro, later to become General Secretary of the WCC, was asked how one is to discover what God is saying and doing in the world. With but slight hesitation he responded, "Listen to

what the poor of the world are saying and watch what they are doing. God is always on the side of the poor."

Given that approach, it is not surprising that at that same conference one seminarian stood to his feet and announced to the attendees that as a result of the gathering the direction of his life had been changed. Previously he had thought that God was calling him to go somewhere in the world and urge people to believe in Christ. Now he was persuaded that his mission was to stay in the United States and do everything possible to destroy the multinational corporations!

Neither is it surprising that in 1970 the WCC allocated its first grants to nineteen antiracist organizations and that there are recurring reports to the effect that it has subsequently provided *mission monies* to a variety of revolutionary causes in Third World countries.

Nor is it surprising that WCC spokesmen loudly denounce U.S. foreign policy while soft-pedaling criticism of the policies and practices of Marxist governments—a posture that has repeatedly been noted in the annual meetings of member communions.

Of course, not all Ecumenist leaders, Protestant or Catholic, are in agreement with this approach and these activities. Pope John Paul himself has found it necessary to come down rather hard on liberation theologians. Nor do all subscribe to the *missio Dei* approach as defined by Hartenstein. But, though not necessitated by a *missio Dei* understanding of mission, the above approach is quite clearly consistent with the very broad view of mission that it sets forth.

Missio Christus *and the Cry of the World*

Traditionally, mission has been seen as growing out of the person and work of Christ in the world, though Father, Son, and Holy Spirit are, of course, directly involved. Christ's coming, his cross, his commission—these have furnished the incentive, the message, and the agenda for missions. In short, we might say that *missio Christus* rather than *missio Dei* (in the WCC understanding) has been the focus. And it is fair to say that this remains the primary focus of most Evangelical mission leaders today.

Of course, this does not answer all the questions and solve all problems. The very fact that Evangelical "front runners" sometimes disagree with each other and sometimes change their own position *may* signal a tendency to interpret Christ's commission in accordance with the Ecumenical or other understandings. For this very reason, "ordinary" believers must exercise their priesthood and, like those early Bereans, search the Scriptures for themselves. However, we repeat that, far from the caricature often drawn, conservative Evangelicals have usually responded to Christ's command to love their neighbors of the world, not only to his commission to disciple them. Various types of data support this contention.

1. *The cry of the world for food, medicine, education, development.* Evangelicals continue to respond to the cry of the world for food, medicine, education, and development on an unprecedented scale. Such well-known agencies as Medical Assistance Program; World Vision International; Compassion International; World Concern; the Samaritan's Purse; Food for the Hungry; Steers, Inc.; Farms, Inc.; and many others have been initiated by Evangelicals. The NAE has its own relief arm—World Relief Corporation. The vast majority of Evangelical missions have educational, relief, and/or developmental programs. When news of a famine in Ethiopia or Burkina Faso reaches Evangelical ears, there will be an immediate and positive response. And, on the part of leadership at least, this response is not mindless compassion. There is an awareness that locals must be enabled to produce what is necessary to supply local needs, for example. Development programs have therefore become commonplace. Especially since Lausanne in 1974, the emphasis on the relationship between social action and evangelism has increased among Evangelicals. Jon Bonk and Ronald J. Sider have called for careful stewardship by Western Christians in this age of need and hunger.

Souls with ears? Hardly. Evangelicals see men and women as whole persons. C. Peter Wagner calls attention to one EFMA-related mission that published a list of personnel needs. Of fifty categories, only two related to evangelism, both of which focused on youth evangelism. Categories included were agronomy, music teaching, nursing, and ecology, among others.[8]

Some years ago I visited a typical Evangelical mission in the heart of Africa. The mission had been there for over half a century and had fifty missionaries scattered throughout some eight or nine stations. In the course of my survey I categorized the personnel according to their assignments and found that all but three or four of them were primarily engaged in educational and medical ministries. Only two had evangelism and church planting as their primary task! The challenge faced by that mission was to translate its stated priority into actuality! Not a few Evangelical missions face the same challenge.

2. *The cry for justice and peace.* Paralleling the increased involvement of conservative leaders in United States politics which is noted by Snyder and Runyon,[9] missions people have also become increasingly concerned and involved in the cry for justice and peace. Michael Cassidy and others in African Enterprise have brought black, white, and colored Christians of South Africa together to face apartheid head-on. After writing *Serving Our Generation,*[10] Waldron Scott left his post as executive director of the World Evangelical Fellowship to found Holistic Mission International. Both Harvie Conn in his *Evangelism: Doing Justice and Preaching Grace,*[11] and Miriam Adeney in her book *God's Foreign Policy*[12] relate God's concern for the poor and disenfranchised and the mission of the church. During the past decade the *EMQ* has given space to women's concerns (see Appendix 2). The role of woman in missions—always a significant one—is being redefined and enlarged. The writings of people such as Jim Wallis and the pronouncements of groups such as the Radical Discipleship Group have been accorded a wide hearing.

3. *Sensitivity to trends.* Evangelical missions are very sensitive to data on world trends of every type. When population experts pointed out that the world's population will have more than doubled in the last half of this century (from 2.5 billion to 6.1 billion as updated in *USA Today*),[13] population statistics and graphs, and their import for world evangelization, became common fare in mission publications of all kinds. When it was noted that our world is rapidly becoming an urban world and it was projected that there would be at least ten cities with populations of over 13 million by the year 2000, the LCWE appointed Ray Bakke to lead an Evangelical response to the challenge; significant attention was given to David B. Barrett's *World-Class Cities and World Evangelization;*[14] and scores of missions adjusted their strategy in response to the urbanization trend. Increas-

ingly the focus of modern missions strategy is on the city rather than the bush country and the jungle. When it became apparent that legal immigration to the United States was increasing dramatically (570,000 in 1985 according to *Insight*),[15] Evangelicals began to organize conferences and consultations around the challenge posed by ethnic America. The EFMA's annual executives' study retreat in 1986 studied world and church trends in order to decide what steps to take to get ready for the 1990s. Futurist Tom Sine has been featured at recent mission meetings. Evangelicals are among the most avid readers of such books as *Future Shock*,[16] *Megatrends*,[17] and *The Re-invented Corporation*.[18]

4. *A rethinking of mission.* The challenges of world inequities and the Ecumenical summons to respond to them has evoked a rethinking of mission on the part of many Evangelicals. Although it must be admitted that few Evangelicals carefully analyzed the implications of the *missio Dei* understanding of mission as espoused by many in the WCC orbit, some leading spokesmen translated those implications into *missio Christus* terms and influenced many to rethink their position.

In this connection, though others could be cited, Utuk points especially to John R. W. Stott's new view and his part in the framing of the Lausanne Covenant.[19] Writing in 1975, Stott professed to have undergone a significant change of view. Whereas formerly he thought the Matthew 28 statement of the Great Commission to be primary, he now felt that the simple John 20:21 statement "As the Father sent me, so send I you" should take precedence *because it makes Jesus' mission and ministry a model for our own.* From that point it was a small step for Stott to go back to the fact that Jesus fed the hungry, healed the sick, comforted the downtrodden, and raised the dead and conclude that therefore evangelization and sociopolitical action are partners in mission with the former having a certain priority.[20] Although the *missio Christus* orientation of Stott's missiology is still obvious, the change in direction is evident and will be considered again later in this chapter.

5. *Kingdom-of-God theology.* Closely allied to the previous point is the new emphasis on kingdom-of-God theology among Evangelicals. Except with reference to passages like John 3:3–5, Evangelicals did not, until the 1980s, tend to emphasize this concept. The dramatic increase in the number

of articles on the subject listed in *Religious Index One*[21] and its ranking as number five out of twenty-eight major trends in the church[22] probably reflects Evangelical interest as much as anything. Howard Snyder, Richard Lovelace, Arthur Glasser, and others have put great emphasis on the kingdom of God in recent years. And the Pentecostal Paul Pomerville has written that kingdom theology clarifies the role of the Spirit in mission and reinforces a Trinitarian view of mission.[23] Of course, the implications of this are somewhat different, depending on whom one asks, but that it has reflected a renewed interest in sociopolitical involvement is beyond question. (We will deal with other implications in chapter 10.)

THE REACTIVE TREND:
THE "UNTHOUGHT-OUT" AGENDA IN MISSIONS

It probably cannot be demonstrated to everyone's satisfaction, but missions also react to the agenda of the world in ways that are less consciously thought through. Evangelicals may be especially susceptible to this temptation. More attention is actually given to the theory and theology of mission in the major articles of the *IRM* than is the case in the *EMQ* (18.2 percent as compared to 14.4 percent; see Appendix 2). It may well be that Evangelicals are taking too much for granted. But Ecumenists are not exempt from blindspots. Although our focus here will be on the unthought-out agenda of Evangelical missions, it should be pointed out that the Ecumenical response to injustice especially is often naïve and shortsighted.

The Ecumenical Reaction to Injustice

Perhaps the most flagrantly mistaken "unthought-out" Ecumenical reaction to the cries of the world has to do with the Ecumenists' denunciation of injustices and dehumanizing forces in the Free World on the one hand, and their soft-pedaling of what is happening in Marxist societies on the other. Ask the highest-placed representatives about this and you will probably receive the same kind of answer that I have: "In the Free World we take advantage of a free press. In closed societies we must go about it in another way." If we accept this answer at all, it must be judged as woefully inadequate in view of the impact of the press on *world* opinion. Frustration at this point recently caused Representative Hal Daub, a staunch Presbyterian, to issue a dramatic appeal to the 1986 General Assembly of the Presbyterian Church (U.S.A.) "to restore political and ideological balance to the denomination's statements" and not to "neglect our spiritual needs for the sake of a political debate." [24]

Evangelical Missions and Their "Unconscious Agenda"

Though not ideologically committed to the world's agenda, Evangelicals are liable to follow it unwittingly. Could the following items by instances of this?

1. Geographically, Evangelical missions interest tends to follow the focus of the secular press and its reports of world events. Immediately after World War II when the eyes of the world were focused on war-ravaged and occupied areas, Europe became an option for missions in a new way, and countries like Japan, Korea, and the Philippines were at the center of the mission stage. New missions such as the Greater Europe Mission, the Far Eastern Gospel Crusade (now SEND International), the Japan Evangelical Mission (now merged with TEAM), and others enjoyed instant prominence and support.

With the onset of the oil crisis, the precipitous state of affairs in the Middle East, and Arab immigration, Muslim missions came to prominence in the middle 1970s. Articles on Muslim missions began to appear with increasing frequency, especially in Evangelical literature. (Islam has been prominent in Conciliar publications over a much longer period of time.) Since 1965 over twice as many *EMQ* articles have focused on Islam as have focused on all other major religions (including animism) put together (sixteen as opposed to seven, the majority coming after 1978; see Appendix 2). The imbalance is even greater in the case of the *IRM*, but the articles are more evenly scattered over the entire time period (see Appendix 2). Numerous books on Islam have also appeared. Seventeen books dealing with Islam have been reviewed in *Missiology* as compared to ten on animism, seven on Buddhism, two each on Hinduism and Confucianism, and one each on Shintoism and Taoism (see Appendix 3). In addition, study conferences on ways of reaching Muslims have become popular; classes on Islam that had gone begging for students suddenly have been filled to overflowing; missions that had gone begging for candidates for Muslim areas have begun to receive more and more volunteers.

Few would argue with the assessment that it is about time that missions to Muslims have their place in the sun. But when the headlines in a missions periodical reads, "Muslims are Wide Open to the Gospel," we need to pause and reflect. Some are, but many are not. To mislead volunteers is to court disaster.

2. Missions personnel tend to adopt the values of the larger society. This trend in the larger church is noted by Snyder and Runyon.[25] There are numerous illustrations of it in missions. One example is the anti-institutional bias that was so evident in the 1960s and early 1970s. Those who were teaching missions in our Bible colleges, and especially, our seminaries during those years can testify to the widespread disinterest in church-planting missions. A survey circulated at a large missionary convention listed dozens of types of potential mission involvement but omitted church planting as an option for candidates! The chapter on "Major Functional Ministries in Mission" in the tenth edition of the *Mission Handbook* (published in 1973) began with a section on "aid and relief" and did not even include a section on the planting of churches.[26]

About the middle of the 1970s or shortly thereafter, church planting once again came into the fore, and since that time the number of field missionaries engaged in church planting has slowly but steadily increased. A comparison of statistics on the deployment of American missionaries in 1975 and 1985 reflect this upswing of interest.[27]

It could be cogently argued that the relative disinterest in church-planting mission so evident a decade and a half ago was the direct result of the anti-institutional bias so prevalent in North American society at that time and that the increased interest since that time reflects a softening of institutional bias and an increased interest in world evangelization as I have described it in chapter 2. (At the same time, between 1979 and 1985 there was decreased involvement in nurturing existing churches and increased involvement in "other ministries." This may indicate that Evangelicals are demonstrating heightened interest in sociopolitical involvement simultaneously with evangelization in the 1980s.)

Another illustration of this trend of adopting cultural values in contemporary mission may be the growing preoccupation with self-fulfillment. After man had been reduced to a machine at worst and an animal at best, the postwar psychology of Abraham Maslow and others made man "human"again, though not in the biblical sense, of course. Self-actualization, self-fulfillment, self-worth, self-esteem— these became the key concepts contributing to a meaningful existence. Ultimately, Naisbitt and Aburdene concluded that even work itself had been "re-invented." They wrote, "There is a new ideal about work emerging in America today. For the first time, there is widespread expectation that work should be fulfilling—that work should be fun."[28] Whether work has been "re-invented" or not is open to question. Karl Marx proposed a very similar statement about work a century ago! But there can be no question that a radically different self-oriented assessment has become common, even in missions.

Chart 3.2

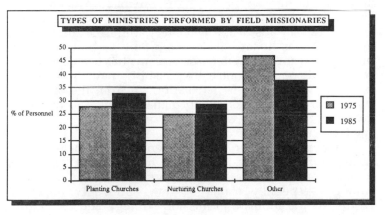

A thoughtful analysis of the trend toward short-term service (presently there are almost 28,000 short-termers from North America alone, representing some 41 percent of the total number of overseas workers and their rate of increase greatly outstrips that of career missionaries)[29] may well reveal that this phenomenon results from the new approaches to self-fulfillment and to the nature of work itself. That it does not result from mission effectiveness is obvious in most cases. *Exceptions there are, but the consensus is that the*

benefits of short-term service accrue more to the missionary than to the nationals. (The same conclusion has been responsibly voiced in relation to the Peace Corps.) Most missions validate their short-term program on the number of career candidates that are forthcoming from the short-term ranks rather than on the basis of field results. As a matter of fact, some missions are now limiting the percentage of their total force that can be short-term. And, as we have seen, more and more short-termers now gravitate toward missions like Youth With a Mission and Teen Missions, International— missions that are programmed to serve and deploy them.

However one might evaluate the trend to short-term missions, any analysis that does not relate it to the larger reactive trend in missions will fall short. *Ideas of self-worth and fulfillment have their positive side of course. But divorced from biblical understandings of depravity, cross-bearing, and self-denial, they will prove to be deadly foes of missions.*

Still another example of the adoption of world values may well be the recent emphasis on mission teams of all kinds. True, Paul was the leader of a mission team. But in its *modus operandi* his team was very different from many mission teams today. It is important to note that the prominence now given to mission teams has been concurrent with a phenomenon noted by Naisbitt—namely, that "the small-group structure is percolating up from the office and shop floor to the ranks of top management. . . . In the re-invented corporation, we are exploring the idea of the CEO chief executive officer as a team. . . ."[30]

In mentioning this, I do not intend to argue against team strategy and certainly not against international teams and cooperation in missions. But before concluding that team strategy—especially teams of one nationality or ethnic group—is the ultimate in mission strategy and committing an imbalanced investment in it, it may be well to analyze its weaknesses as well as its strengths and be patient enough to test its track record. A number of "end-all strategies" such as mass evangelistic crusades (evangelism-in-breadth!), Evan-gelism-In-Depth, and Theological Education by Extension have taken more proper places as partial answers to world evangelization in recent years.

Finally, the most arresting example of adopting the values of the larger society may be the success orientation of missions. Twenty-five years ago J. I. Packer wrote, "The way to tell whether in fact you are evangelizing is not to ask whether conversions are known to have resulted from your witness. It is to ask whether you are faithfully making known the gospel message."[31]

Theoretically, Evangelicals believe that. But practically, success is what is used to "sell" missions in many instances. It is for this reason that the bandwagon appeals, inflated numbers, and one-sided reporting noted in the preface are so prevalent in the promotion of missions today.

3. Evangelicals often tend to utilize the findings of the social sciences quite uncritically. It could be argued, for example, that as the science of missions has developed, missiologists have tended to apply social science principles and ideas without *first* subjecting them to the judgment of Scripture. To take an example elaborated elsewhere in this book, it is an open question as to whether "people group," "homogeneous unit," "group decision," and related notions in modern church growth theory were objectively analyzed in the light of Scripture early on. Be that as it may, it is almost certain that most participants at the Congress on World Evangelization at Pattaya in 1980 did not really evaluate the basic claim that when they looked at the world as composed of "people groups," they were "seeing the world as God sees it." This claim was based on the idea that *ethnē* in the Great Commission really means people groups rather than Gentiles. As I have said, various Evangelical scholars have concluded that that may not be the case at all. In one sense it is not important whether it does mean that or not, because people-group strategizing is good strategizing. In another sense it is a very important point, because the Bible can be made to say most anything if we insist on reading our meanings into its words.

4. Finally, there is a tendency among Evangelicals to overreact to the conclusions of Conciliarists and Ecumenists. Initial reactions are usually negative. Later reactions are often positive. Liberalism, after all, does not make a large number of converts from the world. Most of its converts are made from the more conservative sections of the Christian church and as the results of a liberalizing process.

It may be that Utuk's conclusion that Evangelicals have consciously *or* unconsciously responded to world events and the Ecumenical movement by changing their position so as to make sociopolitical action an essential part of mission should be modified. More than likely, the response has been both conscious *and* unconscious. There can be little doubt that those who framed the Lausanne Covenant *consciously* substituted a statement that the Bible is "without error in all that it affirms" and the "infallible rule of faith and practice" for the Wheaton Declaration statement that the Bible is "the inspired, the only authoritative, inerrant Word of God." The Lausanne affirmation is still an excellent one, but it does leave room for a wider interpretation.

Likewise, there can be no doubt that they had Uppsala and Bangkok and other Ecumenical discussions and documents in mind, not only when they affirmed that "reconciliation with man is not reconciliation with God, nor is social action evangelism, nor is political liberation salvation," but also when they decided on the statement that "evangelism and social action are both part of our Christian duty." It is doubtful, however, that the majority of those who signed the Covenant (2,000 out of 2,700 attendees; 50 percent from the Third World) were conscious of the nuances and implications of this way of uniting evangelism and social action. Utuk's conclusions may be more nearly correct than some Evangelicals would like to think.

"YOU CAN'T STEP INTO THE SAME RIVER TWICE"

The ancient Greek philosopher Heraclitus concluded that "you can't step into the same river twice." Everything in the world being in a state of flux, the river itself has changed before you can step into it the second time. Nothing in the world is so certain as change. One must look to God, his Christ, and his Word to find that which is permanent and unchanging.

The challenge to missions, then, is to keep abreast of a changing world while still embracing the eternal written and living Word. At the very least, that challenge has three aspects.

Missions Must Value Perspicuity

It seems presumptuous to say that people of missions must value clear thinking, but astute Christian observers have noted the confusion that pervades much of church life today.[32] Mission requires a special blend of mind and heart.

When Jesus first sent out his disciples, he charged them to be "shrewd as serpents, and innocent as doves" (Matt. 10:16).

Those who, unlike Christ himself, question the full authority of Scripture, run the very real risk of sacrificing mission on the world's altars. The lostness of humanity, the necessity of conversion, the importance of extending the church, even the uniqueness of Christ—one by one the essentials of mission and even of the faith itself tend to go by the board. After two days of lectures, discussions, and reports at an annual meeting of the North American Academy of Ecumenists several years ago, one participant made a confession that was not at all out of keeping with the tenor of the meeting. He said, "To be brutally honest, I am tempted to give up my Christian faith entirely. But I don't really feel comfortable in doing so." The theme of the meeting had to do with Christian evangelism!

Those who stoutly and steadfastly subscribe to biblical authority are not necessarily out of the woods. Evangelicals have no easy time in keeping head and heart together in mission. No other area of church life is so wedded to enthusiasm, feelings, commitment to the cause, the ability to motivate others, and activism as missions. No other church workers—be they evangelists, pastors, teachers, counselors, or musicians—are recruited in the same way or with the same vigor as are missionaries. No other Christian enterprise is promoted with exactly the same kind of appeal. Those connected with Evangelical missions must consciously choose to love God with heart, strength, *and mind* and to serve Christ and the world accordingly.

Missions Must Establish Priorities

Let it be completely clear: *missio Dei* with its emphases on the action of the triune God in mission and the concern of God for the whole of creation is a positive gain when kept within the framework of Scripture. And as for kingdom-of-God theology, Jesus himself said that it would be preached in all the world as a witness to the nations (Matt. 24:14). The primary meaning of kingdom (*malkuth* in the Old Testament, and *basileia* in the New), after all, has to do with kingship, lordship, and authority rather than with this or that particular expression of God's kingship in time and space.

The Ecumenists' problem in this connection is that they tend to forget that Satan is the god of *this age*; that Jesus said in his Olivet Discourse that wars, pestilence, famine, and the like will characterize this entire age until his reappearing; that our Lord himself invaded a time and a society pervaded by injustice and left behind that same society now facing disaster; that when James warned the rich because of their unjust practices, he urged their believing victims to be "patient . . . until the coming of the Lord" (James 5:7); and that the Old Testament law said, "You shall not be partial to the poor nor defer to the great" (Lev. 19:15). Their problem is that in their passion to realize the peace and justice of God in the world, they tend to forget that God must be recognized, believed in, and worshiped by his creation because of his intrinsic nature as God and not for extrinsic blessings he affords the world. Their problem is that in their impatience to achieve peace, they forget that the sovereign God who makes the wrath of Midianite and Maoist to praise him (Ps. 76:10) does not thereby exonerate either of them. In short, they tend to forget that unless people repent and become converted, *they will never see the kingdom—at least not from within*!

A comparison of Isaiah's prophecy in Isaiah 61:1–2 and our Lord's use of that prophecy in his home town of Nazareth (Luke 4:18–19) reveals God's intentions toward the *spiritually impoverished* ("afflicted," "humble," "poor"), the *physically incapacitated* ("blind"), and the *sociopolitically disenfranchised* ("prisoners," "downtrodden"). Whether or not one interprets this passage in precisely this way, it is apparent from Christ's subsequent ministry that our Lord Jesus had a heart for men and women in all three of these conditions. Ecmumenists, however, have tended to confuse priorities here or at least to erase distinctions. To their credit, Evangelicals have not only retained a priority for ministry to the spiritual needs of mankind, but in their best moments have seen that it is much more difficult to know how best to minister to peoples' physical and sociopolitical needs. Also, they have retained a place for divine judgment—"to proclaim . . . the day of vengeance of our God" (Isa. 61:2).

Quite often the Evangelicals' problem is that they do not want to interpret the Christian mission in such a way that they appear to be indifferent to the cry of the world while being obedient to the call of God. As a result, biblical priorities may become confused in their attempt to define and describe the Christian mission.

Precisely this may be occurring in John Stott's more recent understanding of mission—at any rate, in the way he explains it. He makes it clear that, while making evangelism and sociopolitical action partners in mission, he wants to preserve a priority for evangelism. This, of course, is not easy to do. But it is clear that Stott's concern for social involvement has not resulted in a lessening of concern for evangelism. Nevertheless, a significant problem attends his definition of mission when he concludes that " 'Mission' describes . . . everything the church is sent into the world to do."[33] Not only does this definition fail to clear up the priority question, it also places an unintended but special burden on the missionary. How so?

As is well known, the words *mission* and *missionary* are not in the New Testament. They come to us through the Latin *mitto* from the Greek *apostello* ("to send"). The trouble with defining mission as everything the church is sent to do is that we naturally link "mission" with the missionary. Asked to link the word *mission* with the word that most closely resembles it in a list of biblical designations for church leaders and members, people will link "mission" with "missionary" immediately:

Mission → Missionary ("apostle" in the NT)

Prophet

Evangelist

Pastor-teacher

Elder

Deacon

Believer-priest

There are two consequences of this. First, the thorny issue of priority in mission remains unresolved. Second, the missionary is immediately charged with the responsibility of doing everything.

Now we know that evangelists are evangelists because they have a special task to carry out. Likewise, pastor-teachers, and so on. But when we link "mission" ("everything the church is sent into the world to do") with the "missionary" only, or even primarily, we obscure the special task given to the missionary. Moreover, we may frustrate our missionaries because they work under foreign governments that may curtail what they can do and they work in situations where the needs are often overwhelming. We may not intend this, but that does not change the result. The English language has played a trick on us!

It would be well if, instead of using the word *mission* to describe all that the church is sent into the world to do, we would use a word like *task* instead. Or, if instead of using the word *missionary* we would use the New Testament word *apostle* just as we use the New Testament words *prophet* and *evangelist*. But that is wishful thinking. In any case, let us not allow terminological confusion to undermine the primary task of sending missionaries into all the world to do precisely what the first missionaries did—evangelize and gather believers into local congregations where they can be taught the ways and words of Christ. *That is their specialized task. Whatever else they do by way of doing good to all people (Gal. 6:10), they do, not because they are missionaries, but because they are Christians and belong to the larger church of Christ!*

Missions Must Become Proactive

At a recent meeting of EFMA mission leaders mentioned above, Ted Ward challenged them to become *proactive*, not just *reactive*. By that he meant that they should think ahead to see where the world is going and make their plans accordingly. That is a large order. No one really knows what the world will be like a generation from now or even a decade from now. But Ward was right. World trends are pointers of what the world may be like in the future, if not proofs of what it will be like. And there are those prophesies given by Jesus that are so often discussed but often neglected when we start laying plans for the future! Alternative scenarios for the future can be laid out, and corresponding strategies discussed.

By way of example, had missions been more proactive a generation or more ago, they might have given much more attention to strategies for reaching world-class cities. Although the reaching of rural populations and remote tribes was a legitimate concern then as now, it has long been apparent to futurologists that cities with massive concentrations of people and sociopolitical power will characterize the world of tomorrow.

In regard to the future, mission leaders of today should be responding to a scenario in which AIDS devastates significant segments of the population. This is especially so in the case of missions to Africa because, on the basis of current epidemiological data, some experts predict that 25 percent of the population of that continent will die of AIDS within a decade.[34]

Again, both world trends and Scripture seem to indicate that tomorrow's world will be less free than the world of today (see chapter 10). If so, major adjustments in missionary strategy will be required because most contemporary strategy is based on freedom of speech and worship. What adjustments? To answer that question meaningfully is to be proactive.

OIKOUMENĒ, KOSMOS, AND AIŌN

The word *ecumenical* comes from the Greek word *oikoumenē*. The Greek word, of course, has a long history. It was used by Herodotus. It means "the land where people dwell" or "the inhabited earth." It likely had reference to the Greek, Roman, and then the Mediterranean worlds. It has not been a significant word in the church throughout history. But it was used in the Oxford (1937) conference to join the ideas of unity and mission, and it has come to be widely used since that time. The Methodist historian of church and mission, Cecil Northcott, once said in my hearing that the word *ecumenical* will eventually replace such words as Catholic, Protestant, Orthodox, Baptist, Methodist, universal, and so on as *the single word* identifying the church in the world.

Oikoumenē is used only fifteen times in the New Testament (eight times in Luke-Acts), and in none of these instances is it used as a modifier of the church. That, of course, does not mean it is disqualified from such usage. After all, to the chagrin of many, modifying words such as Catholic, Protestant, Charismatic, Baptist, and Presbyterian are not used in the Bible either—at least, they are not used in the way we use them. But the inhabited world is certainly where the "church militant" is to be found and constitutes the sphere in which our mission is to be carried out.

It is most likely that the word *kosmos* ("cosmos") comes from *kosmeō*, which means "to put in proper order" or "to decorate." It is used quite widely in contemporary theology and missiology to call attention to the breadth of God's workings in the universe and (sometimes) the "suprahistorical" such as might be the case when reference is made to the "cosmic Christ." The word is widely used in the New Testament. It is used in ways that recognize that the world and its peoples have been created—"put in order"—by God and are the objects of his love and provision in the sending of his Son (John 3:16) and need to know of that provision (Rom. 1:8). But it is also used in ways that recognize that the world is askew and "off its true Center"—having been "put out of order" by the entrance of sin and therefore transcient and passing. It is with that in mind that John exhorts believers not to love the world or the things that are in the world (1 John 2:15). Faithfulness and fruitfulness in mission require that we do not confuse these "two worlds."

Aiōn is translated properly as an "age," but also by implication as the "world" and, by extension, as "the ages." So there is something of temporality *and* eternality in the word, depending on how it is used. Paul warns believers that Satan is the "god of this age" (2 Cor. 4:4), that the wisdom of this age is foolishness with God (1 Cor. 1:20), and that we are to be delivered from "this present evil age" (Gal. 1:4). But this age of blindness and unbelief will give way to a far different state of affairs. So Paul writes:

> Now to Him who is able to do exceeding abundantly beyond all that we ask or think, according to the power that works within us, to Him be the glory in the church and in Christ Jesus to all generations forever and ever [lit., of the age of the ages]. Amen (Eph. 3:20–21).

All three words—*oikoumenē, kosmos,* and *aiōn*—are used within the context of that great missionary passage in Romans 10:1–12:2. Speaking of missionaries and their message, Paul says, "Their voice has gone out into all the earth, and their words to the ends of the world [*oikoumenē*]" (10:18). Speaking of the setting aside of the Jewish nation until all—Jews and Gentiles—have had an opportunity to accept the Savior, Paul says, "For if their rejection be the reconciliation of the world [*kosmos*], what will their acceptance be but life from the dead?" (11:15). Urging believers to give themselves unreservedly to the plan and purposes of God, Paul says, "And do not be conformed to this world [aiōn], but be transformed by the renewing of your mind, that you may prove what the will of God is, that which is good and acceptable and perfect" (12:2).

When we rethink these passages and review contemporary discussions, it becomes apparent that mission today and tomorrow requires understanding as well as action. What we understand will determine what we will choose to do. *And what we choose to do will make all the difference in the world!*

4

AMBIVALENT POLARIZATION—CONVERGENCE AND DIVERGENCE IN MISSIONS

Our discussion of the "reactive trend" demonstrates that after almost two thousand years the church is still discussing the nature of its mission on earth—and evidencing no little disagreement in the process. Theologically and organizationally Christian missions are separated from one another. But they are not standing still. They are moving. So the question that cries out for an answer is this: Are the missions moving in a direction that will cause them to converge at some point in the future or in a direction that will assure continued divergence? Only the future can answer that question. For the present, the trend is toward polarization, but which missions will end up traveling which road in not entirely clear. Ambivalence and ambiguity characterize contemporary polarization.

THE SEARCH FOR UNITY

In 1900 there was a global total of 1,900 denominations, seven confessional councils, and only one multidenominational council of churches—the World Evangelical Alliance formed in 1846. By 1980 there was a world total of 20,780 denominations (increasing at the rate of 270 denominations per year, or over five a week), 550 national councils of churches, 55 regional or subcontinental councils, 27 continent-wide councils, 45 world confessional councils and three international or world councils of churches.[1] The overlapping and competition that sometimes result from such a profusion of ecclesiastical organizations provides a motivation to many to labor for cooperation and unity. But there is another—and for some, an overriding—motivation. It is to be found in the relationship between unity and the worldwide mission of the church itself.

Conciliar Protestantism and the Ecumenical Movement

Conciliar church leaders have long been persuaded that success in the Christian mission is intimately related to Christian unity. Early on it was believed that a preoccupation with doctrinal differences deterred the church and its missions from the more urgent concern of world evangelization. Somewhat later many came to feel that the very fact that there were so many divisions within Christendom militated against witness in a fragmented world. Their rallying cry was John 17:23: "They may be perfected in unity, that the world may know that Thou didst send Me, and didst love them, even as Thou didst love Me."

It is significant that the Ecumenical movement in Protestantism really grew out of missions involvement. John R. Mott, Joseph H. Oldham, and other architects of the first World Missionary Conference, which met at Edinburgh in 1910, were fearful that doctrinal division would deter conferees from the kind of unity and cooperation they believed essential to the fulfillment of the Great Commission. They therefore decided that doctrinal and confessional discussions concerning, for example, the meaning of the Great Commission and the nature of mission itself were outside of the purview of the conference. In effect, each participating church or mission was free to define mission in its own way. Thus began a tradition of excluding doctrinal issues from the agenda of Christian councils insofar as practicable.

Of course, church doctrines and confessions are not so easily pushed into the background. Edinburgh subsequently gave birth to *three* organizations—one on mission (the IMC or International Missionary Council), one on Faith and Order, and one on Life and Work. The latter two merged into the new World Council of Churches, which was organized in Amsterdam in 1948. When the IMC became the missionary arm (the DWME or Division of World Mission and Evangelism) of the WCC in New Delhi in 1961, it seemed to many that a new day had dawned for the mission of the church. All had agreed on a minimal confession of faith, and member communions could now concentrate on unity and mission. The confessional statement reads:

> The World Council of Churches is a fellowship of churches which confess the Lord Jesus Christ as God and Saviour according to the Scriptures and therefore seek to fulfill together their common calling to the glory of the one God, Father, Son and Holy Spirit.[2]

The incorporation of the Trinitarian formula and the phrase "according to the Scriptures" was not unopposed but was insisted on by the Eastern Orthodox Church as a condition of membership in the WCC.

The atmosphere at New Delhi was euphoric. Pictures of church leaders of various countries—each attired in his culturally and ecclesiastically appropriate regalia and all marching shoulder to shoulder—appeared in newspapers around the world. Delegates fanned out across the world heralding the coming of a new day for the church and its mission.

Paralleling this larger history of the world church and mission, of course, was the development of national councils. In the United States, for example, the Foreign Mission Conference (FMC) of North America formed in 1911 and was integrated with the Women's Board of Foreign Missions in 1934. Another major step was taken when the FMC became the Division of Foreign Missions (DFM) of the National Council of the Churches of Christ (NCCCUSA) in 1950. Finally, the DFM and the Central Department of Church World Service integrated to become the Division of Overseas Ministries of the NCCCUSA in 1965. Organizationally, at least, the history of Conciliar churches and their missions prove that the stated desire for cooperation and fraternity is more than rhetoric.

Conservative Protestants and Cooperation

Fundamentalists and Evangelicals responded to what they believed to be doctrinal indifference and deviation in the Ecumenical movement by scheduling their own conferences and forming their own associations. In the United States, the earliest of these associations to be formed was the Interdenominational Foreign Mission Association (IFMA) in 1917. Next came the Evangelical Foreign Missions Association (EFMA, affiliated with the National Association of Evangelicals) formed in 1945. The Associated Missions of the International Council of Christian Churches (TAM) organized in 1948 is ostensibly an international association but for practical purposes can be considered to be North American. Finally, the Fellowship of Missions (FOM) was organized in 1950. Neither of the latter two organizations has grown appreciably in the recent past. The IFMA and the EFMA are the most significant in size and most representative of the conservative Evangelical wing of Protestantism. They cooperate in mission projects and meet jointly at least every three years.

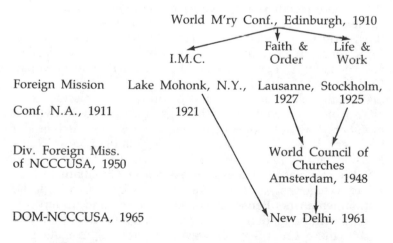

The Stream of Ecumenicity—
Conciliar Protestants

United States   *World*

World M'ry Conf., Edinburgh, 1910

I.M.C.   Faith &   Life &
                 Order   Work

Foreign Mission   Lake Mohonk, N.Y.,   Lausanne,   Stockholm,
                                          1927   1925
Conf. N.A., 1911   1921

Div. Foreign Miss.   World Council of
of NCCCUSA, 1950   Churches
                                    Amsterdam, 1948

DOM-NCCCUSA, 1965   New Delhi, 1961

Internationally, Evangelicalism has given rise to two associations that are especially important to world missions—the World Evangelical Fellowship (WEF) with its

Missions Commission initiated conjointly by the NAE of the United States and the British Evangelical Alliance in 1950, and the Lausanne Committee for World Evangelization (LCWE) inaugurated under the aegis of the Billy Graham Evangelistic Association in 1974. Many Evangelicals who are part of the WEF (and the IFMA and, especially, the EFMA) are also involved in the LCWE. The latter organization, however, also includes many representatives of the mainline Conciliar denominations who nevertheless are of a more Evangelical persuasion.

In addition to these cooperative bodies are to be found both national and international associations of Pentecostals and Charismatics. In fact, this stream represents the most active and rapidly growing major segment of Christianity. For the most part these movements are theologically conservative, but some Pentecostal groups are members of the WCC, and other are extremely separatistic. Charismatic Christians are found across the ecclesiastical spectrum. The most significant international gathering of Pentecostals has been the Pentecostal World Conference, which has held numerous conferences since they were first inaugurated in 1947. More recent years have witnessed various other such gatherings of Pentecostals and Charismatics as, for example, the World Conference on the Holy Spirit, the International Conference on Charismatic Renewal in the Catholic Church, and the Latin America Catholic Charismatic Renewal Leaders Conference.

Finally, there are a significant number of missions that are not affiliated with any of these groups (though individual members may be). Some of the largest missions such as the Southern Baptists, Wycliffe Bible Translators, New Tribes Mission, and Youth With a Mission come in this category.

We can place theological conservative Christians in four broad categories for the sake of simplicity: Evangelicals, Fundamentalists, Pentecostal/Charismatics, and independents. It will be evident that there are significant differences within these groupings, however. Therefore, to state that conservative Protestant mission bodies have not been able either to demonstrate overall unity or to present a unified alternative to the World Council of Churches is to state the obvious.

The Stream of Ecumenicity—
Conservative Protestantism

Independents	Pentecostals Charismatics	Evangelicals	Fundamentalists
So. Baptists,	World Pentecostal Conference (1947), et al.	IFMA (U.S.), 1917	TAM (U.S./Int), 1948
Wycliffe,		EFMA (U.S.), 1945	FOM (U.S.), 1950
YWAM, et al.		WEF (Int.), 1950	
		LCWE (Int.), 1974	

The Roman Catholic Church

Although the primary focus of this book is on the Protestant—and especially the Evangelical—churches, it is necessary to highlight certain developments in the Catholic and Orthodox sectors as well. The official position of the Roman Catholic Church has changed dramatically during the past generation or two. During the latter part of the nineteenth and the first part of the twentieth centuries its relationship to Protestant churches and missions was hardly cordial. Toward the middle of this century, however, attitudes began to change so that observers were exchanged at various gatherings—unofficially at first, and then officially. In 1960 the Secretariat for Christian Unity was established.

Vatican Council II (the Twenty-first Ecumenical Council) held in Rome from 1962 to 1965 marked a major change in the position of the Roman Catholic Church. A joint committee composed of representatives of the Vatican and the WCC was established in 1965. The "Decree on Ecumenism," which came out of Vatican II, indicated that non-Catholic Christian groups are not the object of mission work but instead are invited to participate in dialogue. The "Decree on the

Church's Missionary Activity" stated that missions are to be concerned with preaching the gospel and planting the church among people who do not yet believe in Christ. Disturbing to many was the "Declaration on the Relationship of the Church to Non-Christians." It seemed at odds with the missionary calling of the church by adopting a conciliatory stance toward non-Christian religions rather than calling attention to idolatry and the need for repentance.

These decrees—along with the changes that resulted in the giving of the Bible to its members, the translation of the Bible for others, and the introduction of the vernacular in the liturgy—guarantee that the Roman Catholic Church will never be the same. The question its hierarchy must now answer is, Have the doors to innovation and change been opened too widely? and if so, how does one go about closing them in an age of religious pluralism and widespread doctrinal indifference? Although some observers say that Ecumenical concerns are not a top priority for Rome currently, we can be confident that Catholic leaders and laity will walk through those doors frequently.

Streams or a River?

The search for unity does not end at this point. W. J. Hollenweger speaks of over 80 million adherents of non-white indigenous (nativistic) churches around the world— "churches that many Western Christians have difficulty in even recognizing as churches."[3] Fearing that their alienation will entail a total reversal of twentieth-century Ecumenism, he calls for a new kind of unity based on an "intercultural theology" that admittedly will not be conceptually uniform or governed entirely by faithfulness to the historical heritage of the church. In his view, the alternative will be another split between the churches in the northern and southern hemispheres that will be more catastrophic than the division between Catholicism and Protestantism.

Again, within both the Roman Catholic Church and the World Council of Churches a very concerted effort is being made for a kind of meaningful relationship with adherents of the great non-Christian faiths. Within the WCC a Director of the Dialogue Programme has been appointed and a series of dialogues with leading representatives of the major non-Christian faiths has been initiated. The door having been opened during Vatican II, on October 27, 1986, Pope John

Paul invited representatives of twelve major religions (including African animism) to Assissi to pray for world peace. The momentum to achieve a new kind of ecumenicity has gradually picked up steam. The common ground is not doctrine, of course. Rather, it is spiritual experience.

*The Stream of Ecumenicity—
Roman Catholicism*

Roman Catholic Actions	*World Council of Churches*
Warning against pan-Christian activities, 1928	
Una Sancta Brotherhood for Ecumenical Cooperation, 1938	Utrecht, 1938 (Faith & Order)
Unitas, Ecumenical center founded in Rome, 1945	. . . . Amsterdam, 1948 . . . . Lund, 1952
Secretariat for Christian Unity, 1960	. . . . New Delhi, 1961
Vatican II, 1962–1965	

Joint Committee, 1965
Consultations and Exchange
of Observers on Regular Basis

What does this brief historical overview reveal? Convergence? Most assuredly. Divergence? Without a doubt. Unification? Yes, to a certain degree. Polarization? Yes, a case is easily made for it. But which trend is the major trend *currently*? Let us explore that question further.

SIGNS OF CONVERGENCE IN MISSIONS

If the observer can see both a coming together and a pulling apart in the history that brings us to the present hour, what evidence is there that the forces that make for unity and ecumenicity might prove to be stronger than those that make for division?

First, some see changes in the attitudes and positions of

Ecumenists and some Evangelicals as indications of convergence. As we noted in the previous chapter, the Nigerian scholar Efiong S. Utuk believes that significant changes occurred in Evangelicalism between the EFMA-IFMA–sponsored congress in Wheaton (1966) and the Billy Graham Evangelistic Association–sponsored Congress on Evangelism in Berlin held some five months later, on the one hand, and the congress in Lausanne in 1974, which was also sponsored by BGEA, on the other. Although the Wheaton meeting was billed as a counter-WCC gathering, and Lausanne constituted an Evangelical response to the WCC meeting in Uppsala in 1968 and especially the DWME "Salvation today" conference in Bangkok in 1972–1973, Utuk notes that Lausanne moved closer to Conciliar positions on such issues as church-mission relations, unity, social action as a part of mission, and even on dialogue with representatives of other religions.

Utuk makes pointed reference to the Anglican John R. W. Stott's revised position, which makes social action a partner of evangelism (though he does not mention other areas in which Stott's position is very different from that of most Conciliarists) and his role as an architect of the Lausanne Covenant. He also mentions the challenge presented to the Lausanne Congress by René Padilla and the members of the Radical Discipleship group, Howard Snyder's insistence that the church is the only divinely appointed agency for the spreading of the gospel, and papers presented by a number of others whose views he feels pointed in the direction of Conciliar positions. He concludes that the "new missiological fact of our time" is that "there is an emerging consensus on many missiological questions" and that " 'Evangelicals' are becoming more 'ecumenical' than ever, while 'Ecumenicals' are becoming more 'evangelical.' "[4] Utuk believes that, given time, the unresolved issues between the two movements can be settled, including questions concerning the Christian attitude toward non-Christian religionists.

Second, the tendency to give priority to the experience of the new birth over doctrinal and ecclesiastical considerations has resulted in a blurring of the latter. This is evident in the approaches of organizations such as the Billy Graham Evangelistic Association and Campus Crusade for Christ (both non-Charismatic) and Youth With a Mission (Charismatic). In the past, the inclusivistic sponsorship of the Billy Graham crusades occasioned a good deal of controversy among Evangelical and Fundamentalist Christians. That controversy is now largely a matter of history, and most Evangelicals at least have accepted the Graham position that if the gospel is preached and people are won to Christ, the cause of world evangelization has been well served. Mass crusades around the world tend to reflect this position.

Currently, a similar type of controversy centers on the approach to be taken in evangelizing nominal Christian populations. Should missionaries seek to introduce nominals to a personal relationship with Christ and then disciple them within their traditional churches? Or should those who come to Christ in a personal way be formed into new congregations where Reformation doctrines and biblical authority are maintained? A strong case is being made for the former position, and, to the extent that it prevails, the Ecumenical cause will be enhanced.

Third, the Pentecostal/Charismatic emphasis on another type of spiritual experience—that of a "second blessing" or "baptism of the Spirit" and in some cases a third and fourth experience—also signals convergence. This phenomenon cuts across not only denominational but also Catholic-Protestant and Conciliar-Evangelical divergences. Hollenweger divides Pentecostalism into three streams: classical Pentecostal denominations (including their mission churches), the Charismatic movements in the traditional churches (including their mission churches), and the newly emerging indigenous nonwhite churches in the Third World. He accepts David Barrett's total of 115,096,239 Charismatics in these three streams in 1980 but thinks that Barrett's projection of almost a quarter billion in the year 2000 is high. In any case, with regard to the Ecumenical trend he says of Charismatics:

> Initially the Charismatics accepted the theology of pentecostalism along with the pentecostal experience. This has brought them into conflict with their own traditions. At the present time great efforts are being made to interpret Pentecostal spirituality within the categories of their own denominational traditions. . . . In general the argument runs like this: Since we have become Charismatics we understand our own (Catholic, Reformed, Anglican, Lutheran) tradition better. There is

no need for a critical review of the theological position of
our church.[5]

Interestingly enough, then, this emphasis on a second
spiritual experience (and recurring experiences such as
tongues, dreams, healings, exorcisms, and the like) on the
part of Western Charismatics has already occasioned a new
kind of Ecumenism. (I recall posters that were prominently
displayed in Manila several years ago, inviting missionaries,
priests, pastors, nuns, and church workers to "leave your
doctrines at home" and come to a conference seeking a
spiritual experience that would bring unity.) Similar, but
much more broadly interpreted experiences in nativistic
churches call for a still newer Ecumenism!

Fourth, with the growth of missiology as a significant
theological discipline, a number of organizations, programs,
and publications that bridge doctrinal and denominational
lines have emerged. The American Society of Missiology is
by far the most prestigious of several academic organizations
promoting the interests of missiology as a discipline. In its
leadership, committees, and publications it consciously and
carefully provides for equal input from Catholics, Protestant
Conciliarists, and Evangelicals.

The interests of missiology have also undergirded the
programs and publications of the Overseas Ministries Study
Center (recently moved from Ventnor, N.J., to New Haven,
Conn.) and its publications, *The International Bulletin of
Missionary Research.* Authors such as Ralph R. Covell,
Charles Kraft, and Orlando Costas have recently had works
published by Orbis Books. Orbis is the publishing arm of the
Catholic Foreign Mission Society of America (popularly
known as Maryknoll). Its publications include numerous
book promoting liberation theology and the humanization
missiology prominent in the WCC and it has been accused
by White House communications director, Patrick J. Buchanan (a Roman Catholic), and others of promoting Marxist
causes.[6] Obviously, for these authors the interests of missiology as a discipline and a possible wider readership take
precedence over any concerns growing out of identification
with Orbis.

Fifth, in recent years the World Evangelical Fellowship
with its more complete and traditional statement of faith has
had to take a back seat to the more inclusive Lausanne

Continuation Committee as far as being at the cutting edge of missions is concerned. In his recent book *The Dream That Would not Die* Executive Director David Howard has chronicled the story of the WEF and has prophesied that it will have a significant role in the future of world missions.[7] At this point, however, the more adequate financing, the self-perpetuating nature, and the more limited evangelistic and missionary purpose of the LCWE have accorded it more international prominence. Since the LCWE is answerable only to itself and not to national Evangelical organizations, it is free to include evangelically inclined people from the various church traditions. Therefore also it is much more flexible and free to change in accordance with the spirit of the times and inclinations of its leadership. This helps to account for the changes that Utuk believes take an Ecumenical direction.

Sixth, increasingly Evangelicals have joined Conciliarists in emphasizing the kingdom-of-God theme as it relates to the Christian mission. Snyder and Runyon point out that "the number of articles on the kingdom of God catalogued in *Religion Index One: Periodicals* increased from 56 in the decade 1960–70 to 139 in the decade 1970–80 (a 150 percent increase) and well over that number since 1980."[8]

It is significant that the first international conference on the *nature of the church* called by Evangelicals (Wheaton, 1983) featured a keynote address on the kingdom of God. The make-up of the conference was selective, and it cannot be said to have been entirely representative, but it did signal the fact that one of the most prominent themes of Ecumenical *missio dei* has come to be prominent in some Evangelical circles as well.

Seventh, it has now become more clear that privately as well as publicly there has been a continuing effort on the part of certain leaders of *both* Ecumenical and Evangelical persuasions to bridge the gap that separates them. Some of this effort has taken place behind the scenes. When the long-time WCC leader, John Coventry Smith, published his book *From Colonialism to World Community: the Church's Pilgrimage*, it became known that a group of church leaders, including an "unnamed Fuller Seminary professor," had been holding regular periodic meetings with an eye to unity.[9] But some of the effort has been up front and public, as when Richard Lovelace and Arthur Glasser led a small group of Evangelicals in calling for the participation of Evangelicals in the WCC at the Vancouver meeting in 1983.

Numerous other signs of convergence—particularly as they relate to the broader types of Ecumenism involving nonwhite nativistic movements and representatives of other religions—will emerge as we proceed. Here we have concentrated on those relating to the relationship between Ecumenists and Evangelicals. *In doing so, the intent has not been to judge or recriminate, but merely to point out that these changes and occurrences give the appearance of convergence between the two.*

SIGNS OF DIVERGENCE IN MISSIONS

R. Pierce Beaver's assessment is that the years up to World War II witnessed a remarkable unity among the various Protestant missions.[10] In view of the fact that the rhetoric of the debates has toned down considerably in recent years and taking the above signs of convergence into consideration, it may seem that the current trend is also in the direction of unity. Actually, both assessments are debatable. Currently, at least, there are signs of polarization in missions—a polarization that may not be transcended in the near future, if ever. Why? Because many Evangelicals look past the signs of unity to differences that they view as growing out of some of the deepest of theological commitments. The evidences for divergence (concentrating on Protestantism at this point) are of various sorts.

First, Evangelicals (including Pentecostal and Charismatic Evangelicals) have found it necessary to schedule numerous conferences and consultations in order to discuss and promote mission as they understand it. Out of these conferences have come significant publications and declarations as to the nature of the Christian mission—declarations that have uniformly maintained the uniqueness of Christianity, the authority of Scripture, and the priority of evangelism despite the changes and ambiguities mentioned previously. In this connection (and in addition to the "Wheaton Declaration," the Berlin position, and the "Lausanne Covenant") the "Frankfurt Declaration on Mission" promulgated by fourteen Evangelical Lutheran theologians in Germany in 1970 should not be overlooked. It brought to light a clear and continuing opposition to the humanization posture of the WCC within the Lutheran Church in Germany.

Second, there has been a declining interest in world evangelization on the part of Conciliarists at the same time as Evangelicals have experienced an accelerated interest. The repeated Conciliar declaration that evangelization is the responsibility of the churches (as opposed to the mission agencies and their missionaries) should not be allowed to obscure this fact. Statistically, the number of missionaries associated with the Division of Overseas Missions of the National Council of Churches in the United States, for example, was surpassed by the number of Evangelical missionaries in 1960. Since that time the gap has widened. The DOM has only about half as many missionaries today (4,349) as in 1969 (8,279). The number of missionaries related to the Evangelical associations (such as the Evangelical Foreign Missions Association and the Interdenominational Foreign Mission Association) and unaffiliated (but largely Evangelical) boards has shown a steady and dramatic increase over the same period (25,011 to 35,620).[11] Similarly, the number of Conciliar crosscultural missionaries sent out by Third World churches is but a small fraction of the total.

Third, divergence on the specific issues that have plagued missions in the postwar period is still apparent. Writing in 1974, R. Pierce Beaver noted some of the most important of these as of that date. He wrote:

> If unity is to be fostered, it is imperative that a tremendous effort be made to eradicate the polarization which has cursed Protestants in mission during the past quarter century. Terms and slogans have been set up, one after another, and two parties have rallied around these banners and assailed each other. First we had the watchwords; presence versus proclamation; then Jesus the Man-for-Others versus Jesus Savior and Lord; followed by humanization and development versus evangelization; after that liberation and revolution versus soul-saving; and they have all been caught up in a quarrel as to whether salvation is the redemption of society or of the individual.[12]

In calling attention to these issues, Beaver insisted that in each case the two positions were complementary, that they represented two sides of the one coin called mission, that balance was needed for wholeness in mission, and that Ecumenists and Evangelicals could indeed unite if they could see that a synthesis is possible.

Beaver's concern was and is commendable. But another decade has passed, and these issues are still topics of debate. Why? Many would answer that it is not because either side is blind to their nature but for precisely the opposite reason. When viewed clearly, these issues reflect the kind of dispute that is not resolved by compromise but only by capitulation on the part of one side or the other.

Fourth, there are signs that when "the chips are down," Ecumenists themselves may back away from the Conciliarism that is part and parcel of the Ecumenical movement. Take the recent case of the charge of illegal proselytism involving Youth With a Mission missionaries in Greece. After drawn-out legal proceedings, the missionaries were exonerated by the Court of Appeals in Athens, but

> the defense argued that essentially the doctrines of Eastern Orthodoxy are compatible with Evangelical Protestant Christianity, . . . [but] the priest and the Orthodox theologian said that the differences are fundamental and that all Protestant Christianity cannot be reconciled with the true Church of Jesus Christ, Eastern Orthodoxy. While the Eastern Orthodox Church is a member of the World Council of Churches and receives large amounts of money from Christians of other confessions, her representatives in court maintained that there is no ground for cooperation with Protestants, who are dangerous heretics.[13]

Fifth, Ecumenical and Evangelical theologians differ markedly on those very doctrines that traditionally have been intimately intertwined with motivation for world mission. Adoniram Judson said that he would not have gone to the mission field had he not believed in the lostness of the heathen, but contemporary Ecumenical theology is deeply indebted to the conclusions of theologians who not only deny that doctrine but also the very existence of hell itself. "Listen to these theologians," urges Kenneth Kantzer:

> Paul Tillich says that all existing humanity, like Christ, will eventually be absorbed into the eternal ground of all being. Nels Ferré puts forth the sentimental hope that in the end love must dissolve all evil. Rudolf Bultmann speaks vaguely of the infinite triumph beyond human history. Emil Brunner despairingly compromises with the annihilation of all who are not redeemed. And Karl Barth opts finally for a radical break with Reformation tradition.

In spite of unequivocal scriptural statements teaching eternal punishment, he argues that these are only divine threats to keep us from arriving at such a destiny.[14]

Kantzer goes on to say that although he is impressed by such arguments, he prefers to go to Jesus Christ as his authority on such a subject! As long as he does—and as long as other Evangelicals do—it is difficult to conclude that polarization can be overcome.

Finally, as implied in the previous paragraph, there is the underlying and continuing disagreement as to the authority of the Bible. The heart of the matter can be simply and succinctly stated. It is this: Conciliar-Ecumenists tend to view the Bible as a mixture of truth and error, though *in some sense* the Word of God. And they tend to interpret the Bible and Christian mission horizontally in terms of the reconciliation of people to people. Most Evangelicals, on the other hand, view the Bible as being the completely trustworthy Word of God. And they tend to interpret mission as being concerned first of all with the reconciliation of people to God. To put it another way, Evangelicals tend to emphasize the biblical insistence on conversion as a matter of highest priority, whereas Conciliar-Ecumenists do not. This results in the difference in priorities that we noted in the previous chapter. In fact, it results in differing views on the very nature of the mission of the church.

Divergence between Evangelicals and Catholics is somewhat more complicated because Catholic insistence on the authority of the Bible and church tradition often brings Catholics closer to Evangelical positions. Nevertheless traditional Catholic understandings of such doctrines as those relating to Mary, auricular confession, and the sacraments on the one hand, and the newer liberalism harbored within the Catholic Church on the other, may well indicate that differences will be deep and abiding.

It is significant that while the WCC hesitated to put even the vague phrase "according to the Scripture" in their statement of faith, Evangelicals have always given priority to an article on the authority of Scripture in their own statements. Granted that the Lausanne Covenant statement, which speaks of that which "Scripture affirms" and of the "infallibility of Scripture," does give some "wiggle room" for varied interpretations, nevertheless the intent of the statement is to assert the full authority of the Bible. In his argument for convergence referred to above, Utuk chooses not to mention this part of the Lausanne Covenant. He should have, because in the final analysis it could be argued that differences on the authority of the Bible will fuel other differences and assure polarization for some time to come.

IMPORTANT CHOICES IN MISSIONS TODAY

Which Kind of Ecumenism?

Various types of Ecumenism must be identified and distinguished. Even an overly simplified categorization reveals at least five types:

Ecumenism One—an Ecumenism including all who adhere to the complete authority of Scripture and cardinal Christian doctrines.

Ecumenism Two—an Ecumenism of Protestant and Orthodox churches with a minimal statement of faith.

Ecumenism Three—an Ecumenism of Roman, Orthodox, and Protestant churches that transcends historical divisions, the basis still to be worked out.

Ecumenism Four—an Ecumenism that also includes the diverse newly merging nonwhite indigenous churches; the basis being a validity accorded to the religious experiences and expressions of all churches.

Ecumenism Five—an Ecumenism that embraces the sincere adherents of all living religious faiths, that allows for a limited validity of all major teachings and doctrines, and that is based on a validity accorded to all sincerely sought spiritual experiences.

In the Ecumenical movement there is a "slippery slide" that extends from Ecumenism Two to Ecumenism Five. Evangelicals who seem willing to settle for an Ecumenism based on the present minimal statement of faith of the WCC should take into account the fact that many in that organization are already hard at work on an Ecumenism that embraces the sincere adherents of other religions. It is difficult to imagine an Ecumenism that would be more inimical to the Christian mission!

Will We Learn the Lesson From Edinburgh?

More than two generations have passed since that momentous missionary conference in Edinburgh in 1910. There can be no question but that the organizers of that gathering possessed a great heart and vision for the Christian mission. But the question that must be asked today is this: Were they right or wrong in thinking that by omitting discussion on doctrinal issues such as the nature of mission and the correct interpretation of the Great Commission they could best foster cooperation and the actual carrying out of the mission of the church? *However stated, that is one of the most fundamental questions facing Christian missions today.*

It would seem that the verdict of history is clear. Issues of faith and order (and life and work) refused to go away after Edinburgh. Within seventeen years Edinburgh had spawned, not one, but *three* streams: the International Missionary Council, Faith and Order, and Life and Work. It required over half a century and the efforts of all the king's horses and all the king's men to put the three streams together again! And by that time, the majority of Evangelicals had organized their own cooperative associations, consultations, and endeavors on the basis of more conservative and exclusivistic statements of faith.

Which Kind of Ecumenicity?

The Chinese ideograph for crisis is made up of two characters. One means opportunity. The other means danger. In the Chinese view, a crisis is a time of opportunity *and* danger.

There is a crisis in Christian missions today—a crisis composed of opportunity and danger. Missions are not static. They are changing. Evangelicals tend to divorce themselves from the old Fundamentalism. They are more open to diverse interpretations and broader relationships. Conciliarists give more recognition to Evangelicals on the one side and to representatives of other faiths on the other. Catholics attempt to maintain their authority over the faithful while holding out open hands to erstwhile "heretics and schismatics" and even to non-Christians. In short, there is considerable movement up and down the "Ecumenical scale." What seems to be fairly constant is a continuing concern for *some kind of ecumenicity.*

Over the years from 1965 through 1986 the WCC-sponsored *International Review of Missions* has devoted a larger percentage of its space than has the IFMA-EFMA-sponsored *Evangelical Missions Quarterly* to discussions of unity and cooperation (8.3 percent as compared to 2.6 percent). Moreover, in the case of *EMQ* all of these discussions had to do with distinctly Evangelical cooperation. As concerns the amount of attention devoted to international, regional, and national conferences of all kinds, the *IRM* percentage was 8.9 percent as compared to 5.8 percent in the case of the *EMQ*. This attention was focused almost entirely on Ecumenical conferences in the case of the former and Evangelical gatherings in the case of the latter (see Appendix 2).

These results are not altogether surprising. There is more of a special and continuing concern for ecumenicity and Ecumenical-type gatherings in WCC circles than among Evangelicals. However, two things must be said. First, gatherings of all sorts are becoming the order of the day in both camps. Second, by and large the interest among both is in gatherings displaying *their own distinctive type of ecumenicity*.

Roman Catholics in mission today have a new freedom to study the Bible for themselves. Conciliar Protestants can and do spend a great deal of energy and time discussing the nature of the Christian mission—a subject concerning which both their forebears and the Bible have much to say. Conservative Evangelicals espouse a fully authoritative Bible and come together on the bases of excellent, if imperfect, statements of faith and purpose. Thus for all who find themselves within these (and still other) branches of Christendom there is a great potential for discovering or rediscovering the biblical view of faith and mission. Therein lies the real opportunity for unity in mission.

But if there is opportunity, there is also danger—danger that the sons and daughters of Rome will not turn from tradition to the Scriptures so recently made available to all, or that they will become enamored with one or another form of secularism, or that they will take refuge in some Charismatic experience without ever discovering the great truths recovered by the Protestant Reformers.

There is danger that Protestant Ecumenists will betray

the Reformation and will extend the bounds of cooperation and unity so as to embrace since adherents of *any* faith.

There is danger that Pentecostals and Charismatics will aspire to acceptance and unity either by gradually neglecting Spirit-born experience or by glorifying it at the expense of Scripture authority.

There is danger that other Evangelicals will take too much for granted and, resting in the security of long-cherished but seldom reevaluated doctrine, will "get on" with mission until they belatedly discover that the faith that fueled mission in the first place has eroded away.

There is danger that the lesson of Edinburgh 1910 where doctrinal concerns were sacrificed to activism and the lesson of Jerusalem 1928 where this sacrifice led to the surrender of biblical mission vis-à-vis non-Christian religionists will be forgotten. There is danger that history may be repeated and with even less recourse to anchors that could arrest the drift toward Ecumenism Five!

THE "LORD'S PRAYER" FOR UNITY

It would be naïve to think that the lines between the groupings we have dealt with in this chapter are clear and straight. Conservative Evangelicals would likely embrace most Fundamentalists as being one with them, though most Fundamentalists would exclude even conservative Evangelicals from their Fundamentalism. Many neo-Evangelicals are found within the Ecumenical movement. Many Pentecostals make it clear that they are not in agreement with the inclusivism of the Charismatic movement. And so on. Moreover, there is the continuous movement and change in most sectors of the church and missions that we have already noted. Therein lies the ambivalence and ambiguity of contemporary convergence and divergence.

It would be presumptuous to think that any one group or individual has a corner on the truth. Some must be closer to the truth than others. But no doubt all of us have our blind spots. Perhaps it would be appropriate, then, for all who can agree that it was indeed our Lord who actually prayed the prayer recorded in John 17 (others may as well turn elsewhere) to examine that prayer again.

When our Lord prayed, "May they [all who believe through the Apostles' message] be brought to complete unity to let the world know that you [God the Father] sent me and have loved them even as you have loved me" (John 17:23 NIV), for what kind of unity was he praying and how does it relate to contemporary missions?

By and large, Conciliarists and Ecumenists have interpreted this as a prayer for organizational unity such as that expressed in the WCC, whereas Evangelicals have insisted that it is the mystical unity that already exists in the body of Christ.

But is there not a third possibility? I refer to the Pauline teaching that the ascended Christ gave "person gifts" (apostles or missionaries included) in order that people might come to God and that God's people in the several churches might be prepared for service and reach a unity of faith and maturity so that they would not be blown around by every wind of doctrine but would grow up in Christ (cf. Eph. 4:1–16). *In other words, when we engage in our mission to disciple the nations and, by God's grace, give rise to the kind of churches where believers espouse sound doctrine together, grow together in Christlikeness, and serve together, our Lord's prayer and plan is being realized and the world comes to know that God indeed has sent his Son!*

When one realizes that the overwhelming majority of this world's peoples down through the centuries, and multiplied millions today, have been and are far removed from the great Ecumenical gatherings of the church, it is not likely that the world will be greatly impressed by an organization of churches. And we can be quite sure that the world will not be impressed by a unity that is invisible!

What unity is left? A biblical unity—a unity-in-Christ and a unity-in-truth! These are found together in John 17. As Klaus Runia says:

> . . . the . . . contrast between truth *about* and truth *of* Christ is utterly foreign to the N.T. Admittedly . . . the personal relationship is primary. . . . Yet the N.T. (and this is equally true of the O.T.) never separates the personal and doctrinal aspects. Jesus' own discussion with the Jewish leaders nearly always concerned doctrinal issues; in some cases the right understanding of Jesus Himself was the topic of discussion. The epistles of the apostles all consist largely of expositions of God's revelation in Jesus Christ, the Christ-event and its doctrinal implications. In His "letters" to the seven churches of

Asia Minor (Revel. 2 and 3) the exalted Lord refutes various doctrinal errors, which destroy the personal relationship with Him.

The same combination of the *personal* and the *doctrinal* is found in John 17. There can be no doubt that the personal element is in the foreground. . . . But this is immediately linked with "keeping the word," which Jesus had received from the Father and transmitted to His disciples (vv. 6, 8, 14, 18).[15]

It is not easy to justify the birth of five new *denominations* in our world every week. It is impossible to justify the disregard that Christian missionaries sometimes display toward other missionaries and existing churches in the areas in which they work. Courtesy and kindness are always in order. But beyond that, it is unity-in-Christ and unity-in-truth that will please God and attract men and women to the gospel, whether displayed within the churches or among the churches and whether displayed within the missions or among the missions! But it must be unity-in-Christ *and* unity-in-truth. Only *that* unity is *Christian* unity!

5

"THIRD FORCE" EMERGENCE— THE ROLE OF PENTECOSTALISM IN CONTEMPORARY MISSIONS

The Brazilian pastor pushed past one or two inquiring parishioners, unlocked the padlock that secured a roughly constructed door barring believer and unbeliever alike from the huge sanctuary still under construction, and ushered me inside.

"No one except the architects, construction workers, elders, and myself are allowed inside until the dedication," he said. "But you are my special guest. I want you to see what God has given to us."

"God's gift" was impressive to say the least. In its incomplete state the sanctuary was more reminiscent of a sports arena than of a sanctuary as such (it was designed to seat over fifteen thousand people), but it featured a long platform that was bounded on one side by a large "waterfall" from which water cascaded into a huge trough and coursed to a baptistry on the other side.

Within an hour or two the regular Saturday evening service had begun. The old sanctuary, which seated perhaps four to five thousand people, was quite comfortably filled with an enthusiastic crowd. The service continued for almost three hours and featured a small but skilled orchestra, special musical groups, testimonies, lots of congregational singing, and an hour-long sermon from the pastor.

The pastor's name was Manoel de Melo. The church was the *Brasil para Christo* (Brazil for Christ) church in São Paulo. I was witnessing part of a phenomenon of profound importance to the church and its missions—the rapid growth of what is sometimes referred to as the "Third Force in missions" (the first two being Roman Catholicism and Protestantism). In two short generations since its beginnings the Pentecostal Movement has come to a place where many of its leaders confidently prophesy—and plan for—a worldwide revival that will be climaxed by the coming of Christ. Henry P. Van Dusen's 1958 appraisal to the effect that the movement is emerging as a Third Force in Christendom does not seem to have been far afield when we consider Pentecostalism's growth and influence.[1]

IDENTIFYING THE "THIRD FORCE"

Four Streams of Pentecostalism

Pentecostalism is not easy to define. At least four streams are quite clearly identifiable, however:

1. Classical Pentecostalism, which had its beginnings in the early part of this century and formed its own churches and denominations;

2. Neo-Pentecostalism (Charismatic Pentecostalism), which dates to the post–World War II experiences of numerous people within the mainline Protestant churches—people who, after receiving the baptism of the Spirit and related gifts, elected to stay in those churches;

3. Catholic Charismatics (Catholics often use the designation "Renewal"); and

4. the Pentecostal movement within the nonwhite indigenous churches throughout the Third World and especially in Africa.

As indicated earlier, there are various ways of dividing up the movement. The *World Christian Encyclopedia* differentiates between Pentecostals (capital *P*) or those in Pentecostal denominations of white origin, and pentecostals (lower case) or Charismatics in non-Pentecostal denominations and in the nonwhite indigenous Pentecostal denominations. However, the *Encyclopedia* makes other distinctions that make a final categorization somewhat difficult.[2]

In spite of numerous differences, that which tends to be characteristic of all of these streams is an emphasis on the postconversion baptism of the Spirit attended by speaking in tongues (sometimes distinguished from the gift of tongues as such) and the reception of one or more *charismata* or gifts of the Spirit such as *glossolalia* (tongues), prophecy, healing, power over evil spirits, and the interpretation of tongues. Issues that tend to divide Pentecostals/Charismatics have to do with (1) their relationship with those in church traditions where the fundamentals of the Christian faith are deemed to have been forsaken, (2) the number and character of special postconversion experiences to be sought, (3) teachings concerning the Trinity, (4) practices of water baptism, and (5) the proper ways of exercising spiritual gifts.

The Development of a Movement

Pentecostalism as we know it today is often traced to the devotional practices of certain Roman and Anglo-Catholic divines as they were interpreted by John Wesley and in the eighteenth century; to the Irvingite Movement, which began in England in 1830; to the leaders of the nineteenth century American Holiness movement such as Charles G. Finney, Dwight L. Moody, Hannah Whitehall Smith, A. B. Simpson, and Thomas Upham; to Charles Parham's Bible School in Topeka, Kansas; and, especially to the Azusa Street Revival in Los Angeles in 1906. It has usually produced a deepseated missionary motivation, and it is this motivation that has propelled it to its present role as perhaps the most missionary-minded segment of world Christianity.

Many of those who received the tongues gift in the revival on Azusa Street went to nations that were indicated when the particular language of their gift was revealed. (The disappointment that followed their discovery that they were not exempt from the normal process of language learning was not sufficient to dampen the missionary zeal of the movement.) English Pentecostals early on gave so much money and energy to foreign missions that local growth was affected adversely. For several years, Dutch missionaries were sent out under English auspices, but as early as 1909 Dutch Pentecostals founded their own society, and six years later a missionary training school was begun in Amsterdam.

Stories such as these were to be repeated in country after country until today most branches of the Christian church and most areas of the non-Christian world have felt the impact of one or another form of Pentecostalism.

A LOOK AT THE RECORD

Few other emergent phenomena relating to the twentieth-century church and its missions are so readily established by simple statistical measurements as those relating to the impact of Pentecostalism, but, of course, there are other types of indicators as well. In one form or another, Pentecostalism has grown to proportions that continue to amaze supporters and critics alike. On the one hand, it has invaded church after church, denomination after denomination, institution after institution, and mission after mission with a challenge to spiritual renewal by seeking the baptism and empowerment of the Spirit and by appropriating spiritual gifts. On the other hand, it has invaded the world with a gospel message authenticated by "signs and wonders."

Consider the record:

First, Pentecostalism is the most rapidly growing segment of the Christian church in the twentieth century, now constituting approximately 150–170 million or more believers world-wide, depending on how many offshoots are included. (Some estimates go even higher.)

Second, perhaps as significant as the statistics on overall growth is the rate of growth of some of the Pentecostal groups in the Third World. Dividing African Charismatics into Roman Catholic Pentecostals, non-Roman Catholic Pentecostals, and neo-Pentecostals, for example, the *World Christian Encyclopedia* gives *yearly* growth rates as follows: Catholic Pentecostals 45 percent; neo-Pentecostals 27 percent; and Anglican Pentecostals, 25 percent.[3] Figures for some other continents such as Latin America are almost as arresting. David Barrett writes that he would not be surprised if the bulk of Roman Catholic laity in Latin America is predominantly Charismatic by the year 2000.[4]

Third, as many as nine of the world's twenty largest churches are Pentecostal/Charismatic.[5] This list includes the world's largest church (by far)—the Full Gospel Central Church in Seoul, Korea, led by Paul Yonggi Cho; it has well over 500,000 members!

Fourth, although one of the best known and most successful of the Pentecostal missions has been that of the

Assemblies of God (U.S.), the movement has spawned other groups with effective missionary enterprises as well, such as those of the Pentecostal Assemblies of Canada, the Pentecostal Church of God, the International Church of the Foursquare Gospel, the Open Bible Standard Churches, and Elim Fellowship. This in addition to parachurch ministries such as Youth With a Mission, Christ for the Nations, Last Day Ministries, and Jimmy Swaggart Ministries. Youth With a Mission (YWAM), which may have as many as twenty thousand career and (primarily) short-term missionaries, is the world's largest Christian mission in terms of sheer numbers.[6]

Fifth, although often neglected by the secular and even the religious press, Pentecostals/Charismatics have staged some of the most broadly ecumenical and representative (world representation) religious enclaves in the post–World War II era. The World Pentecostal Conference has been held in various nations every second or third year since 1947, when one hundred delegates from twenty nations met at the first such conference in Zurich, Switzerland. Other such conferences include the World Conference on the Holy Spirit, the Latin American Catholic Charismatic Renewal Leaders Conference, the International Conference on the Charismatic Renewal in the Catholic Church, the Conference on the Charismatic Renewal in Christian Churches, and the International Charismatic Pilgrimage to Lourdes (on the Shrine's one hundredth anniversary in 1979), among many more.

Sixth, in spite of the fact that the *EMQ* and the *IRM*, the two journals specially analyzed in preparation for this study, have not featured the Pentecostal movement as much as its growth might seem to warrant (the *IRM* has actually devoted more space to it, especially in very recent issues; see Appendix 2), church and mission scholars generally have shown increasing interest. *Missiology* book reviews do reflect some interest in the movement, though not nearly as much as in Roman Catholic and Conciliar Protestant missions (see Appendix 3).

No doubt the perception that it is a "fringe" movement and the fact that it produces few scholarly works accounted for the lack of serious attention accorded Pentecostalism in earlier days. But in the 1950s Henry P. Van Dusen was joined by Lesslie Newbigin in noting its potential.[7] Then in the late

1960s and early 1970s the writings of Assembly of God missiologist Melvin Hodges, the work of Vinson Synan showing Pentecostal communities to be the fastest growing world-wide,[8] a history and survey of the movement by Walter Hollenweger entitled *The Pentecostals*,[9] and a number of books analyzing the growth of Pentecostal churches on the various mission fields by such scholars as Donald Palmer, Donald McGavran, and William Read highlighted Pentecostal growth. One of the most widely circulated books in the latter category was C. Peter Wagner's *Look Out! The Pentecostals Are Coming*, a sympathetic analysis of Pentecostal vitality and growth, subsequently republished as *Spiritual Power and Church Growth*.[10] Excellent new books by Pentecostals Gary McGee and L. Grant McClung, Jr., are also available.[11]

WHICH ROAD TO TRAVEL?

There can be no doubt. The Pentecostals are not just coming. They have arrived! More than that, they are going places. Over a decade ago Martin Marty predicted that Pentecostalism would become the major form of Christianity in the Third World.[12] Current statistics indicate that Marty is a good prophet. But what about the future? Which road will Pentecostals and Charismatics travel? How will Pentecostal/Charismatic growth make an impact on the churches and missions of tomorrow?

While I was growing up in a Pentecostal church in southern Wisconsin, the church members were very committed, but we were not thought of as the religious and social elite of the community. In fact, our successive pastors took no umbrage at the recognition accorded pastors of mainline and prestigious churches. True Christians are, after all, a "peculiar people," and the road that leads to eternal life is admittedly a narrow one. We Pentecostals entertained some doubts as to the road "nominal Christians" were traveling, but we had no doubts at all about the road that we were traveling. We regularly engaged the services of powerful evangelists to help us persuade locals to join us in our pilgrimage. And we dutifully participated in the sending forth of missionaries to persuade people around the world to start on the narrow road as well.

Although my present identification is not with that denomination, I have through the years counted some of my most committed family members and friends within that same communion of the Pentecostal movement. And I am happy to do so. For even though my affiliation has changed, I still owe a debt to my Pentecostal upbringing that will never be fully repaid. And I am persuaded that for a variety of reasons we all are indebted to the Pentecostal churches and missions for their contributions in the past, and we may incur an even larger debt in the future. Whether we will or not depends in large measure on the direction they take in tomorrow's mission *because it is in the Third World that Pentecostals have the potential for their greatest impact.*

I will not ask here whether or not Pentecostal doctrines are correct or whether Pentecostal experiences are genuine. Neither will I ask whether Pentecostally induced church schisms are defensible. As with all our communions, when the record is ultimately set straight neither side of the ledger will be devoid of entries. In any case, though these are important questions, they would take us far afield. *Rather, putting the best possible construction on mainstream teachings and experiences, we will be concerned here with the directions the Pentecostal/Charismatic movement might take in the world mission of the future.*

Progress in the Christian Mission

Certain aspects of the Pentecostal movement augur well for the future. If they continue and, indeed, become more characteristic of all of our missions and mission churches, the Great Commission cause will be greatly aided.

First, the movement needs to continue to give a large place to the Holy Spirit and his work. Of course, Pentecostals have not been alone in underscoring the place of the Holy Spirit in mission. The Anglican missiologist Roland Allen has carefully linked the spontaneous expansion of the church with the work of the Holy Spirit.[13] The Reformed missiologist Harry Boer has painstakingly shown us from the Acts record that the Holy Spirit is the Missionary Spirit who fulfills the Great Commission through us and that our treatment of the Great Commission as though it were a fiat command rather than an organic law of the Spirit is a regrettable misunderstanding.[14] But in the final analysis it has been our Pentecostal friends who have been almost univocal in emphasizing the truth of Zechariah 4:6: " 'Not by might nor by power, but by My Spirit,' says the Lord of hosts." Apart from the Spirit, the mission will flounder. Increasingly, we will need that reminder lest we become overly dependent on our strategies or flag in the face of the opposition.

Second, in their presentation of the gospel, Pentecostals often break through the ethnic, national, and class barriers that separate people. There is some justification for the insistence of church-growth specialists that "homogeneous unit" churches grow better than heterogeneous churches, especially when we are thinking of planting new congregations. But critics have a case when they point out that ethnic and class churches do not really reflect the New Testament teaching that such distinctions do not really exist in the body of Christ. In this respect, Pentecostal churches often exemplify the biblical ideal.

Concerning the Azusa Street Revival, Hollenweger writes, "White bishops and black workers, men and women, Asians and Mexicans, white professors and black laundry women were equals [1906!]."[15] In a world where the races and tribes and classes and genders continue to entertain prejudice and even war against each other, Pentecostals may well be in the forefront in demonstrating that the gospel entails both a vertical conversion to Christ and a horizontal communion with our neighbors.

Third, the Pentecostal movement has been called a grass-roots ecumenism that brings believers of various historical and confessional traditions together in Christ-honoring, Spirit-infused worship and witness. Although more will be said about this shortly, let me say here briefly that there is both truth and significance to this appraisal.

Within recent months I have preached the Word at YWAM-sponsored Sunday evening meetings in Germany and Switzerland, among other places. In both of these countries believers and unbelievers came from far and near. In a meeting in Germany, the pastor of a denominational church testified that the leaders of his congregation were not in favor of a Sunday evening service, so he and a small group of his people attended as often as possible in order to share in the blessings. I was told that the Switzerland meeting was the best attended Sunday evening service in that part of the country, with attendees coming from a radius of thirty to forty miles and representing many different denominations and several missions.

What will the bishops and pastors, the elders and deacons, of churches with minimal witness and muffled prayers answer to those of their congregations who are willing to travel many miles in order to participate in services where the Word of God is preached, the songs of Zion are sung, prayers of faith are uttered, and a challenge to take Christ to the nations is shared? Insofar as Pentecostals provide otherwise unoffered opportunities for God's people to gather around Christ, his Word and his work, the churches around the world will be blessed by their zeal.

Fourth, this movement challenges the church of Christ to fulfill the Great Commission. We have already noted that the revival on Azusa Street and other Pentecostal beginnings were characterized by a mission vision from the very first. Speaking specifically of the Assembly of God, William Menzies claims that it was out of concern for mission that the aversion to organization was overcome and churches banded together.[16] He also notes that this denomination is one of the few that actually includes a statement on the mission of the church in its affirmation of faith:

> Since God's purpose concerning man is to seek and to save that which is lost, to be worshiped by man, and to build a body of believers in the image of His Son, the priority reason-for-being of the Assembly of God as part of the Church is:
>
> a. To be an agency of God for evangelizing the world (Acts 1:8; Matthew 28:19, 20; Mark 16:15, 16)[17]

We can only pray that this vision and faith will continue to characterize not only this part of God's family, but also the larger Pentecostal movement and the larger church of Christ.

We should also note that Pentecostal Holiness leader Vinson Synan headed up a forty-member steering committee for the July 1987 General Congress on the Holy Spirit and World Evangelization in New Orleans. The committee was composed of Pentecostals and Charismatics from a variety of backgrounds. Speaking concerning the thrust of the Congress, Synan said:

> We've been in the upper room with our spiritual gifts. But we are supposed to go to the streets with our tongues and healings and prophecies. We believe the Pentecostals and charismatics have been raised up by God

as the shock troops for the greatest final assault on the enemy.[18]

Fifth, while we must admit to differences within the movement, Pentecostalism generally has had a most effective ministry among the poor and disenfranchised while at the same time holding to the priority of an evangelizing mission in the world. Although the theology of their approach has often not been spelled out clearly, those who know the movement from the inside will almost certainly accept Paul Pomerville's defense of the Pentecostal position as being representative, even though it has seldom been as well articulated.[19]

Pomerville, formerly a member of the Assemblies of God, takes issue with Ronald Sider and all who hold that God somehow has a preference for the socioeconomically poor. This, he says, "approaches a theological absurdity, especially in the context of the New Testament."[20] In reference to Luke 4:18-19 which speaks of Christ's ministry as one of proclaiming release to captives and setting free the downtrodden, Pomerville notes that the kingdom portrayed in the Gospels was not a political kingdom and that political and social deliverances were not the thrust of Christ's ministry, but that the Gospels are replete with exorcisms and deliverances from demon possession.[21] He insists that, while both Old and New Testaments do make reference to the socioeconomic poor, the "significance of the poor . . . in connection with the Kingdom is that they are ready to respond to the gospel because of their humility and probable positive affective disposition toward repentance and faith. . . ."[22]

The point is not that God is unconcerned for the needy and suffering people of the world. Nor is it that Christians have no responsibility toward them. Assuredly not. Rather, the point is that in its New Testament and present expression the outworking of the kingdom is primarily the liberation of people of faith from the bondage imposed by their sin, Satan, and Satan's emissaries of evil, not by oppressive political and economic structures.

Numerous Pentecostals today join in urging increased concern for the needy, the sick, and the "marginalized" of the world, thereby indicating that their record in this respect has not always been unreproachable. But the genius of the movement has been that it gives priority to the gospel mandate and to the still deeper need of the spirit. In the missions and the churches of the Third World much depends on the retention of that priority.

Sixth, as much as any church, mission, or movement—and far more than most—Pentecostals have been successful in inculcating a positive attitude toward church growth throughout their movement. When the most forceful and articulate advocate of church growth of recent times, Donald McGavran, wanted someone to write a chapter entitled "Creating Climate for Church Growth" in one of his edited works, he chose the Pentecostal Melvin L. Hodges for the task.[23] If anything is generally characteristic of Pentecostal churches world-wide, it is an ethos of growth. In a time of defeatism, stagnation, and retreat in many churches, a growth climate may prove to be one of the great bequests of Pentecostalism to the larger church of Christ.

Some Cautions

We have by no means done justice to the inherent potential of Pentecostals/Charismatics when we have outlined their potential for blessing the missions, the churches, and the world of tomorrow. Like every movement, theirs also must be steered around certain pitfalls that even now loom large on the horizon.

First, classic Pentecostalism runs the danger of cultural accommodation. Perhaps it is those who have been close enough to the Pentecostal churches to detect the changes that have occurred over the years—but not so close as to be unaware of their gradual incursion—who are in the best position to call those changes to the attention of Pentecostals. As is true in many of our churches, the altar of many a Pentecostal church nowadays is infrequently visited—especially on Sunday mornings. Services may be somewhat free, but they are far more formal and predictable than they once were. Appeals sometimes tend to partake of the approaches suggested by Madison Avenue rather than being wholly prompted by the Spirit. And those gifts historically claimed to be the normal bestowal of the Holy Spirit are less in evidence.

The point is not that the churches of classic Pentecostalism a generation ago were altogether commendable and the churches today are blameworthy. Nor is it my intention to indicate that change is altogether bad. Not at all. The point is that the churches of classical Pentecostalism a generation ago were different. No doubt some of the changes represent a response to the Spirit's injunction that all things be done decently and in order. But it may be that some of these changes result from the desire for cultural acceptance and from less willingness to be "peculiar"—to be different. To the extent that this is true, classic Pentecostal churches suffer from a malaise that is the common affliction of many a contemporary church. To the extent that this is true, the world has invaded Pentecostal churches, and they will be weakened in their attempt to invade the world. To the extent that this is true, the world mission of tomorrow will suffer.

At the same time, classic Pentecostalism must produce the first-rate scholars and strategists who will lend more credibility to the movement and direction to its missionary practitioners.

Second, Charismatics run two risks: that of *doctrinal perversion* and that of an *aborted mission.*

To the degree that any Christian movement elevates the authority of spiritual experience above that of Scripture revelation, it runs the serious risk of doctrinal perversion. An occurrence comes to mind that may serve to illustrate the point.

A number of years ago, a newly arrived Charismatic missionary neighbor in Japan appeared in the *genkan* (entry) of our home with an animated invitation. His excitement was born out of some local meetings with leaders of a variety of churches and missions, some of whom were quite well known nationally. He said that the night before one or two of the most prominent of these ecclesiastical leaders had received the baptism of the Holy Spirit accompanied by the gift of tongues. He was persuaded that the Holy Spirit was about to do an entirely new thing in the churches of Japan and fairly insisted that I must join in these meetings if I wanted to be a part of it.

The ensuing conversation lasted an hour or two, and during that time it became apparent that some of the group had been involved in the compromise with State Shinto that characterized a portion of the Japanese church during the war. In the wake of that compromise these leaders exhibited no signs of remorse. Moreover, indications were that at least one or two of them questioned not only the authority of the

Bible but also the deity of Christ. My questions proved to be an embarrassment to my neighbor: How can one subscribe to the authority of the Spirit in an ecstatic personal experience while refusing to submit to the authority of that same Spirit in God's inspired Word? How can we test the spirits in accordance with 1 John 4:1–4 if we cannot discuss the biblical meaning of the lordship of Christ?

Since the meetings did not really allow for a consideration of such fundamental concerns, my friend withdrew the invitation in some confusion. Later on, he himself ceased to attend, and finally the gatherings were discontinued. In one sense, that was unfortunate because it seemed obvious that they reflected a spiritual hunger. In another sense, it was propitious because ultimately that hunger could be satisfied only by coming to God in a way prescribed by his Word.

As for the risk of an aborted mission, that possibility is implicit in the foregoing propositions and illustrations. But there is a further consideration as well. One highly placed and respected Pentecostal leader recently reminded me that the Charismatic movement as such has never given birth to a significant missionary thrust. Moreover, he insisted that the missionary emphasis of the 1987 General Congress on the Holy Spirit and World Evangelization mentioned previously represents a Pentecostal influence in the planning committee, not a Charismatic one. Perhaps the presence of Charismatics around the world should not be too readily interpreted as evidence of a missionary vision and involvement. Charismatics should ask themselves whether they are really more interested in making converts to Christ from the pagan world or converts to a particular spiritual experience from this or that segment of the professing Christian church.

It is not too late for Charismatics to reconsider. A Spiritless Christianity is no Christianity at all. A doctrineless Christianity is no Christianity at all. Charismatics will have to decide how far they will go in pursuit of spiritual experience at the expense of biblical doctrine. Much rests on their choice.

Finally, nonwhite indigenous (nativistic, independent) churches, many of which exhibit decidedly Pentecostal and Charismatic characteristics, run the very real risk of a syncretism that could lead to reversion. There are perhaps seven thousand of these groups in sub-Saharan Africa alone, most of them led by prophets who command the reverent following of their members.

With reference to these groups, Paul Pomerville takes strenuous exception to the views of B. G. M. Sundkler and G. C. Oosthuizen, both of whom entertain a very negative view of them. He insists that both Sundkler's view that these churches constitute a "bridge to paganism"[24] and Oosthuizen's very similar view that they are a "bridge to nativism"[25] emanate from a rejection of Pentecostalism itself rather than from a willingness to accept it and its manifestations as a work of the Spirit.[26]

Pomerville has a point, but it could be argued that he overlooks the negative potential of the syncretism that abounds in many of these churches. Consider for a moment Philip Steyne's words:

> The nomenclature *African Church Independency* covers a variety of forms of religious expression. It ranges from orthodox Christian sects to neo-pagan cults. . . . The demarcation line between blatant syncretism and Christian independency is notoriously difficult to draw, for in the process of change from animism to Christianity it is well-nigh impossible to determine when a person has crossed, within his inner consciousness, the boundary line between the two.[27]

Speaking specifically of the Zionists who constitute more than half of all black Christian churches in South Africa (in addition to many more in neighboring countries), Steyne notes that they became syncretistic almost from the first:

> It was one Daniel Bryant who baptized, in 1904, the first group of twenty-seven Zionist African believers in South Africa. In 1908, P. L. le Roux, a prominent European worker in the group, received the "baptism of the Holy Spirit." Africans in the group were not slow to follow. The African Zionist churches, with their strong pentecostal leanings and practices, had been launched. It was not long before they incorporated within their structures traditional religious forms that characterized their faith, at times, as being more nativistic than Christian.[28]

Much depends on whether or not millions of Zionists and others "on the bridge" between paganism and biblical Christianity actually make it to the Christian side. And, although a responsibility for this crossing rests on all of our missions, there can be little doubt that Pentecostal missions and missionaries have an unusual opportunity to teach the members of nonwhite indigenous churches around the world all that our Lord has commanded.

THE THIRD FORCE AND THE LAST REVIVAL

Not a few Christians interpret the Scriptures as prophesying the coming of a great world-wide revival before Christ returns. Some see at least the beginnings of that revival in events occurring in the church today. One survey of church leaders ranked a major revival as number six out of a list of thirty possible trends.[29] Vinson Synan's view is representative of Pentecostal thinking:

> Today . . . millions of people . . . believe that the church is now in the "latter-rain" stage of God's dealing with mankind. They believe that the greatest miracles and victories in the history of the church will come just before the appearing of the Lord. They fervently believe that all gifts of the Spirit have been restored to the church and that the bride of Christ will be caught up in a shout of victory rather than in a moan of defeat.[30]

The questions of whether or not we are witnessing the beginnings of such a revival and whether or not such a revival is in the immediate offing must for now remain open. But that the choices of well over 100 million Pentecostal and Charismatic Christians today will vitally affect the direction of world missions tomorrow is beyond debate. We can only pray that they will humbly look to the Holy Spirit for direction even as they look to him for power.

6

A SCIENCE ORIENTATION— THE DEVELOPMENT OF THE DISCIPLINE OF MISSIOLOGY

When, over twenty years ago, I returned to the seminary classroom as a professor, the experience was nothing short of overwhelming. During my days as a student the seminary curriculum had included one general course in missions. Now there were more than thirty such courses, and I was the only full-time professor in the department. More than that, like so many others who are called upon to teach missions, I found my credentials inadequate: they consisted of little more than theological studies, successful field experience, and specialization in a related but secular discipline.

My feel for the challenge was hardly dispelled by the well-intended remark of an older and experienced colleague, Professor George Peters, when he informed me that he taught missions "as a science." At the university, science generally connoted the formulation of empirically verifiable laws. As he proceeded to explain, it became clear, of course, that that was not what he meant. "Science" comes from the Latin *scientia*, meaning "that which is known." Professor Peters had this more basic meaning in mind. He taught missions as a systematized body of knowledge relating to the Christian world mission.

That reordering of my thinking helped. But it did not dispel my frustration completely. After all, although certain libraries contained a number of missions-related titles, the number of up-to-date and helpful textbooks was abysmally small. And there were those thirty plus courses listed in the catalogue—all waiting not so much for students as for helpful textbooks and adequate instruction.

What has happened in the discipline since that time could hardly have been predicted by anyone. And it can be fully appreciated only by those who have some sense of relevant history.

A DISCIPLINE IN SEARCH OF A HOME

Standing Room Only?

As Johannes Verkuyl says, "There was a day when missiology was accorded no place in the encyclopedia of theology. She was not even given standing room."[1] Recognition did not come easily in either Europe or the United States. The year that Alexander Duff assumed his duties as a missiologist at the New College in Edinburgh (1867) was an important year for the introduction of mission into Protestant curricula.[2] From that year there were efforts to initiate serious missions training in a number of schools. Alexander Duff in England, Carl Plath in Germany, and Rufus Anderson in the United States spearheaded those efforts. In Europe, Gustav Warneck was the first to receive an official appointment to a chair of missionary science (at the University of Halle, in 1896). Eventually, the subject came to be offered at almost all theological schools in Germany and in many such schools in other European nations.

In the United States, a proposal was made to include instruction in missions at Princeton as early as 1811. Nothing came of it for almost twenty years, and when missions instruction was introduced, it was short-lived. Toward the end of the nineteenth century, however, a number of schools added the study of missions to their offerings. Then, fueled by the response to the missions challenge within the Student Volunteer Movement and the World Missionary Conference in Edinburgh (1910), interest in the discipline increased. In 1911 the Hartford Seminary Foundation established the Kennedy School of Missions—the first and most prestigious school for missionaries in the United States. Not long after, in 1918, Union Theological Seminary in New York appointed Daniel J. Fleming as a full-time professor and gave missions a permanent place in the curriculum. Yale Divinity School, McCormick Theological Seminary, and other schools soon followed suit.

But already theological liberalism was conspiring against biblical mission. Gradually over the years, the Student Volunteer Movement lost both its vision and its power to recruit new missionaries. Some believed that the placing of missions professors in the schools would turn the tide. But, as James Scherer has shown, it did not.[3] Today, most of the historical theological schools in the United States that still have tenured professors of missiology on their faculties find it difficult to populate their missions classes. Kennedy School of Missions has long since closed its doors. And in Europe the few professors of missiology who still remain on the theological faculties of state church–related universities double as professors of such subjects as church history and world religions.

Standing Room Where?

The "doubling up" role of some professors raises still another question of historical importance to missiology. From the beginning there have been differing notions as to where the study of missions might belong in the curriculum. Early on, the liberal German theologian, Friedrich Schleiermacher—who had been influenced by Zinzendorf's missions-minded Herrnhutters in his youth—made a small place for it within the area of practical theology. The Princeton proposal referred to above teamed it with pastoral theology. Abraham Kuyper and J. H. Bavinck basically agreed by categorizing missions as one of the practical theological disciplines, though they found a much larger place for the subject, and Bavinck, at least, argued for a greater degree of independence for the subject.

Still others, such as Gustav Warneck and Kenneth Scott Latourette, placed missiology within the discipline of church history. Often referred to as the "father of the science of mission," Warneck, however, divided the subject in such a way that part of it also fit into the biblical disciplines and part into practical theology.

As one might suspect, any body of subject matter that is integrated into a separate discipline loses its own identity. Lamenting this, such European missiologists as Walter Freytag, O. G. Myklebust, Manfred Linz, and now Verkuyl have made a strong case for independence. The latter scholar calls it a "complementary science."[4]

MISSIOLOGY COMES OF AGE

Definition

We have spoken of missiology without defining it. Verkuyl defines it as "the study of the salvation activities of the Father, Son, and Holy Spirit throughout the world geared toward bringing the kingdom of God into existence."[5] It will be apparent, however, that such a definition presupposes a certain view of mission.

The official journal of the American Society of Missiology, *Missiology, an International Review,* defines the discipline as on page 140.

> Missiology, the science, is the systematic study of the theory and practice of Christian missions, combining such disciplines as anthropology, cross-cultural communication theory, ecumenics, history, intercultural studies, methodology, religious encounter and theology.[6]

The *World Christian Encyclopedia* defines it very succinctly as "the science of missions, missionary history, missionary thought and missionary methods."[7]

Perhaps it is best to stay with the neutral phrase that is used repeatedly in writings that refer to the subject. Simply put, missiology is the science of the Christian world mission. If one understands science in the broad sense of the word, this definition helps to free the subject from implicit theological biases. It also helps us to understand the present state of the discipline.

Development

One controlling term in this definition, then, is the word "science," thought of as systematized knowledge. As such, contemporary missiology has many precursors, whether one thinks of Origen's writings against Celsus, Augustine's *City of God,* Boniface's missionary methods in Germany, Lull's approach to Muslims, or any of a number of theorists and practitioners dedicated to organizing Christian truth in such a way as to make it persuasive to unbelieving peoples the world over. But perhaps it suits our purposes better to acquiesce to the general notion that the German Gustav

Warneck (1834–1910) was the founder of the Protestant
science of missions. Even though he was not the first to deal
with mission questions in a scientific manner, he was the
first to produce a massive (five-volume) systematic treatment
of the subject.
W. Holsten finds two aspects of Warneck's missiology to
be of particular importance. In the first place, Warneck's
work was based on both Scripture and experience, "but it is
carried out in such a fashion that in many cases the validity
of the basic Scriptural exposition is established from the
practical experiences."[8] In the second place, Warneck saw
mission as a process of education so that, though he did not
lose sight of the conversion of individuals and the establishment of churches, his aim was the establishment of "people's
churches" and the eventual christianization of pagan societies to the point where all people are brought up in a
Christian atmosphere and the knowledge of salvation is
mediated to all members of the race.

For the first half of this century and beyond, the greatest
impetus to the science of missions came from those who
were informed by anthropology. The Catholic Father Wil-
helm Schmidt founded the influential journal *Anthropos* in
1906 and otherwise promoted anthropological inquiry and
insights among missionaries. After World War II, Eugene
Nida, William Smalley, William Wonderly, Jacob Loewen,
Louis Luzbetak, and others picked up where Schmidt had
left off. Nida published some most significant books on
linguistics and culture, and Smalley became editor of the
journal *Practical Anthropology*. When the American Society of
Missiology was founded in 1967, *Practical Anthropology*
became the official journal of that society and was renamed
Missiology: an International Review. Probably more than any
other single factor, the formation of the ASM has proved to
be decisive in securing a place for missiology in the register
of theological disciplines.

This does not mean that the place currently enjoyed by
missiology will necessarily be an abiding one. Even now its
robustness is attended by a certain malaise. There are various
reasons for this. It is no doubt true, as Scherer says, that in
the United States before 1950 missiology, "unlike its more
academic European cousins, failed to develop a genuinely
scientific and academic character, and was 'plagued by a
certain immaturity with regard to definition, methodological

basis and objectives.' "[9] Alas, all too often that is still the case. But that does not account for the virtual demise of missiology in the state church–related educational institutions of Europe nor in many mainline seminaries in the United States.

The fact of the matter is that even more important than the word "science" is the word "mission" in our definition of missiology. *When a sense of mission is lost, missiology begs for students and becomes of little account. When mission becomes everything the church does or is supposed to do in the world, missiology loses its focus and becomes whatever reflects the mood of the hour. Protestant Conciliarism and Evangelicalism run both risks, but the evidence is that Conciliarism has already run afoul of the former risk and Evangelicalism is having trouble with the latter.*

It is important, therefore, that even as we celebrate the coming of age of this "new" science, we examine the state of its health with a view to preserving its tremendous potential for the fulfillment of the Great Commission.

Data

What we have said about unprecedented development of the discipline needs the reinforcement of some hard data if the significance of this major trend is to be appreciated. Let's look at some of it.

1. *A look at the schools.* As we have seen, missions have had a share in the curricula of certain theological schools since the last part of the nineteenth century, but the subject has never had the wide acceptance it enjoys in North America today. In 1985 the Association of the Professors of Missions conducted a survey on the theme "The Future of Missiology as an Academic Discipline in Seminary Education." The results represented a marked improvement over a similar survey conducted just a decade before. Replies were received from sixty-six member schools of the Association of Theological Schools (plus two others). When one takes into account the fact that missions in the classical sense is not a priority item in some ATS-related seminaries, the results become even more significant and encouraging.

At the doctoral level, some schools have offered the subject as one track within D.Theol. or Ph.D. programs. Kennedy School of Missions offered a Ph.D. degree in missions. Then in 1932–33 two Catholic schools in Europe began to offer the D.Miss. (doctor of missiology) degree.

After the initiation of a School of Mission in 1965, Fuller Theological Seminary offered the D.Miss. to those involved in crossscultural ministries. Subsequently, Fuller inaugurated the Ph.D. in missiology as well. Trinity Evangelical Divinity School, Asbury Theological Seminary, Columbia Graduate School of Bible and Missions, Wheaton Graduate School, Dallas Theological Seminary, Moody Bible Institute, and other schools offer advanced degree programs in missions.

Status of Missiology in Sixty-Six ATS-Related Seminaries[10]

Some course(s) in missions offered?	Yes—55; No—11
Increase in number of courses?	Increase—32; No change—15; Decrease—1
Number of courses?	Over 40—1; 20 to 40—4; 9 to 15—15; 1 to 3—20

If one were to include Bible schools and Bible colleges in a survey such as the one conducted by ATS, the results would show a continuing high interest in missions subjects. The Bible-school movement especially has been a primary training ground for missionary candidates reaching back into the nineteenth century. Nor should it be overlooked that, largely because of the impetus and materials provided by Ralph Winter and his colleagues at the U.S. Center for World Mission, a special course on missions perspectives is now offered at numerous secular colleges and universities across North America. As many as 2,200 students were enrolled in this course in 1987 alone.

2. *A look at professional societies.* Confining ourselves to North America, we note that three primary associations composed of teachers of missions and related subjects have been inaugurated since World War II. The Association of Professors of Missions (APM) was founded in 1950 in an attempt to reinforce missiology as a discipline in the schools. It continues to exist, though it is periodically called on to defend its existence in view of the attrition in missions

interest in some mainline seminaries and the creation of other associations.

The Association of Evangelical Professors of Missions (AEPM) was initiated by Evangelicals in 1965. It has had its ups and downs. But the 1980s has seen a revived interest so that its present membership is close to two hundred. It is significant that the AEPM is the only association of mission professors that requires its members to sign a statement of faith (either the statement of the EFMA or that of the IFMA).

The association that has contributed most to the recognition of missiology as a bona fide academic discipline is the American Society of Missiology (ASM). Founded in 1967, the ASM has not fulfilled all the hopes of those Evangelicals who were counted among its founding members. This is because, composed as it is of Roman Catholics, Conciliar Protestants, and Evangelicals, the views of mission demanding recognition are widely divergent. Nevertheless, the ASM has over seven hundred members and, through its annual meetings and publications (especially the journal *Missiology*), the ASM is currently the most prestigious of the three associations.

3. *A look at the research centers.* Still another factor in the rise of missiology has been the rapid increase in the number of centers where the Christian mission is researched and studied. Undoubtedly the most widely known of such centers are the Overseas Ministries Studies Center, the Billy Graham Center, the U.S. Center for World Mission, and the Missions Advanced Research Center (MARC). Darrell Dorr of the U.S. Center has compiled a listing of twenty-eight such centers world-wide, some of which are just beginning to make significant contributions to missions and missiology. The Midwest Center for World Mission in Oak Park, Illinois, is a case in point. Furthermore, Dorr indicates that his listing is only a partial one. There are more such centers—perhaps many more!

4. *A look at the available information.* To those who have been intimately involved in missionary education over the last thirty or forty years one of the most astounding developments in the entire enterprise has been the dramatic increase in missionary literature. A generation ago mission professors were hard put to find suitable materials even for the relatively few courses offered in most schools. Today the major problem is not to find materials but to sort them out. Bibliographies for most courses fill many pages.

We should recognize the contributions of those publishers, compilers, and distributors who are dedicated solely to the dissemination of mission materials. In addition to the contributions of the research centers mentioned above, William Carey Library in Pasadena has published many a book of missions, books that apart from that publisher would never have seen the light of day. The Association of Church Mission Committees (ACMC) in Wheaton has performed yoeman service in providing relevant materials (and conferences and seminars) for students and leaders of mission efforts in the local churches.

Perhaps just as important to missiology as journals and books and the like, is the current "emergence of total and complete global Christian information."[11] Given the development of extensive databases and the multiplication of personal computers being put to Christian uses (29 million computers are reported to be owned by Christian individuals and organizations world-wide!),[12] this may prove to be one of the most significant developments in modern missions.

AMERICAN MISSIOLOGY—WHICH WAY?

Three Sources of Missiology

There are three primary sources of the materials that go to make up the discipline of missiology. They can be referred to in various ways, but I choose to identify them as Revelation (the Old and New Testament Scriptures), research (the findings of the social sciences), and reflection (on the results of previous missionary experience). (This schema leaves the position of history somewhat ambiguous. Obviously, general history belongs to the social-science category. Missions history may go under either the research or the reflection category, depending on whether it is carefully reconstructed from the past or is more personal and immediate.)

We can diagram these sources and their relation to each other and to the discipline as on page 140.

It is important to keep these sources in proper balance. Since the mission is first of all God's mission and then becomes ours, it is imperative that the Bible be given priority in missiology. Augustine was correct in saying that knowledge from Scripture takes precedence over that from other sources. But he was also correct in asserting that all truth is God's truth and therefore can be used in Divine service.[13]

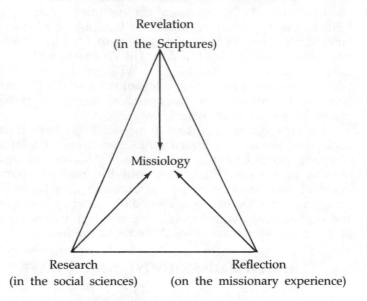

Revelation
(in the Scriptures)

Missiology

Research   Reflection
(in the social sciences)   (on the missionary experience)

The Sources of Missiology and Contemporary Writings

Perhaps more important than the number of missions and mission-related books is their nature. Book after book and article after article highlight the material of the social sciences—anthropology, linguistics, crosscultural communication, psychology, sociology, and history. A thematic content analysis of book reviews in the journal *Missiology* between 1973 and 1986 is revealing in this regard. (See below and also Appendix 3.)

Note that about one out of every four or five books reviewed focused on the social sciences. If one adds up the books highlighting theological themes on the one hand and those focusing on the sciences and missions history on the other, the former is outnumbered 83 to 133.

This concern for what can be learned from the various sciences is also evident in the *International Review of Missions* and, even more so, in the *Evangelical Missions Quarterly*. (See below and Appendix 2.)

Number of Books (of a Total of 444) Reviewed in Missiology
Which Focus on Aspects of Theory and Theology of Missions

Aspect	Number of Books	Percentage of Total
Contributions of the sciences	79	17.8%
Theology *and* mission	60	13.5%
History of missions	47	10.6%
Theology *of* mission	29	6.5%
Introduction to mission/missiology	18	4.1%
Missions bibliography, statistics	17	3.8%

Number of Articles (of a Total of 949) in IRM
Which Focus on Aspects of Theory and Theology in Missions

Aspect	Number of Articles	Percentage of Total
Theology *and* mission	90	9.5%
Theology *of* mission	55	5.8%
History of missions	34	3.6%
Contributions of the sciences	14	1.5%
Introduction to mission/missiology	14	1.5%
Missions bibliographic data, statistics	9	.9%

It is noteworthy that, on a percentage basis, the *IRM* gives considerably more attention to theological subjects and the history of missions than it does to the contributions of the sciences. The *EMQ*, on the other hand, gives a much higher priority to the contributions of the sciences than does the *IRM* and proportionately less to theological subjects and the history of missions. One explanation of this disparity may be that the theology of *IRM* authors and readers is more pluralistic and therefore comes in for more discussion, whereas *EMQ* authors and readers assume a basic agreement on theological matters and therefore give more attention to other aspects of mission theory. The editors and editorial board of the *EMQ* would be well advised to ponder how long this assumed theological consensus might hold if theological subjects related to mission continue to be neglected. Of what lasting significance is the Evangelical commitment to the authority of the Bible if biblical teachings do not explicitly inform our missiology?

Number of Articles (of a Total of 604) in EMQ
Which Focus on Aspects of Theory and Theology of Missions

Aspect	Number of Articles	Percentage of Total
Contributions of the sciences	38	6.3%
Theology *and* mission	26	4.3%
Theology *of* mission	19	3.1%
History of missions	8	1.3%
Missions bibliographic data, statistics	7	1.6%
Introduction to mission/missiology	4	.7%

Lessons from German Missiology

Edward Rommen reports that he recently asked a prominent Norwegian missiologist, Professor L. Munthe of the University of Oslo, to characterize the major difference between European and American approaches to missiology. Munthe replied without any hesitation that while much of American missiological thought has been dominated by the social sciences, Norwegian missiologists at least start with Scripture.[14] Given the Evangelical commitment to the authority of Scripture and in view of his interest in European missiology, Rommen (who was in the process of completing a doctorate at Munich), set out to see what could be learned from the course of German missiology and missions during the past one hundred years.

In the nineteenth century, the German conviction that target cultures should be understood thoroughly led to a great interest in ethnology (today considered to be a division of anthropology), the non-Christian religions, and other related disciplines. Actually, the social scientists of the time seem to have reciprocated by showing interest in the contribution that missionaries were making to their own disciplines. In the International Conference of Orientalists held in 1874, for example, the well-known Max Müller openly expressed the desire to have ten times as many missionaries in attendance because "in these missionaries we have not only apostles of religion and civilization, but at the same time the most valuable pioneers of scientific research."[15]

For Gustav Warneck—and other missiologists as well—this "friendly pact between mission and science" outweighed any possible risk.[16] Warneck appealed to the readers of his missions journal to support ethnographic research being undertaken by an anthropologist at Leipzig. In fact, he envisioned an exchange of information between missionaries and anthropologists that would aid "the propagation of the faith through science."[17]

This special appreciation for the role of the social sciences in missiology played an increasing role in German missiology during the first part of the twentieth century. By post–World War II days, however, the legitimacy and benefits of this approach were increasingly called into question, and German missiology became more oriented to theology once again.[18] The question is, Why? Several possible reasons may be adduced.

First, Rommen notes that as early as the 1920s there was a controversy in German missiology as to the extent to which biblical moorings had given way to applied anthropology. It is likely that this was a lingering concern for some.

Second, German missiologists were accused of using sociological and anthropological techniques in order to impose European civilization and church structures on unsuspecting peoples abroad. This was viewed by some as replacing mission with propaganda.[19]

Third, the Australian missiologist and former missionary to Indonesia John McIntosh suggests that the German approach yielded mixed results on the very field where it had one of its best tests. He believes that syncretism reared its head very early on in the Batak church (Rhenish Mission) precisely because the missionaries were overly confident in their anthropological understandings. This outcome may have contributed to the turnaround in German missiology.[20]

Whatever the reasons for the change in direction of German theology, Rommen's conclusion is worth pondering:

> Although contemporary German missiologists have not completely abandoned the social scientific aspects of mission strategy, they have indeed shifted the focus of their attention to a rethinking of the theological foundations for the mission task. North American evangelicals, on the other hand, seem to presuppose a kind of theological consensus, the existence of which "frees" the missiologist for unencumbered pursuit of the more practical issues. Now, we may not necessarily agree with the outcome of European theological deliberation, but their emphasis is probably legitimate since sound and active theology is the only effective safeguard against the potential misuse of the social sciences.[21]

THE MISSIOLOGY OF TOMORROW

Not a few European churchmen and missiologists have a tendency to look down their noses at much of American missiology. Undoubtedly there are various reasons for this, but the one that is most often heard is that American missiology is simply too pragmatic. Whatever works is right and good. Ironically, in many respects European missiology tends to be in decline. Chairs of mission in the major educational institutions of Europe (where theological studies are often under the aegis of these institutions) are gradually disappearing. Increasingly, whatever of missiology may be available to students is being taught by professors of church history, comparative religion, and so forth. North American missiology, on the other hand, is flourishing—especially in Evangelical institutions. For good or for ill, it seems likely that North American missiology will play a large role in pointing the way to the future.

If this reading of the situation is at all accurate, it is time for mission leaders and missiologists in North America to consider some hard choices.

Missiology is a science. That is, it represents a significant body of knowledge. But it is also eclectic. That is, it selects much of that knowledge from related disciplines, seeks out its significance for missions, and applies it to field situations.

The use of biblical controls in the processes of selection, interpretation, and implementation is extremely important. We neglect them at the peril of the very mission that missiology has been raised up to promote. *American missiology must choose. Will biblical theology control Evangelical missiology? Or will missiology go its own way? In large measure, tomorrow's mission depends on our choice.*

Not all the signs are entirely encouraging. In addition to the red flags to which we have already pointed, there are some disturbing questions raised by the approaches of prominent missiologists. Harvie Conn, for example, sees contemporary missiology as taking significant steps in the direction of a new kind of "trialogue" between theology, anthropology, and mission.[22] Well and good. Let us hope that such a trialogue becomes more evident and intense. It has great potential for good. But in his discussion of the agenda of such trialogue, Conn seems to think that the risk of overlooking anthropological insights is greater than the risk of compromising biblical authority. That is both doubtful and disturbing.

Charles Kraft insists that the insights of anthropologists and linguists are better suited than those of historians and philosophers for the tasks of interpreting and contextualizing Scripture.[23] It is true that anthropology and linguistics make substantial contributions to both missiology and Bible interpretation; but let us remember that if the Lord tarries, the anthropology of the twentieth century will no more be the anthropology of twenty-first century than nineteenth century anthropology is the anthropology of today. As for linguistics, that science is beset by some deep-seated controversies. Moreover some linguists are now pointing out that there has been an overdependence on the dynamic-equivalence approach to translation—the approach to which Kraft is deeply indebted. Missiologists highly value the insights of anthropologists and linguists, but the notion that grammatico-historical analysis should be relegated to a secondary role in Bible translation is not only doubtful and disturbing; it is also dangerous.

David Barrett indicates that the prophets and implementers of the new era we are entering "will be, not evangelists or missionaries or church executives, but global researchers. And the major tools seem likely to be personal computers with access to vast databases of missionary and global information."[24] Let it be that futurologists be consulted and that research be encouraged, but let us remember that the only sure guide to the future is God's prophetic Word and that apart from his direction the results of human inquiry may be misapplied or not applied at all. The best prophets are still the divinely appointed ones.

In 1980 two important mission conferences were held almost concurrently. One was the World Missionary Conference sponsored by the DWME (WCC) and held in Melbourne, Australia. The other was the Consultation on World Evangelization sponsored by the LCWE and held in Pattaya, Thailand. The theme of the former was "Your Kingdom Come." The theme of the latter was "How shall they hear?" Much has been written about those two conferences. Much more could be written. But an ironic twist of missiological history became apparent when, toward the end of the Pattaya consultation, a DWME leader came from the already completed meeting at Melbourne. His report brought to light that a significant part of the DWME program had been devoted to regular small-group Bible studies. The LCWE program had not featured any similar studies and only a very few of the major addresses had concentrated on the biblical text in any serious way!

All truth indeed is God's truth. But the truth that exists in undiluted and untainted form is discoverable in only one Book! Of the many choices that must be made in doing missiology, those made as a consequence of that fact loom as the most important. In our missiologizing will we, in effect, substitute the changing word of man for the eternal Word of God? The social science corpus for the Scripture canon? The seemingly pragmatic for the clearly apostolic? The scenarios of people for the scenario of the Lord? Those are the questions—and the choices—that confront missiology today!

7

BRIDGE-BUILDING—
RELATING TO PEOPLE OF
OTHER CULTURES AND
RELIGIONS

Thanks to modern technology, today's missionaries find that the first ten thousand miles in mission are relatively easy. It is the last eighteen inches that are difficult!

What does that mean? It means that international travel today presents relatively few problems. Of course, there are places on planet earth that are reached only by transferring from an international jet to a JAARS or MAF single-engine Cessna. But the fact remains that the vast majority of missionaries can reach their chosen field in a matter of hours.

It also means that once the missionary has arrived, the communication problem begins. To relate meaningfully to people of a very different culture and religion, to attain mutual understanding, to secure more than superficial change—these constitute the tough part of missions today just as they did in the first century.

Currently men and women in missions are being made profoundly aware of the challenge of those last eighteen inches! To an unprecedented degree every effort is being made to bridge them. To understand missionary bridge-building is to go a long way toward understanding missions today.

In a sense, bridge-building is not new. Down through history some have been greatly concerned with it. Numerous controversies have arisen over right and wrong ways of going about it. What is new is the extent of the contemporary concern and the intensity of current controversies.

BRIDGE-BUILDING IN EARNEST

Even before missiologists and theologians went to work on bridge-building in earnest in the 1970s and 1980s, it was apparent that missions needed rethinking and retooling. Traffic between Western and non-Western worlds had become two-way. Easterners had no qualms about exporting their ideologies and religions to the West. But Western missionaries were under fire for exporting Western culture and the Christian gospel to the East. Christian missionaries had begun to pay attention to the journal *Practical Anthropology*, Eugene Nida's *Customs and Cultures* and *Message and Mission*, Donald McGavran's *Bridges of God*, and Edward Hall's *Silent Language*. Some even went back to Kraemer's *Christian Message in a Non-Christian World* and his later book *The Communication of the Christian Faith*. Later the doors to "new understandings" of other religions were opened for Protestants at New Delhi in 1961 and for Roman Catholics at Vatican II in 1962–1965. For those who could read it, the handwriting on the wall conveyed a clear message: Christian missions must take other cultures and religions more seriously and relate to them more meaningfully or run the risk of being bypassed and left speaking to themselves in a language only they can understand.

In the late 1960s, and especially after an interreligious consultation and a consultation on contextual theology at the beginning of the 1970s, bridge-building began in earnest. Thenceforth missions would never be the same. In fact, the church would never be the same.

Consider the evidence:

1. Almost one-fifth of the books that have been reviewed in *Missiology* over almost a decade and a half have dealt directly (or perhaps indirectly in the case of books dealing with the non-Christian religions) with bridge-building.

2. Between 1964 and 1986, well over 10 percent of all major articles appearing in the *International Review of Mission* and the *Evangelical Missions Quarterly* focused on these same areas. (We will comment on the differences later.)

3. Within ten years or so of a major interreligious

dialogue and the initiation of the contextualization concept, numerous major conferences and consultations reflecting these concerns were scheduled:

Number of Book Reviews in Missiology (of a Total of 444)
Focusing on Aspects of Bridge-Building

Non-Christian religions	58	(13.1%)
Interreligious dialogue	6	(1.4%)
Communication/ contextualization	19	(4.3%)
Total	83	(18.8%)

Number of Articles (out of 949) in the IRM
and the EMQ (out of 604)
Focusing on Aspects of Bridge-Building

	IRM	EMQ
Non-Christian religions	84 (8.9%)	27 (4.5%)
Interreligious dialogue	24 (2.6%)	3 (0.5%)
Communication/ contextualization	24 (2.5%)	37 (6.1%)
Total	132 (14.0%)	67 (11.1%)

1970—Ajaltoun Consultation (WCC dialogue between Buddhists, Hindus, and Christians)

1971—Consultation on Dogmatic or Contextual Theology (WCC)

1972—"Salvation Today"—CWME Assembly in Bangkok

1973—"Seoul Declaration" by All-Asia Mission Consultation in Seoul

1974—"Lausanne Declaration" by International Congress on World Evangelization in Lausanne

1976—Consultation on Theology and Mission, Trinity Evangelical Divinity School—School of World Mission and Evangelism.

1977—Consultation on the Gospel and Culture in Bermuda (LCWE)

1980—Consultation on World Evangelization in Bangkok (LCWE)

4. Numerous publications featured these themes. In addition to the short-lived *Gospel in Context*, mission journals highlighted bridge-building themes. Books on the subject came off the press in record numbers. A sampling of titles will serve to illustrate the continuing concern:

1970—*Latin American Theology: Radical or Evangelical?*

1971—*Dialogue Between Men of Living Faiths*

1972—*Ministry in Context—The Third Mandate Program of the Theological Education Fund (1970–1977)*

1974—*Truth and Dialogue in World Religions: Conflicting Truth Claims*

——*Christianity Confronts Culture: A Strategy for Cross-Cultural Evangelism*

1975—*What's Gone Wrong With the Harvest?*

1976—*Asian Voices in Christian Theology*

1977—*Dialogue: The Key to Understanding Other Religions*

——*How Can I Get Them to Listen?: A Handbook on Communication Strategy and Research*

1978—*Communicating Christ Cross-Culturally: An Introduction to Missionary Communication*

1979—*Christianity in Culture: A Study in Dynamic Biblical Theologizing in Cross-Cultural Perspective*

Gospel and Culture

1980—*Contextualization of Theology: An Evangelical Assessment*

New Paths in Muslim Evangelism: Evangelical Approaches to Contextualization

1981—*Towards a World Theology*

1982—*Doing Theology Across Cultures*

Destroying the Barriers: Receptor Oriented Communication of the Gospel

1984—*Communication Theory for Christian Witness*

1985—*Preparing Missionaries for Intercultural Communication: A Bicultural Approach*

Counseling Cross-Culturally: An Introduction to Missionary Counseling

1986—*Ministering Cross-Culturally: An Incarnational Model for Personal Relationships*

Pastoral Counseling Across Cultures

BRIDGE-BUILDING AND RISK-TAKING

Missiologists often speak of the risks involved in relating to people of other cultures and religions. These risks are of various kinds.

The Risk of Being Misunderstood

Almost two hundred years ago the "Serampore Trio" (Carey, Marshman, and Ward) were misunderstood because of their efforts to understand the culture and religion of India. In fact, they devoted so much attention to this that some of their supporters back in England accusingly reminded them that they had been sent to convert the heathen, not to be converted by them! But those gifted and intrepid missionaries knew precisely what they were doing. You can be sure that if Carey thought that Baptist convictions were important enough to try to convince Judson of them, then surely he thought that the Christian gospel was important enough to convince Indians of the lordship of Christ. Indeed he did. And that is what he and his colleagues were about—learning about India in order to adapt the presentation of the biblical gospel most effectively.

The Risk of Going Too Far

Charles Kraft believes that at least half of the so-called heresies identified by the church councils of the early centuries were not really heresies at all but, rather, were legitimate attempts to contextualize the gospel for pagan peoples of the time.[1] That is highly questionable. Given the great minds and hearts of the church fathers and examining the doctrines in question, a much fairer estimate is that heresy was the right name for them. But it is likely that at least a number of those teachings did represent attempts to bridge the gap between Christianity and non-Christian populations. And to the extent that that was so, the fact that some of those attempts were labeled heresies alerts us to the risk of going too far in bridge-building. It is ironic that the gospel itself can be lost in the effort to accommodate it to other cultures and religions. But precisely that sometimes happened in the early centuries and precisely that is happening today. The risk of going too far is very real.

Ⓐ The Risk of Not Going Far Enough

Recognizing the risks of being misunderstood and going too far, not a few missionaries and theologians have refused to make any adjustments whatsoever. Edward F. Hills, for example, not only takes exception to any translation of the Bible other than the now rather archaic King James Version, he even suggests that this translation (English though it be) will bind together true Christians from all cultures for many decades to come![2] Similarly, in one way or another, many Western theologians seem to insist that the only really valid theology (and the only valid way of doing theology) is to be found in their Western cultures. By the same token, many evangelists and even missionaries attempt to communicate the gospel and teach the Bible in the Third World by using the same sermons and textbooks that were developed in their own cultures (usually translated into the local language, of course). And for their part, Western authors are often commended for the number of languages into which their books are translated—sometimes, at least, a rather dubious distinction.

Several years ago I was invited to speak in a newly planted congregation in an East African city. Both missionaries and nationals had been involved in the effort. Preceding the preaching service was a Sunday school with "classes for all ages." I joined the adult Bible class, which, for the size of the church, was amazingly small despite probable cultural factors militating against a large adult class. The missionary teacher was teaching the Book of Romans. His outline, content, illustrations, and approach could as readily have been used in East St. Louis. He seemed oblivious to the fact that the entire lesson, and probably the choice of Romans itself, grew out of his upbringing, theological training, and ministry experience in a culture far removed from Africa. When class members introduced themselves later, it became apparent that only those who were interested in Western culture (largely for professional reasons) had bothered to join the class. (That is discouraging because African believers desperately need biblical instruction that is relevant to their world view!)

In large measure, missions must assume the responsibility for the widespread appeal of nativistic movements in Africa, many of which combine the beliefs and practices of tribal religion with those of Christianity in a syncretistic mix. Generally speaking, Africans live with a fear of spirits, respond to sickness, resort to witchcraft, engage in worship, and otherwise experience life and death in ways that can be appreciated by most Westerners only by dint of great effort. But apart from that understanding and appropriate adaptation, the missionary form of the Christian message does not seem to answer local questions or fit local situations. Reversion to the "old way," or at least revision of the "new way," should not, then, come as a surprise.

The time has come to give serious consideration to the growing volume of criticism that is coming from Christian leaders in non-Western cultures. To take but one illustration from many, consider the words of the Seoul Declaration noted earlier:

> Western theology is by and large rationalistic, moulded by Western philosophies, preoccupied with intellectual concerns, especially those having to do with faith and reason. All too often, it has reduced the Christian faith to abstract concepts which may have answered the questions of the past, but which fail to grapple with the issues of today. It has consciously been conformed to the secularistic world view associated with the Enlightenment. . . . Furthermore, having been wrought in Christendom, it hardly addresses the questions of people living in situations characterized by religious pluralism, secularism, resurgent Islam, or Marxist totalitarianism. . . . Consequently, we insist on the need for critical reflection and theological renewal. We urgently need an Evangelical theology which is faithful to Scripture and relevant to the varied situations in the Third World.[3]

BRIDGE-BUILDING AND ABERRANT CONTEXTUALIZATION

A number of terms and concepts relate to bridge-building in missions—identification, adaptation, accommodation, indigenization, inculturation, and dialogue, to name some of the major ones. (And various strategies have been proposed with a view to accomplishing this—using "eye openers," finding "redemptive analogies," and establishing "common ground," among others.) All of these terms have their own nuances, but the one term that at one time or another has been applied to all of these and other bridge-building efforts is the new term "contextualization." That is therefore the one we will focus on in connection with the present trend.

The origin of the neologism "contextualization" is usually associated with a consultation ':'Dogmatic or Contextual Theology" held in Bossey Switzerland, in 1971 at which Bishop Nikos Nissiotis presided, and with the Third (Reform) Mandate Program (1970–77) of the Tehological Education Fund (WCCdsponsored) and its director, Shoki Coe. These leaders made it clear that they wanted to go beyond indigenization (the establishment of self-supporting, self-governing, and self-propagating churches proposed by Henry Venn and Rufus Anderson in the nineteenth century) and similar approaches to both missionizing and theologizing. "Contextualization" has been the "in word" in missiology ever since. It does not represent a fad. It represents a major trend. It will not go away—either as a term or as a missionizing and theologizing approach.

Elsewhere I have attempted to deal in some detail with the underlying presuppositions and varied outcomes of differing understandings of contextualization.[4] Here we can no more than highlight them, but it is absolutely essential that we do at least that much because these understandings chart very different roads into the future of missions.

Contextualization as "Prophetic Accommodation"

From an Evangelical point of view it is unfortunate that those TEF initiators of contextualization were not bound by an absolutely authoritative biblical text. This is apparent in the following words of one of them (Shoki Coe):

> . . . in using the word *contextualization*, we try to convey all that is implied in the familiar term *indigenization*, yet seek to press beyond for a more dynamic concept which is open to change and which is also future-oriented.
>
> Contextuality . . . is that critical assessment of what makes the context really significant in the light of the *missio Dei*. It is the missiological discernment of the signs of the times, seeing where God is at work and calling us to participate in it. Authentic contextuality leads to contextualization . . . and this dialectic between contextuality and contextualization indicates a new way of theologizing. It involves not only words, but actions.[5]

The TEF initiators called for a kind of contextualization that would begin, not only or primarily with a study of the Bible, church creeds, and classical texts of theology, but also with involvement in the contemporary situation. In particular, they focused on participation in today's struggles against economic and political oppression. Taking the Old Testament prophets as their models, they insisted that God's voice is to be heard, and his acts are to be seen, in the human situation—especially that of the downtrodden and disenfranchised of the world. If the church is to communicate "good news" to such people, they must be able to recognize it as good news. If Christian theology is to be *relevant* to them, it must be *rooted* in their existential situation. Of course, it should also be *related* to the Bible.

The architects of contextualization were not creating something out of nothing. Several of them were informed by a Marxist interpretation of history, Moltmann's "theology of hope," Cone's "Black theology," the historical-critical approach to the biblical text, and much else. But they succeeded in directing the attention of both the church and its missions to the critical need for breaking the Western mould that had informed and formed the ways in which Christianity was both understood and practiced in much of the world. And they helped to fuel still more efforts to make the gospel and Christian theology "relevant" to people of other cultural and religious backgrounds. "Liberation theology," "Third-eye theology," "waterbuffalo theology," "Yin-Yang theology," "African theology"—these and other contextualized theologies became focal points of discussion. The political theologies among them became especially popular. A new "theology of theology"—ethnic theology (ethnotheology)— became prominent. People of mission were challenged to think beyond traditional geographical boundaries to cultural, religious, and sociopolitical boundaries.

But informed as it was by a liberal understanding of Scripture, contextualization as initially proposed went too far in the direction of accommodating cultures, religions, and existential situations. Authentic contextualization was "prophetic." *This did not simply or even primarily mean to communicate the message of the biblical prophets. It meant to attempt to reenact the ministry of the prophets.* It meant to go among peoples in their various contexts and deliver a divine message that speaks to their situation. However—and this is a critical point—it also meant that the message could be discerned only *by listening to, and joining in the struggles of, the poor.* The prophet is one who is able to hear God's voice and see his acts in human affairs. He then articulates what he sees and hears.

There are various versions of this type of contextualization, but if one were to hazard a simple definition that would apply to most of these versions, it might be "prophetic accommodation." And if one were to try to describe the method that would apply to most of them, it would center on the method of dialectic with a view to discerning the truth (what God is saying and doing) in any given situation. With this in mind, it is easier to understand Emilio Castro's conclusion (mentioned earlier) that God is saying and doing what the poor are saying and doing.

Contextualization as "Syncretistic Accommodation"

If the contextualization proposed by Nissiotis and his colleagues seems to point in the direction of an unbiblical *relativism* rather than biblical *relevancy*, still other bridging proposals go even farther in that direction.

E. C. Dewick notes three attitudes that have characterized the church's attitude toward other religions:[6] (1) the attitude of hostility that refused validity to the truth claims of other religions, (2) the insistence that Christianity is the fulfillment of the partial truths presented by other religions, and (3) the willingness to affirm that valid truths are taught by all religions and the desire for interreligious cooperation. In his opinion, there was little or no evidence of the third attitude in the church right up to the middle of the twentieth century. Commenting on this, Donald Swearer says:

> If Dewick's assessment of the attitude of the Christian church toward non-Christian religions by and large is true, then we would have to say that the past twenty-five years represent a departure from precedent. Today, many prominent Christian spokespersons profess an attitude of interreligious cooperation. As F. S. C. Northrop put it, "The unique religious fact of our century is its universal ecumenical mentality." Meetings have been held and publications have appeared from the World Council of Churches Program on Dialogue with People of Living Faiths and Ideologies, and from the Vatican's Secretariat for Non-Christian Religions. Scholarly conferences on

truth claims and interreligious dialogue have also been held (e.g., Conference on the Philosophy of Religion, University of Birmingham, 1970). And publications of experts on non-Christian religions, who as committed Christians also write about dialogue with the worlds' living faiths (e.g., Wilfred Cantwell Smith), all bear witness to a burgeoning interest in this area.[7]

It is a rather simple thing to illustrate further precisely what Swearer has in mind.

In 1970, about the time that the direction of the TEF consultation mentioned above was being determined, the WCC sponsored a most significant interfaith consultation in Ajaltoun, Lebanon, that was destined to set the stage for others still to come. Called a "Dialogue Between Men of Living Faiths," it brought Christians, Buddhists, Hindus, and Muslims together for ten days of conversations and joint (voluntary) worship. At the end of the consultation participants were invited to write down their impressions. Among others who wrote in a similar vein, one wrote:

> The dialogue . . . introduced most of us to a new spirituality, an interfaith spirituality, which I mostly felt in common prayer: who actually led the prayer or medita- tion, a Christian or a Muslim, or a Hindu, or a Buddhist, did not much matter. . . what we really became aware of was our common human situation before God and in God.
>
> We were thus led gradually into a new relation with God, with our own selves, and with others, and this new relation was perhaps to what entire human history was moving. . . . A new day was dawning not on a new earth, or in a new sky but on a new work of man, on man doing something new. This day is just begun. Our dialogue was therefore not an end but a beginning, only a step, there is a long way to go.[8]

Again, John Hick, who is professor of theology at the University of Birmingham and who edited a book based on the Birmingham conference mentioned by Swearer, writes in that book: "We live amidst unfinished business; but we must trust that continuing dialogue will prove to be a *dialogue into truth*, and that in a fuller grasp of truth *our present conflicting doctrines will ultimately be transcended*"[9] (emphasis mine).

More recently, Hick has helped edit a book that includes contributions representing the Buddhist, Hindu, Jewish,

Muslim, Sikh, and Christian faiths. The essays vary but exhibit two strands of thinking that seem to be common to them all. First, all view the different religious faiths as varied but valid ways of perceiving the Ultimate Reality. Second, all are concerned with the kind of transformation of human existence that replaces self-centeredness with "Reality-centeredness" via the religious experience afforded by the various religions.[10]

Swearer also mentions Wilfred Cantwell Smith in this connection. Smith commends the church for moving away from its "erstwhile monologue of proselytizing missions" to contemporary dialogue. But he finds that dialogue still to be too occasional and polarized. He proposes a "colloquy" in which there is a "side-by-side confronting of the world's problems." And he suggests that in this way we can move toward an entirely new theology, which he calls a "world theology."[11]

What is being proposed here can be thought of as another (aberrant) form of contextualization—*syncretistic accommodation*. The *context* is the interfaith meeting of religious progressives seen as a microcosm of *seemingly* diverse cultures and religions. The *method* is to pursue (new) truth by means of nondisputational dialogue (or colloquy in the case of Smith). The *result* is a new syncretistic "gospel" that will eventuate in a "new day" of "new relationships" between God and man, and man and man.

BRIDGE-BUILDING AND BIBLICAL CONTEXTUALIZATION

As can be seen from the above, there are two dangers inherent in bridge-building. One danger is that of underestimating the possibility of losing the truth of divine revelation as it is in the Scriptures. Absolutely nothing can be gained, and everything can be lost, by compromising the gospel in an attempt to communicate it. The other danger is that of overestimating the value of such truth as may be found in human cultures and religions. No one who understands either the cultures or the religions of humankind would say that they are devoid of all truth. But neither would anyone who understands the Scriptures say that *as cultural and religious systems* they lead people to God. If in our quest for common ground we leave the impression that God and his

Son and his salvation can be found within those systems and apart from a radical conversion, nothing is gained and all is lost.

Bridge-Building in the Bible

The greatest gap ever bridged was the gap that existed between a holy God and sinful man. And the best bridging ever accomplished occurred when the great "Apostle and High Priest of our confession" (Heb. 3:1) invaded our planet and lived and labored among us as the Man Christ Jesus. Philippians 2:6–8 recounts the gigantic downward steps taken by our Lord: from equality with the Father to manhood to servanthood to a grievous death. Nevermore could any man say, "I have no way of knowing—really knowing—what God is like." Look at Jesus the Son, and you see God the Father.

The Bible is replete with examples of divinely undertaken and divinely directed contextualization. But for present purposes we confine ourselves to several instructive examples from the ministries of the Lord Jesus and the apostle Paul.

In the ministry of our Lord a most obvious demonstration of what we are talking about is to be found in John 3 and 4. In chapter 3 Jesus spoke to the Jewish teacher Nicodemus, who by every human measurement must have had few peers when it came to religious knowledge and moral character. But Jesus spoke of the need for a change so radical that it can be said to be a new birth without which no one can apprehend or enjoy the kingdom of God. As was the case with so many Jews encountered by Jesus, Nicodemus desperately needed to know that to be physically born and morally enculturated as a progeny of Abraham was not sufficient for salvation.

Turning to the episode with the Samaritan woman in chapter 4 we see that the conversation began and developed very differently. In that case the analogy between physical water and the "water of life" served to initiate a lengthy dialogue. Then the rival claims of two religions—one centered in Gerizim and the other in Jerusalem—quickly came to the fore when the woman said, "Our fathers worshiped in this mountain, and you people say that in Jerusalem is the place where men ought to worship"(v. 20). Jesus responded with two assertions that speak volumes today. First, true worship is not ultimately to be tied to any geographical location but is a matter of spirit and truth (v. 23). Second, Samaritan worship was devoid of a knowledge of God, whereas Jewish worship was of God (v. 22). In this latter connection the phrase "we worship that which we know" is quite remarkable. It is the only case where Jesus used this precise expression and by it spoke *as a Jew*, though, significantly enough, he said something similar in answering the Canaanite woman (Matt. 15:24, 26).

As we turn to the apostle Paul, it is instructive to analyze Luke's account of his early encounters with various types of audiences when he embarked on his missionary ministry. In Acts 13:14–50 we find him addressing Jews, proselytes, and Gentile God-fearers in the synagogue at Pisidian Antioch. Accordingly, he began by saying, "The God of this people Israel chose our fathers" (v. 17) and proceeded to argue from Old Testament history and prophecy that Jesus indeed was the Christ. In Lystra (14:8–18) the missionaries encountered animistic people who made ready to sacrifice to them as gods. There Paul found it necessary to insist on their own humanity, to contrast idols and the living God, and to overview a very different sort of history stemming, not from special, but from natural revelation. Later, during his second journey, Paul *disputed* with Athenian Stoics and Epicureans (see Acts 17:18 NASB margin) and addressed them in a way that recognized their religiosity and revealed a knowledge of their poets, but which insisted on repentance and faith in Christ (Acts 17:22–31).

Biblical bridge-building reveals a profound knowledge of human nature, culture, and religion on the one hand, and a significant effort to adapt to them on the other.

Contextualization as "Apostolic Accommodation"

The Bible does more than provide precedents and perspectives for bridge-building. It also defines the parameters. Christ commanded the apostles (and us) to *disciple* the world's peoples (to enroll them as his learners or followers) by *going* into the whole world, by *teaching* all that he commanded, and by *baptizing* them in the name of Father, Son, and Holy Spirit. Any accommodation that is made to the cultures and religions of the world must be consonant with that commission—its requirements, its message, its means, and its ends. That is why in biblical bridge-building

communication always centered on what God had said in his
Word; the call was always to conversion; the demands were
never adjusted to human preferences; and dialogue often
entailed disputation.

Bruce Nicholls has defined contextualization as "the
translation of the unchanging content of the Gospel of the
Kingdom into verbal form meaningful to the peoples in their
separate cultures and within their particular existential
situations."[12] That definition is unnecessarily restrictive, for
it confines contextualization to verbal forms, whereas lifestyle, theologizing, programming, and much else can be a
part of it. But it recognizes two elements that are absolutely
essential to authentic contextualization efforts: the supracultural nature of the biblical gospel and the cultural requirements of meaningful communication.

Of course, the biblical gospel is not acultural. It was
given to and through prophets and apostles—men who
received and reported the divine message in linguistic and
cultural frames of reference. But the sovereign God ordered
the cultural circumstances, the prophetic and apostolic
personnel, and the linguistic forms in such a way that in both
the revelational and inscripturation processes it was *his
message* that was transmitted. The biblical message, therefore, is unique. The impingements of circumscribed cultures,
imperfect authors, and human languages are transcended in
such a way as to provide a perfect gospel.

Of course, we often fail in many respects as communica-
tors. But, relying on God-given abilities and the ever-present
Spirit, we are called on to translate, adapt, adjust, interpret,
and apply the gospel to people in their respective cultures in
such a way as to preserve as much of its original meaning
and relevance as possible.

This approach can be called "apostolic accommodation."
It is *apostolic* because it is especially but not solely the
responsibility and privilege of those who are sent to other
peoples in other cultures. The *context* is the arenas of non-
Christian belief systems. The *method* is to establish a common
ground in which unbelievers can be *taught* the truth of the
supracultural gospel. The *result* will be both the transformation of those who place their faith in Christ and the
confirmation in unbelief of those who refuse so to do.

If the reason for the current emphasis on bridge-building
in such journals as the *IRM* and the *EMQ* is now more

apparent, so must the differences in approaches be more clear. The preoccupation with the non-Christian religions and with interreligious dialogue in the *IRM*, which we noted above, sometimes stems from the desire to transcend differences coupled with a willingness to downgrade the necessity of conversion. As Willard Oxtoby so pointedly puts it:

> The Gospel authors said, "Believe," but they also report Jesus as saying, "Love." The core of Christian identity lays on us an obligation to love our neighbor—including our non-Christian neighbor—that must be weighed against the obligation to assert the truth of our creed. What, then, if our insistence on preaching our belief is an offense to the integrity and identity of our non-Christian neighbor? Christ's commandment to love that neighbor may imply that we curtail our insistence on our own rightness. Put simply, to tell the Hindu, for example, that he cannot find salvation or fulfillment in his own tradition and community *is morally a very un-Christian thing to do*[13] (emphasis mine).

Oxtoby goes on to point out that this approach is not new, having been proposed by such men as William Hocking over half a century ago, by E. L. Allen in 1960, and more recently by Wilfred Cantwell Smith. Indeed, it is not new. What seems to be new, however, is the rapidity with which it is being embraced by so many both within Christian and non-Christian traditions.

Conservatives, on the other hand, are much more concerned with a kind of contextualization that results in a clear communication of the claims of Christ and the call of the gospel. They tend to understand dialogue in the New Testament sense of confronting unbelief with the necessity for repentance and faith. The Lausanne Covenant speaks of dialogue "whose purpose is to listen sensitively in order to understand" (para. 4), but the understanding gained is with a view to present the gospel in more meaningful and persuasive ways.

Perhaps it would be helpful to chart the major positions on bridge-building (summarized above) on a "contextualization continuum," which ranges from a high view to a low view of biblical revelation on the one hand, and a high view to a low view of human culture and religion on the other.

The Contextualization Continuum[14]

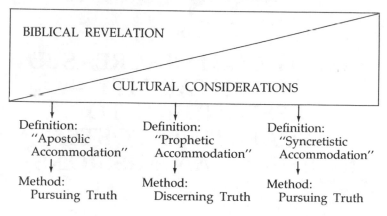

Definition: "Apostolic Accommodation"	Definition: "Prophetic Accommodation"	Definition: "Syncretistic Accommodation"
Method: Pursuing Truth	Method: Discerning Truth	Method: Pursuing Truth

BRIDGES TO MEN AND THE "BRIDGE" TO GOD

During his earthly ministry our Lord taught his disciples, saying, "Truly, truly, I say to you, I am the door of the sheep. All who came before Me are thieves and robbers, but the sheep did not hear them. I am the door; if anyone enters through Me, he shall be saved, and shall go in and out, and find pasture. The thief comes only to steal, and kill, and destroy; I came that they might have life, and might have it abundantly" (John 10:7–10).

So much for all those pretending profferers of salvation who *preceded* Christ in the world, irrespective of their insistences and even their insights.

Just before his passion, resurrection and ascension while there on the Mount of Olives our Lord said, "See to it that no one misleads you. For many will come in My name, saying, "I am the Christ," and will mislead many" (Matt. 24:4–5).

So much for all those who *succeeded* Christ and have laid claim—or yet will lay claim—to being God's Anointed, irrespective of their persuasive words and even their powerful works.

Bridges to God? There is but one, and it is God's "Son Gift" and not any product of human culture or religion.

Bridges to the world and its people? He built them, and so must we.

8

RISING COSTS/INCREASED ACCOUNTABILITY— RESPONDING TO ESCALATING COSTS IN CHRISTIAN MISSIONS

The really critical question traditionally posed by the missions to potential candidates has been a simple one: "Are you *willing* to obey the Great Commission and go to a foreign land with the gospel?" More often than not this issue of willingness to engage in missionary service was the critical issue. If potential candidates were willing to go, then it was time to tackle the next major hurdle: finances. If candidates could raise their support, the missions were ready to send them out. Several assumptions undergirded this approach.

First, it was assumed that we would go forward in missions if only we could send out missionaries in sufficiently large numbers.

Second, it was taken for granted that almost any Western missionary, quite irrespective of educational background and the abilities that she or he might possess, would be both appreciated and effective on the mission field.

Third, it was assumed that missions would not cost very much. The American dollar set the standard for world currencies. And, since missionaries are the most dedicated among Christ's servants, they would labor sacrificially with whatever support God's people in affluent America might be led to provide.

Of course, these and similar assumptions have been

rather severely tested at various times down through the years. A classic and almost humorous case in point is the agreement worked out between A. B. Simpson and Fredrik Franson in response to Hudson Taylor's plea for volunteers to go to China. Since Franson in Scandinavia found it possible to find recruits but difficult to get enough money to send and support them while Simpson in America found the reverse to be true, they agreed that Franson would provide Scandinavian volunteers and Simpson would collect the American dollars required to send them to China.

It all seemed logical enough—given the assumptions above. But the plan backfired. Swedish volunteers were indeed sent to China with American dollars. But objections were soon forthcoming from China. Franson's dedicated but uneducated Scandinavian lumberjacks somehow did not really mesh with China's highly developed culture! Simpson withdrew support. Some of Franson's recruits were left in the lurch. Simpson and Franson had a falling out of sorts. Looking back, we can understand why both of these missionary-minded leaders were justifiably piqued at the results of their experiment. Missions require a special kind of culture-sensitive dedication and logic!

In spite of problems, old understandings of the nature of missions and the characteristics of missionaries have enjoyed a remarkable longevity. Today, however, though the old assumptions and their attendant errors are by no means a thing of the past, there is a growing trend toward higher accountability. Moreover, as the cost of missions continues to spiral upward, we can expect to see an ever-increasing attention to cost-effectiveness in the future.

THE SKYROCKETING COST OF MISSIONS

Before me is a letter from a former advisee in the seminary. He now has his Ph.D., is married, has two children, and is bound for Europe with a well-known faith mission. The letter says that he is in need of $36,000 yearly support and $23,000 for outgoing outfit. That is the *current* support level. It would not be at all unusual if one to two years of deputation were required to raise that amount. And by that time, the amount of yearly support needed will likely increase by several thousand dollars.

When adjusted for inflation, statistics indicate that the

support of foreign missionaries has not really increased in recent years.[1] But in terms of the sheer number of dollars involved, the cost factor is at least psychologically somewhat overwhelming. Until very recently, inflation has seriously affected the economy of the United States itself. But to a far greater extent it has plagued many a foreign country where our missionaries are working. There the inflation rate has sometimes been as high as ten to twenty times that of the United States. And recently the inflation problem has been compounded by the fact that the American dollar has taken a beating on international money markets.

Again, it is now widely felt that missionary support levels should be somewhat commensurate with those of other Christian workers. Many missions build the cost of health insurance, retirement plans, children's education, and even a vacation allowance into their support structure. (At least one mission even allows candidates to raise monies required to pay off debts incurred in the process of getting their education!) Then too, the cost of maintaining a home office and staff, and of promoting the work of the mission, must be taken into consideration.

As a result of these and other relevant factors, the support required to send my former advisee and his family to Europe is thirteen times that allowed my family of four when we were sent to Japan just one short generation ago in 1950! And their outfit allowance is forty-six times as much!

The calculations of an executive officer of one of our large Evangelical denominational missions reveal that from the time of acceptance until the completion of one term of service and the first furlough period, the mission has made an investment of just under a quarter million dollars in their average missionary family.

No wonder the pastor of the average Evangelical church is deluged with requests to allow a representative of this or that mission organization to make a presentation in his church! No wonder that a true "World Christian" friend of mine reports that he regularly receives from ten to twenty letters a week requesting financial support, and that before the ink is dry on his check another appeal has arrived, sometimes from the same mission! No wonder that a significant number of Christian young people have reservations about a support system that seems to require that they spend many months traveling from church to church in order to raise their support! *Missions cost money!*

PATTERNS OF MISSIONS GIVING

How have Christian churches in general, and mission is particular, responded to the escalating cost of carrying on the mission of the church? As we would expect—and as we will see—the responses are many and varied. In fact, it is because of the wide variety of proposals that intelligent and Spirit-directed choices have to be made by Christian leaders and laypeople everywhere. But there are at least two trends that seem to be both general and significant. First, people in the churches are responding with a sense of increased stewardship. Second, leaders in missions are responding with a higher sense of accountability.

Global Giving for World Missions

Extreme caution must be exercised in interpreting and comparing statistics on Christian finances. Problems connected with reporting, inflation, fluctuating exchange rates, giving outside of normal channels, and so forth plague statisticians. Even though the editors of the *Mission Handbook*, for example, attempt to make those adjustments that will make figures as comparable as possible, they themselves indicate the difficulties that are faced in interpreting the data.

Although comparisons should not be made between the two sets of figures, it is instructive to see recent patterns of missions giving world-wide and in North America.[2]

From the charts below it will be apparent that while global Christian *income* was about thirty times as great in 1987 as compared to 1900, total Christian *giving* was only seventeen times as much in 1900. Giving for *foreign missions* during those eighty-seven years increased until it was forty times as much as in 1900. This is an encouraging sign. However, when one realizes that the per-member weekly mission giving has increased only tenfold, is no more than ten cents, and is not projected to go higher during the next few years, one is tempted to ask how serious Christians really are about fulfilling the Great Commission.

It is also important to note that while church income has increased by little more than 50 percent during the seventeen years from 1970 to 1987 and is projected to stay about the same for the next thirteen years, parachurch and institutional giving has increased 300 percent and is projected to increase 600 percent over the thirty years between 1970 and the year 2000! This may well prove to be one of the most significant trends in global Christian giving patterns.

Chart 8.1

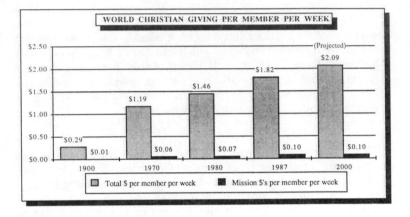

Chart 8.2

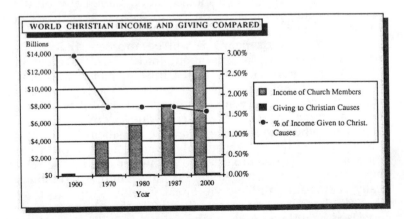

North American Patterns of Missions Giving

Turning from global to North American data, we take note of four significant aspects of missions giving.

Chart 8.3

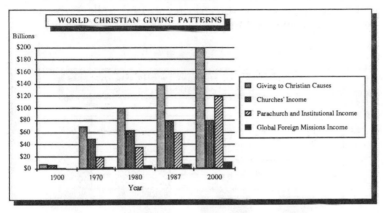

First, missions giving in North America has now topped the one billion dollar mark. (See chart 8.4.)

Chart 8.4[3]

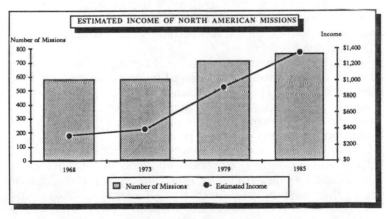

Note: The missions totals represent the number included in the *Mission Handbook;* the income figures include reported plus estimated giving and are adjusted to indicate the amount going for overseas ministries.

Second, when adjusted for inflation, the increase in giving is not great. The increase in the six-year period between 1979 and 1985 is 48 percent. When adjusted for the real value of the dollar (based on the 1967 dollar), the actual increase amounts to only 3 percent. (See chart 8.5.)

Chart 8.5[4]

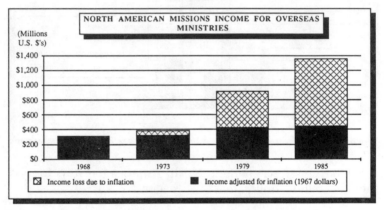

Third, between 1968 and 1979 the percentage of missions income as compared to total church income grew to 13 percent. Since that time it has actually declined to 11 percent. (See chart 8.6.)

Fourth, while income in every grouping of missions increased significantly, unaffiliated missions experienced the largest increase. This more than offsets the rather modest gains of IFMA (interdenominational) missions and correlates with the unprecedented gains world-wide of parachurch and institutional income that we noted above. See chart 8.7.)

We conclude that although missions giving around the globe and in North America appears to be increasing significantly along with rising missions costs, it is doing little more than keeping pace with those costs. Insofar as world evangelization is dependent on financial stewardship, Christians must give more sacrificially if the world is to be evangelized and the Great Commission is to be fulfilled.

Perhaps just as important is the fact that churches and

denominational missions seem to be lagging behind independent and unaffiliated Christian organizations (though the unaffiliated status of the Southern Baptists offsets this factor somewhat). Various reasons may be cited for this: the increasing number of such organizations, the sophisticated appeals being used by them, the newness of many of these organizations, and the innovativeness and vitality of their leadership. But the trend may also signal a lack of confidence in, and concern for, the older churches and their missions. Insofar as this may be the case, Christian leaders and believers should seriously consider the implications of this trend for the future of the church and its missions.

Chart 8.6[5]

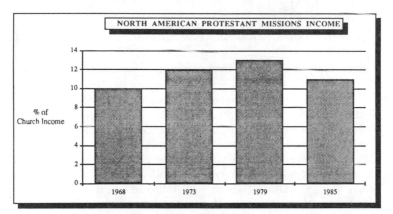

MISSIONARY PERSONNEL—THE PRIMARY RESOURCE

Along with the rising costs in missions there has come to be an increased appreciation for the really primary resource in missions—the missionaries themselves. Perhaps the rising costs have been a factor in this trend, though there are certainly other factors as well.

Great Expectations

The missionary task is one of the most challenging tasks on planet earth. Today more and more missions leaders recognize that fact and are attempting to attract qualified candidates and increase the effectiveness of field missionaries.

Chart 8.7[6]

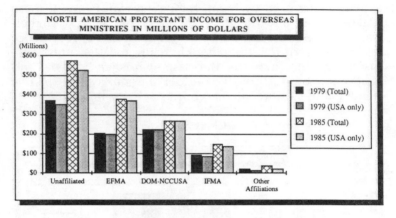

To understand something of what is involved in missionary work, imagine yourself to be a missionary on furlough. Candidacy, itineration, orientation, departure for the field, arrival, language study, involvement, reentry into the home culture, deputation in the churches—all of these experiences and more are now behind you. You have learned many things. Among them you have learned that in every place and at every turn of the road new expectations and demands are made of the missionary. Putting aside stereotypes (missionaries always wear pith helmets; missionaries are backnumbers; if you can't do anything else, you can always become a missionary; missionaries are super holy), think of those expectations that have been put forward with more seriousness and study:

1. The mission board expected you to be spiritual, to be certain of your missionary call, to be adequately prepared, and to have good references.
2. Pastors and potential supporters in the churches expected you to be winsome, a good communicator, gifted, able to report significant success on the field, and the parent of disciplined children.
3. Fellow missionaries expected you to be a good team

member, to learn the language well, and, especially,
to keep your opinions to yourself for a few years.
4. Nationals expected you to be like the pioneers with
one small difference: you should understand that
nationals are now in control and you should conduct
yourself accordingly.

Of course, you are now in a position to reflect on the
expectations you have had of yourself and others as well: the
mission board should provide direction and freedom in just
the right proportions; supporters should pray for your
specific requests and make sure that all needs are adequately
met; fellow missionaries and nationals should appreciate
your education and abilities; and you yourself should attain a
high degree of self-fulfillment in the missionary calling.
Depending on your field and type of service, you undoubtedly feel somewhat overwhelmed by the needs you have
encountered during your time of service. You have often felt
that the resources are meager in view of the cries for help.
You have often wondered if anyone is sufficient for the task
you have undertaken. Sometimes in times of quiet reflection
or while waiting for sleep these thoughts come back to haunt
you.

In any given case the above may seem to be overdrawn.
But perhaps not greatly so. And anyway, the list is by no
means complete, so on balance it may be considered to be
rather representative. *The questions that come to those engaged in
missions today have to do with how much can be expected, not how
little.*

From "People Movers" to "People Helpers"

The time was when mission agencies were largely
thought of as facilitators. That is, their main responsibility
had to do with making it possible for missionary candidates
to get from North America (or wherever) to their field of
service and back and to relay donor funds to them. No more.
As a matter of fact, more and more mission leaders, authors,
and teachers exhibit a growing concern for missionary
personnel—for all aspects of their lives and service from
selection and training, to their effectiveness in field service,
to their retirement. Although there are many evidences of
this, we will confine ourselves to several of the most
significant.

First, missions literature, especially of the Evangelical

variety, reflects this concern. Although our study of 949 major articles appearing in the *International Review of Mission* did not reveal this trend (only 46 articles majored on such topics, and 13 of them had to do with missionary moratorium), the *Evangelical Missions Quarterly* exhibited a great and growing interest in topics having to do with missionary personnel (see Appendix 3).

Over one-third of all the articles appearing in the Evangelical Missions Quarterly *from the first issue until today highlight personnel concerns. Moreover, this type of article has appeared with increasing frequency* (see below and Appendix 2). *This indicates a major trend in the direction of a growing sense of accountability for both their person and their ministry.*

There are indicators of this trend in other missions literature as well. In addition to the classical books on missionary life and work by J. Herbert Kane, Harold Cook, and others, numerous specialized works have appeared in recent years—many of them sponsored or at least encouraged by missions themselves and many of them having to do with the total family and missionary experience. A complete bibliography would take us far beyond the bounds of this work, but a sampling will give an indication of the types of works that have been made available in recent years:

James Romaine Beck, *Parental Preparation of Missionary Children for Boarding School* (1968)

Marjorie A. Collins, *Manual for Missionaries on Furlough* (1972)

D. Bruce Lockerbie, *Education of Missionaries' Children: The Neglected Dimension of World Mission* (1975)

Edward E. Danielson, *Missionary Kid—MK* (1984)

Narramore Christian Foundation, *Reentry Seminar for Sons and Daughters of Missionaries* (n.d.)

Other Indicators of Accountability to Missionary Personnel

One does not have to look far to find other evidences of this trend.

First, surveys designed to enhance the missionary experience are numerous. The Training Department of International Resources of Campus Crusade for Christ field tested a reentry guide in 1980. In 1981 six of the larger Evangelical missions cooperated with the Overseas Ministries Studies Center in making a survey of missionaries' furlough patterns. This was followed up in 1984 by a similar survey in which eleven missions cooperated. Phil Parshall has directed a missionary-spirituality survey in which eight hundred Evangelical missionaries serving in thirty-two different countries with thirty-seven different societies were contacted and to which almost 50 percent responded.[7] Currently, Greater Europe Mission is sponsoring a survey designed to indicate strengths and weaknesses of its orientation program.

The Number of Articles (of a Total of 604)
in the EMQ Concerned with Missionary Personnel

Topic Area	No. of Articles	Percentage of Total
Well-being, incl. spiritual	67	11.1%
Qualifications, effectiveness	40	6.7%
Recruitment	29	4.7%
Preparation, education	27	4.5%
Finances	13	2.2%
Call, appointment, sending	10	1.7%
Withdrawal, attrition	10	1.7%
Short-term service	7	1.6%
Deployment	2	.3%
Moratorium	1	.2%
Totals	207	34.7%

Second, a large proportion of new mission agencies are service agencies with no career personnel overseas. The sole purpose of a number of them—Link Care in Fresno, California, is an example—have been inaugurated for one primary purpose: to keep the missionary force as productive as possible for as long as possible.

Third, still another indication of concern for the welfare and effectiveness of missionary personnel is to be found in the *modus operandi* of the mission agencies themselves. No longer do most reputable agencies tell candidates simply, "Get a year of Bible and missions, raise your support, and we'll send you to the field." In more and more cases, adequate training is deemed essential. No longer does the "support package" include only a monthly stipend and minimal outfit and travel allowance. Health insurance, vacation allowance, retirement funds, and more are usually included. No longer do missions send new missionaries who have had no opportunity to gain an acquaintance with general strategy, field operations, receptor culture and religions, and the national churches. Prefield orientation, field orientation, periodic workshops, and even reentry debriefing sessions are commonplace.

Recently I visited the headquarters of a major denominational mission agency. Within a matter of minutes, the personnel secretary was able to show me a training manual complete with information on various stages in the orientation process, a large packet containing assignments to be covered and books to be read by all candidates, and a sample thirteen-screen printout on one of their missionaries containing every conceivable sort of information from church background to service record to personal skills and even hobbies! Indeed we have entered a new day in missions!

ALTERNATIVES IN MISSIONIZING

In view of rising costs and with a view to accountability in a changing and demanding world, certain alternatives to traditional ways of carrying on missions have been proposed in recent years. Some of the best known of them present us with great potential. Some also evidence certain weaknesses because missionary work is seldom as simple as it appears on the surface.

Send Money Instead of Missionaries

Supporting native evangelists from Western churches is not new in missions. Agencies such as Ministry to Internationals, Inc. (formerly China Native Evangelistic Crusade), have been doing this for a generation or more. And there are instances of this approach throughout the history of missions. But it is now being proposed that the role of churches in the West should change. We are told that we should be sending money *instead of missionaries*.

One of the most vocal proponents of this alternative is K. P. Yohannan, a native of India, president of Gospel for Asia, and author of *The Coming Revolution in World Missions*.[8]

His rationale is simple and, at first blush, very persuasive. Yohannan claims that only 20 percent of the North American missionary force is engaged in evangelism and that they are not serving where they are most needed. He says that sending money is much more cost effective than sending Western missionaries in that thirty native evangelists can be supported for the money that it costs to support one American missionary. He insists that nationals are waiting to join missionary ranks and that they are automatically more effective than their Western counterparts. And he claims that this is the only way to evangelize the world.[9]

To the uninitiated, Yohannan's argument may seem to be impeccable. Experienced missionaries and knowledgeable missiologists know that there is another side to this strategy, however. In the first place, many of Yohannan's statistics are faulty (for example, the 20 percent mentioned above as being engaged in evangelism while "nearly 80 percent of all North American missionaries overseas are involved primarily in social work"),[10] and hardly any of them are documented. Second, the most qualified national personnel are usually already involved and are associated with existing churches and groups. Third, although it is true that missionaries from the outside have limitations when it comes to knowing another culture and learning its language, it is also true that foreigners can often make contacts all but unavailable to native evangelists. Fourth, in the light of economic realities and the missionary experience (e.g., in China national Christian workers have often been accused of being lackeys to foreigner interests), it may not be wise to link the enterprise of world evangelization too closely with North American dollars. Finally, to give mission monies to such programs with "no strings attached," as Yohannan proposes, sounds spiritual but may be poor stewardship. Accountability does not end at the water's edge.

The merits of this alternative will be weighed for years to come. Let us hope that mutual respect, sound judgment, and balanced discussion will characterize that process.

Ministering to Internationals

More complementary to traditional mission approaches than an alternative to them, ministering to internationals within the Western world is sometimes promoted as *the* way of carrying on missions today. When claims are too grandiose, a disservice is done.

For example, at the beginning of the 1980s it was often predicted that the number of international students in the United States would increase to one million by the year 1990. The potential of ministries to international students was sometimes based on that projection. However, the Institute of International Education reports that there were 343,777 foreign students in U.S. higher education during the 1986 academic year and indicates that this number is virtually stagnant.[11]

Again, although it is true that many foreign students and even business personnel are open to the gospel, it is also true that the crucial issue for converts is whether or not they can be related to existing churches upon return to their homeland. Apart from this, the pressure to revert may be overwhelming.

When viewed as complementary to foreign missions, and when meaningful communication and relationships can be established, ministries to internationals should become a high priority for churches and Christian organizations throughout North America. Such organizations as Inter-Varsity Christian Fellowship; International Students, Inc.; The Navigators; and Campus Crusade for Christ are to be commended for taking the lead in this kind of outreach. And the Association of Christian Ministries to Internationals (ACMI) merits wholehearted support in their effort to bring such organizations together for purposes of networking and enhancing this type of ministry.

Self-Support: Tentmaking Mission

Still another proposal is that Christians take advantage of employment opportunities in other countries *for the express purpose of using such opportunities to bear witness to Christ*. Some countries—such as China, Saudi Arabia, and Afghanistan are closed to traditional missionaries but are open to tentmakers. Some governments such as those of Nigeria and Indonesia welcome the contribution of Christians in their school systems. Scores of international companies send representatives abroad. Dedicated Christians by the thousands should consider this possibility. But they should do so with full knowledge that in some countries they must be very careful when it comes to talking about their faith. In addition, because they are accountable to their employers they cannot devote the time to study and ministry that a career missionary can. Tentmaking missionaries usually make their best contribution when they link arms with church leaders and missionaries already in place.

A good place to begin a study of this kind is with a careful reading of J. Christy Wilson's informative volume *Today's Tentmakers*.[12]

RISING COSTS, GREATER ACCOUNTABILITY, AND CHRISTIANS TODAY

There can be no question about it: the situation in world missions today demands that some hard choices be made by churches and their leaders; by the leaders of denominational, interdenominational, and parachurch missions; and, indeed, by all Christians. Before concluding this chapter, it may be well to indicate some of the most crucial of these as they relate to the cost/accountability factor.

Hard Choices and Today's Churches

The pastors and leaders of our churches must decide that they exist for mission; mission does not exist for them. One pastor recently told a group of seminarians that without checking out the mission involved, he scheduled a missionary film that was calculated to draw a large audience. The stipulation was that the mission representative be allowed to take an offering for the mission that produced the film. (The offering amounted to over $3,000!) Imagine his shock when he later discovered that the mission actually had no significant work abroad! He told the seminarians that one of the difficult things he had to do in that pastorate was to confess to his elders that he had erred because his primary motive in scheduling the film was to attract a crowd.

More than this, church leaders must take a more active role in the missionary enterprise. It is not enough merely to hold a missionary conference, bring in outside speakers, and refer candidates and monies to the mission agencies. Accountability to both God and man requires that church leaders themselves be informed and involved. It is fortunate that an organization such as the Association of Church Mission Committees (ACMC) has come into existence to provide materials and conferences designed to enhance that goal. And responsible mission agencies, both denominational and interdenominational, stand ready to help.

Hard Choices and Today's Missions

Leaders of denominational mission agencies must take another look at their operations and, even more so, at the ways in which they present their cause in the churches. They may be taking entirely too much for granted. Very often their presentations simply do not compare favorably with those of the interdenominational and parachurch agencies.

For their part, leaders of interdenominational and, especially, the parachurch organizations must take stock of their relationship to the churches. All too often they expect far more support *from* the churches than they give *to* the churches. When a fair assessment reveals this to be the case, they should inquire as to the biblical emphasis on the nature of the church and also as to the long-range effect of their policies. Their choices today will be crucial for missions tomorrow.

Finally, all mission leaders need to take an inventory of the effectiveness of their field operations in terms of permanent results. Some leaders of a relatively new mission recently asked a missiologist to evaluate their overall operation. After careful consideration he replied:

> Perhaps I can best answer your question by resorting to an analogy. I see your mission as a cargo ship. The ship itself is well designed and in good condition. The officers are good leaders and the crew members are dedicated sailors. The cargo is the most valuable cargo in the world. Basically, only one great problem is evident. Once the ship is in port, hardly anyone seems to know how best to deliver the cargo!

In the final analysis, "delivering the cargo" in such a way that Great Commission purposes are achieved is "where it's at." Missions are not ends in themselves. They must be accountable in terms of the divine ends of mission. That requires uncommon integrity and recurrent evaluation.

Hard Choices and Today's Christians

When it comes to missions stewardship, knowledge of the amount of money given for overseas ministries is only a part of the story. Christians need to inquire also as to how that money is actually spent. Unfortunately, at that point overall figures are very difficult to come by. We are largely dependent on the reports made available by the various missions. The editors of the *Mission Handbook* do, however, include some suggestions that are germane to understanding and evaluating the reports of the missions.[13] We will briefly summarize and comment on those suggestions in the following paragraphs.

As concerns fund-raising, the editors note that while many consumer action groups consider 30 to 35 percent of the amount received as a reasonable cost for fund-raising, most Christian groups feel that the cost should be no more than 25 percent. Even 25 percent may seem to be high in view of the fact that mission agencies operate within the context of believing Christians who are already committed to the mission task. At any rate, fund-raising is an important aspect of rising costs in missions.

As concerns converting resources into mission purposes, the editors indicate that while administrative costs constitute a legitimate mission expense, there is no consensus as to what percentage is reasonable. While this conclusion is no doubt true, it is also true that the multiplication of agencies tends to push overall administrative costs higher and higher. This fact should not escape the attention of careful observers.

As concerns the dollars actually spent on the carrying out of ministry, the editors point out that more and more thoughtful administrators are giving attention to the effectiveness of mission programs and not just their cost per se. No doubt this is the area of missions stewardship where it is most difficult for donors to make a judgment. Giving should be based on the counsel of trusted and experienced mission personnel rather than on emotions.

It is not easy to make a determination in regard to some of these questions. Most missions do furnish audited financial reports to their supporters or upon request. And many mission agencies are now members of the Evangelical Council for Financial Accountability (ECFA). This agency has been brought into existence in recent years in order to monitor the financial policies of its members and to provide assurance to their supporting constituencies.

Earlier in this chapter I referred to my "World Christian" friend who received ten to twenty appeals for mission funds each week. Many of us would be "turned off" by this. But he comments:

> Some people take offense at this and wish that missions would be less importunate in their appeals. Not the World Christian. He will not object to the many appeals that come his way. He may not be able to respond to all of them, but he will respond to as many as he can. And those to which he cannot respond will certainly have a place in his thoughts and prayers.[14]

One of the marks of a World Christian is that he or she shares goods, time, talents, wealth, and home. To be a World Christian requires a different lifestyle—more simple, more concerned, more involved. It requires some hard choices that are truly Christian choices, well suited to the day of opportunity in which we live.

"THE LORD CAME AND DEMANDED AN ACCOUNTING"

> Jesus talks much about money. Sixteen of the thirty-eight parables were concerned with how to handle money and possessions. In the Gospels, an amazing one out of ten verses (288 in all) deal directly with the subject of money. The Bible offers 500 verses on prayer, less that 500 verses on faith, but more than 2,000 verses on money and possessions.[15]

When in the Olivet Discourse our Lord told the parable of the talents, it is likely that he was talking about more than money and possessions as such, but he was at least talking about them. Missions too have to do with more than money and possessions. But missions at least have to do with them.

The larger question seems to have to do with how we handle *everything* that is entrusted to us during the absence of our Lord and how we put *everything* to work for kingdom purposes. And it is not simply a matter of *how much*. It is also a matter of *how wisely* our investment is made. After all, when his lord came and demanded an accounting, the servant with one talent returned that talent intact and untouched. It was those whose talents gained something for the kingdom who heard the "well done" of their lord!

9

THE TRANSFERENCE TREND— RECOGNIZING THE WORLD CHURCH AND ITS MISSION

It is not at all difficult to prove that the missionary enterprise has been one of the most altruistic enterprises that the world has ever known. To maintain that it is also one of the most successful might raise some eyebrows. But a strong case can be made for that proposition also. In fact, the strength of the church in the non-Western world where Christian missionaries have been working throughout the period of modern missions must be considered one of the brightest spots on the Christian horizon!

THE TIPPING AXIS

The reality of the increasing weakness of the West at the present moment in history is not easily admitted, especially by Americans. But it is there for all to see.

Economically: John Naisbitt has shown that the United States is beginning to lag behind. Japan has forged ahead of us, but "Japan, in turn, is being challenged by Singapore, South Korea, and Brazil—the dazzling economies of these newly developed Third World nations."[1]

Politically: a report released by the Atlantic Council and the Citizens Network for Foreign Affairs concludes that as a result of steadily decreased spending on international programs (from 15 percent of the budget in 1950 to less than 2 percent today), America's capacity for international leadership has weakened to "crisis proportions."[2]

Religiously: an analogous shift of strength to the churches of the non-Western world is recognized in a survey by Howard Snyder. At the very top of a list of twenty-eight trends in the church today are three trends that relate to this:

1. The rapid Christian growth in the Third World.
2. The internationalization of the world missionary enterprise.
3. The shift in the "center of gravity" and the major leadership of the church to the Third World.[3]

Recognized or not, the evidence for this transference of strength and leadership from the churches and missions of the Western world to those of the Third World is clear from an examination of four dimensions of world church experience in recent years: nationalization and a corresponding change in church-mission relationships; an attitudinal change on the part of Christian leaders in the non-Western world; the relatively greater growth of Third World churches, especially Evangelical churches; and the rise of non-Western missions.

NATIONALIZATION AND THE CHANGE IN CHURCH-MISSION RELATIONSHIPS

Arriving back on the fields in large numbers after World War II, missionaries were soon to discover that they were in the midst of a transition. The old colonial empires were breaking up. (Over the years from 1943 to the present time, no fewer than ninety-six nations gained freedom from colonial rule!)[4] For their part, many of the churches overseas had come through difficult days. In the process they had matured greatly. And as often as not they had done so in the absence of the missionaries.

The 1950s and 1960s witnessed dramatic changes in the relationship between missions and the churches and church-related institutions they had founded. Mission after mission was faced with an identity crisis as non-Western governments and churches insisted on the transfer of administrative authority to their own representatives.

Faced with inevitable change, Conciliar church missions found it easier than the more conservative Evangelical missions did to fold their mission tents and place property, personnel, and authority under the churches of the host countries. In mission parlance Conciliarists generally opted for *fusion* of their missions with the younger churches. The rationale for this approach was quite convincing.

First, the churches that are present on the "mission fields" of the world must be recognized as sister churches.

Second, the mission is to be carried out everywhere. Mission is on all six continents, including the continents of Europe and North America.

Third, the church is mission. In other words, the mission is the task of the church, not just the task of its mission agencies. Moreover, it is the task of the church everywhere. The mission, therefore, is to be carried out by the churches that have been established around the world.

Fourth, insofar as missions and missionaries are present in continents and countries other than their own, they should not be paternalists or even partners. They should be servants of the churches in the host country.

These propositions usually came to be almost unquestioned in Conciliar churches and in the Ecumenical movement, so much so that the recent startling decline in the number of missionaries in the DOM is not really a cause for great alarm in those circles and classic missions tend to be thought of as outmoded and antiquated.

Evangelicals—especially those connected with faith missions—found the establishment of a new relationship with their respective churches to be a much more difficult process. A major conference of over four hundred representatives of IFMA and EFMA missions held at Green Lake, Wisconsin, in 1971 not only pointed up Evangelical ambivalence on the subject but was criticized for discussing it without adequate representation from the churches abroad.[5]

About a decade later, W. Harold Fuller documented the complex dynamics of changing relationships as the Sudan Interior Mission moved through the stages of pioneer, parent, partner, and participant, and its related church, the Evangelical Church of West Africa, achieved independence as a national church.[6]

There were a number of reasons for foot-dragging on the part of many Evangelicals. Some reasons had more legitimacy than others. But one that stands out as being most significant had to do with the mission itself. However effectively one may argue that the Christian mission belongs to the church rather than to mission agencies, the fact remains that without those agencies mission has often been abandoned on the ecclesiastical beaches of the world. Having escaped that fate in the sending nations, the missions were not about to invite it in the receiving nations.

Those who have not actually been involved in foreign service will have some difficulty in understanding the reluctance of many missions simply to place everything under the control of nationals and be done with the problem. But the primary issue was not so much a question of who was boss. It had to do with such questions as the stewardship of funds given, not to the younger churches, but to the missions; the deployment of missionaries in accordance with their gifts, preparation, and calling; and the ability of missions to continue in the kind of pioneer endeavors for which they were formed in the first place.

Attitudinal Change

Concurrent with the pressure for a changing relationship—and intimately connected with it—was a change in attitude on the part of nationals and some missionary spokespeople as well. Missionaries were no longer knights in shining armor. Gradually, the armor was becoming tarnished!

Elisabeth Elliot, the widow of one of the Auca martyrs, administered some shock treatment with her *No Graven Image* (1966), which left the traditional missionary in a rather ambiguous position at best. Lutheran missiologist James Scherer added his *Missionary, Go Home: A Reappraisal of the Christian World Mission* (1964). A Latin leader, Juan Isaias, wrote *The Other Side of the Coin* (1966) in which he pictured the missionary as sometimes viewed by the national. An African leader, John Gatu, proposed a moratorium on missions to allow the younger churches to develop in accordance with their own culture (1971). The members of the Theological Education Fund proposed that theology should be done by Third World theologians but not in ways Western theologians have done theology (1972). As we entered the 1980s David Cho, executive director of the Asia Missions Association and a Korean, called for the de-Westernization of the Asian Christian movement and the reforming of mission structures.

All of the foregoing productions and proposals—and much, much more—have served notice that the future will not be a carbon copy of the past. The proposals were not always clearly understood nor were they always well received. Understandably, the tone and force that sometimes attended them did not always help the cause. But in times like these, Christians of different lands sometimes have to struggle a bit in order to understand one another.

As things worked out, not a few of the churches (and governments) that called for complete nationalization (especially in Africa) later modified their position and requested missions to assume direction of some of the medical and educational institutions once again. And the missionaries generally were busily engaged in evangelism and church development throughout the period. Nevertheless the transition was a real one. Generally speaking, the younger churches are now in full control of their own church affairs, including the theological training of their emerging leaders.

As the postwar generation of missionaries now passes from the missionary scene, it is important to realize that they have lived and labored through that period during which the churches in Asia, Latin America, and Africa not only grew at an unprecedented rate, but also matured and assumed direction of their own affairs. In that respect, theirs has been one of the most significant generations in two thousand years of missionary endeavor.

Church Growth

In chapter 2 I related several important aspects of church growth around the world to the task of world evangelization. Here we must note church growth factors as they relate to the shifting balance in world Christianity that we have already been reminded of.

First of all, for the first time in the history of the world it can be said that a universal religion exists in the geographical sense of the word *universal.*With very few exceptions the Christian church is represented in every area of the world.

Patrick Johnstone indicates that, although Christianity has declined in Europe during the twentieth century, the overall percentage of the world that can be termed Christian (32.4 percent) has remained more or less constant. He attributes this to significant Christian growth in the non-Western world. He goes on to say:

Christianity is the majority religion of five of the eight areas into which the world has been divided in this book [*Operation World*]. Of the 215 states and territories described only 20 have a resident population that is less that 1% Christian. Christianity has truly become a *world* religion in this century. Only a small proportion of this number would actually be born-again Christians; but God alone knows how many! The Lamb's book of life would make fascinating reading![7]

Second, the decline of Christianity in the Western world (especially in Europe) should be a matter of grave concern. Donald G. Bloesch calls this a "dissipation of faith" and puts it in graphic statistical terms: the percentage of the population that regularly attends church services is no more than 6% in England, 4% in Australia, and 4% or less in West Germany, East Germany, and Scandinavia. Over a million Protestants and almost as many Catholics have left the churches in West Germany since 1961. As for the United States, he calls attention to a Gallup Poll of 1983 that indicated that no more the 12% of the population are "highly committed" to religious practice. Bloesch believes that persecution may be the only thing that will serve to turn the church around.[8]

Third, church growth throughout the world is, by and large, Evangelical growth. (Evangelicals are defined as members of denominations that are Evangelical in their faith, the children of these members, and those of other groups who are Evangelical in their theology.) On a percentage basis, Evangelicals have grown somewhat in the West and Eastern Europe during the decade from 1975 to 1985, though not nearly as rapidly as in the Third World.

During that period Evangelicals in the West and Eastern Europe increased by 1.3% annually. The total number was 75 million in 1975 and nearly 86 million in 1985. In the Third World (omitting China) the increase was 6.7% annually, and the total number grew from 68 million to 130 million.[9]

Fourth, the percentage of all Evangelicals who are located in the Western world (including Eastern Europe) has been declining, but it has been rapidly rising in the Third World. *As far as Evangelicalism is concerned, the significant year in the balance between Western and non-Western Christianity was*

1980. At that time Evangelicalism in the Third World gained parity with Evangelicalism in the West. Since that time, the shift has been even more pronounced until Third World Evangelicalism has come to outweigh Evangelicalism in the West and Eastern Europe dramatically.

Chart 9.1[10]

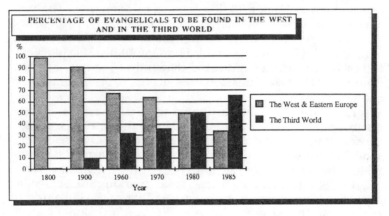

PERCENTAGE OF EVANGELICALS TO BE FOUND IN THE WEST AND IN THE THIRD WORLD

The West & Eastern Europe

The Third World

Year

Fifth, only a small proportion of Evangelicals are thought by Patrick Johnstone to actually have been born again. Third World statistics should not be interpreted to mean that our task is complete in the Third World any more than it is in the Western world. On the contrary, although there is something very positive in all of this, the challenge to the church and its missions remains enormous.

The Rise of Non-Western Missions

Until the middle of this century the success of our missions had been measured almost exclusively on the basis of the number of hospitals, schools, churches, and Christians that resulted from the missionary endeavor. Gradually during the past thirty to forty years a new awareness has surfaced; namely, that the missing ingredient in those churches and schools has been the very thing that made them possible in the first place—a missionary vision. Missionaries had been so preoccupied with the place and people to whom God had called them that they had failed to communicate a concern for reaching still other places and peoples. It was as though the Great Commission had been given to the churches of the West and to no others.

Gradually at first, and then rapidly, the picture began to change. When Lawrence E. Keyes at the beginning of the 1980s had accomplished the most definitive study on the subject up to that time, he calculated that there were at least 368 autonomous, "Third World," crosscultural mission agencies with an estimated 13,000 national missionaries. The vast majority of these missionaries were classified as Evangelical (77 percent), the others being Charismatic (12 percent), Ecumenical (7 percent), and Fundamentalist (4 percent). Keyes' study further indicated that fully 91 percent of the funding of these missionaries came from their own churches.[11]

As arresting as these figures were at the time, subsequent updating has indicated that, if anything, they were too conservative. By the middle of the decade, Overseas Crusades' coordinator for emerging missions, Larry Pate, estimated that at least 20,000 non-Western missionaries belonging to 380 different agencies were working in scores of countries. Furthermore, he estimated that at the current rate of growth the size of the non-Western missionary force would increase to 100,000 by the year 2000.[12]

CAN EVANGELICALS MAINTAIN A BALANCE?

Unless something unusual happens, the die is pretty well cast as far as missions connected with the DOM-NCCCUSA and the WCC are concerned. As we have seen, the number of DOM-related missionaries is in decline. The number of crosscultural missionaries from WCC-related churches in the Third World is extremely low. Evangelicals, on the other hand, are still in the process of making choices today that will vitally affect the cause of world missions tomorrow. Let us see how this is so.

A good place to begin this part of our discussion is to monitor the interest that writers of major articles in the *International Review of Missions* and the *Evangelical Missions Quarterly* and of book reviews in *Missiology* over the past two decades have displayed in various parts of the world, the churches, and their missions (see Appendixes 2 and 3).

The interest of mainline churches in *oikoumenē*, "the land where people dwell," and of the more conservative churches in *world* mission is certainly reflected in these figures. There is tremendous interest in the churches and Christians of the Third World right across the board. However, as yet there is not a corresponding emphasis on Third World missions and missionaries. In the light of the realities of the new situation, it may be timely to ask whether this lacuna is justifiable.

Major Foci Vis-à-Vis World Christianity in 949 IRM and 604 EMQ Articles, and in 444 Books Reviewed in Missiology

	IRM		EMQ		Missiology	
	Articles	*Percent*	*Articles*	*Percent*	*Books*	*Percent*
Geographical Foci						
Africa	71	7.5%	21	3.5%	61	13.8%
Asia (incl. India)	94	9.9%	27	4.5%	77	17.3%
Europe	50	5.2%	11	1.8%	6	1.4%
Latin America	67	7.1%	25	4.1%	36	8.1%
Middle East	5	.1%	3	.5%	4	.9%
North America	36	3.8%	0	.0%	22	5.0%
Oceania	19	2.0%	0	.0%	21	4.7%
Totals	342	35.6%	87	14.4%	227	51.2%
Ecclesiastical Foci						
Third World Churches and Christians	51	5.4%	47	7.8%	28	6.3%
Third World Missions	1	.1%	5	.8%	3	0.7%
Totals	52	5.5%	52	8.6%	31	7.0%

The difference between percentages of material focused on the various geographical areas of the world can probably be explained in part by the fact that the *EMQ* is basically a publication of and for missions people from North America. The lower percentage of articles specifically dealing with Third World churches and Christians in the *IRM* must be understood in light of two facts. First, a significant percent-age of the *IRM* articles are actually written by church leaders from the Third World. Second, the *IRM* has regularly included extensive reports on the status of the church around the world. Since these report articles tend to be very lengthy, the attention given to Third World church and Christians is not necessarily reflected in the kind of content analysis that is based on the number of articles rather than on column inches devoted to the various categories.

Most of the questions that must be faced by Ecumenists are still those that I posed in the chapter on polarization. The considerations of this present chapter, however, present some special questions to be faced by Evangelical churches and missions and their representatives world-wide.

Questions for the Churches

Some of us have the distinct impression that, in spite of the tremendous changes in the world church referred to earlier in this chapter, the leaders of Evangelical churches in the West are slow to recognize Third World leaders as equals and Third World churches as sister churches. Although it does not show up in the thematic content analysis above, it seems that there is a sense in which the churches and leaders of the Ecumenical orbit have modeled a much healthier approach to interchurch relationships. The problem is that they have sacrificed their missions in the process.

One question that still remains to be answered by Evangelicals, then, is this: How can we in the West best demonstrate a true appreciation for Third World churches as full-fledged sister churches and a true regard for Third World leaders as equal partners without sacrificing our missions? Without doubt we are overdue in recognizing that we should be learners as well as teachers. Third World leaders should not be required to master the English language and our Western agendas in order to be accepted by us while we all but ignore their languages and agendas. At the same time, Evangelicals almost by definition will resist interchurch relationships that have the effect of placing their missionaries in a position where they are not free to carry on pioneer evangelism and church extension. Third World church leaders need to recognize this and make allowance for it.

Questions for the Missions

The interest in Europe and North America reflected in the *IRM* (and perhaps in the books reviewed in *Missiology* as well) is probably indicative of the Ecumenical focus on the "church as mission" and on mission as being "on six continents." The Evangelical focus reflected in the *EMQ* on the other hand, while it gives attention to Europe, is almost devoid of attention to North America. This is likely a by-product of the Evangelical tradition of dividing missions into home and foreign missions. The time has arrived to review this division. At one time, and not long ago, it made sense because home missions were basically intracultural while foreign missions were crosscultural. That is becoming less and less true. The West has become home for millions upon millions of Asians, Latins, Middle Easterners, and others. North America is a mission field in this new sense no less than is Europe. To deny home missions the expertise that has come from decades of working in foreign cultures on the basis of a division that no longer squares with the real world would be a major mistake.

Again, although the *IRM* and much other missiological literature as well has almost completely overlooked the interest in the rise of Third World missions, the *EMQ* and the other Evangelical materials have recently highlighted it. The postwar problem of the relationship between the younger *churches* and the Western *missions* will now be resurrected in a new form. What will be the most beneficial relationship between *missions* from all parts of the world in the future? How can a productive relationship be effected? The formation of international teams and similar proposals may be good but do not touch at the heart of the issue. The larger questions have to do with forms of partnership among missions themselves.

Western missions must now face up to the fact that it will seldom be appropriate to devise detailed mission strategies in the Western world and export them intact to other parts of the world. This is especially true in the case of missions headquartered in the United States. Despite our best intentions, such strategies have the words "made in the U.S.A." stamped all over them. Church leaders in the Third World have a right to view our approaches with suspicion in the wake of a series of "end all" strategies that we have exported to them, particularly in the postwar era.

This does not mean that missionaries should be sent with no plan at all for the part they will play in the fulfillment of the Great Commission. That would be the opposite—and equally indefensible—mistake. Our overall approach in the future should have at least three components. First, our missionaries should be equipped with a "macro-strategy." That is, they should have primary and secondary objectives clearly in mind along with a broad outline of the ways in which they can be achieved. Second, they should be equipped in such a way as to be able to develop viable, culturally appropriate strategies in the field situation. Third, they should be prepared to consult and work with national leaders in the development and implementation of field strategy.

Third World missions also must face sensitive issues. While it is true that the difficulties in obtaining visas and exit permits and in exchanging currencies and similar problems often inhibit crosscultural missionizing, the fact remains that there is a strong tendency on the part of Chinese, Koreans, and others to reach only their own people even when they cross geographic boundaries. For example, 51 percent of Korean missionaries cross geographical boundaries but do so in order to reach Koreans in other parts of the world.[13] This is well and good, but since it is true that if the world is to be evangelized, over 80 percent of its people will have to be reached by crosscultural ministry, we must ask if the intention is that this be done by Western missionaries alone.

Third World missions must also ask themselves whether or not they will learn from the mistakes and successes of Western missions. This is not as simple as it sounds. The more acquainted one is with these missions, the more one realizes that they tend to entertain the notion that they will not make mistakes, because they are not Westerners. Actually, however, their missionaries tend to repeat some of our mistakes *and* add a few of their own. We can only hope that this process will not be prolonged.

Questions for Missiologists

Missiologists have some new grist for their mill as well. For example, our study of the journals and book reviews above indicates that, geographically, Asia does receive somewhat more attention than other areas do. But if population and certain other factors (as noted below) are taken into consideration, Asia does not get nearly the attention that it deserves when compared to Africa and Latin America. Actually, the findings corroborate the conclusions of many missionary recruiters who feel that it is easier to get volunteers for Europe, Africa, and Latin America than for Asia.

Perhaps it remains for missiologists to highlight the *missions potential* of a geographical area as a factor in targeting strategy. This is not far-fetched if one takes the long view. Consider the following:

> Asia has always been the sleeping giant. Today, the giant is awake! Pick a subject. Population? Seventy-five percent of non-Western peoples live in Asia. Industry? The Gross National Product and Per Capita Income have both risen faster in Asia during the last ten years than in any other area of the world. Asian industrial and techno-logical advances rival the West in almost every field. Tokyo, Singapore and Hong Kong are among the world's greatest commercial centers.
>
> What about the church? Though much is said about the growth of the church in Africa, few have noted that the church is growing at almost the same rate in Asia (Christianity grew by 38% during the last ten years in Africa, 37% in Asia). What about missions? Forty percent of the non-Western missionary force is Asian, and that figure promises to rise well above 50% by the year 2000 A.D.!
>
> In almost any category, a large piece of the future belongs to Asia. . . . But Asia is a promise, not a guarantee![14]

Western missiologists should also remember that churches and missions abroad are now in the process of establishing their own missionary training schools. Linkages between these schools and the training centers of the West and among missiologists around the world should now become a matter of higher priority.

Questions to Be Faced by the Missionaries

The most obvious questions that have arisen out of the new situation in the world and the church have had to do with the changing role of the missionary. We have asked whether missionaries should be pioneers, partners, or servants. Now we must ask a somewhat different question. We must inquire as to the role of the Western missionary in the mission of tomorrow, not just in relation to the churches and missions but also in relation to a lost world.

Marvin Mayers insists that the traditional missionary is no longer wanted and that the overtly proselytizing missionary will run afoul of anticonversion and similar laws in host countries. But he sees a future for missionaries with specializations needed in those countries, with doctoral level training, and with the ability to creatively minister to felt needs.[15]

Jorge Lara-Braud says few North Americans involved in crosscultural missions possess the intellectual and theoretical tools necessary to deal with the interplay between faith and ideology that is so important in today's world. They should therefore concentrate on reaching the unreached, translating Scripture, and sharing such technological and other skills as they may possess.[16]

John N. Jonsson believes that it is fallacious to define mission in terms of any one role and inappropriate to reduce mission to one role. He believes that each mission role should be viewed as complementary and that all should be acknowledged as part of the body of Christ.[17]

And so the discussion will proceed. As it does, the North American missionary of the future should not lose sight of two basic facts. First, Christ is building this church around the world. Missionaries should be sensitive to whatever local expressions of that church they may find in their sojourn. Local churches and their leaders may or may not be committed to the biblical faith, but as a matter of Christian courtesy they should not be ignored. Second, the primary missionary task is outlined in the Great Commission. That Commission does not change with changing conditions.

THE LIMITED COMMISSION AND
THE LARGER COMMISSION

A colleague in New Testament, Scot McKnight, points out that the first major section of Matthew's Gospel (4:12–11:1) is concerned with the messianic confrontation with Israel *through ministry*. Jesus ministers to his people by teaching, preaching, and healing. Then, with compassion on the shepherdless multitudes (9:36) he calls on his disciples to pray that workers be sent into the harvest (vv. 37–38). Finally, he commissions his disciples to go, not to the Gentiles nor to the Samaritans, but to the lost sheep of the house of Israel (10:5–6). Within those geographical and ethnic limitations they are to "re-perform" his ministry by preaching, healing, and casting out demons (vv. 7–8).

In the next major section, Jesus responds to Peter's confession with a promise to build his church, which the gates of Hades will never overpower (16:18). And not long after, we find him with his disciples on the temple site and then on Olivet. His discourse there crowns his teaching ministry and prepares the disciples for the imminent rejection by Israel and the course of events that will characterize the church age until his return. Central to his program for this entire age are the activities called for by his larger (Great) Commission—namely, the going into all the world and making disciples of all the *ethnē* by baptizing and teaching all that he commanded (28:19–20). *Without geographical or ethnic limitations we are to "re-perform" his discipling ministry.*

It is no wonder, then, that the church has been, is being, and will be built *all around the world and among all peoples. Ours is the larger, the greater Commission. And by his Spirit, he makes possible its accomplishment!*

10

MOUNTING OPPOSITION— THE ENCOUNTER WITH UNBELIEF AND EVIL POWERS

Travel by train along the East German border and observe hundreds of miles of high fencing, the denuded strip inside it, and the spaced observation towers.

Attend one of the prayer meetings in central Europe where, one after another, the gathered believers pray for imprisoned relatives and Christian workers behind the Iron Curtain.

Meet with Christian youth in a Bible school in an Eastern Bloc country where windows and doors are closed to keep the sounds of hymns and prayers from attracting the attention of neighbors.

Share the frustration and fear of a house-church leader in China who has over two hundred names on a list of new Christians awaiting baptism, but who will baptize only four or five at a time lest opposition be increased.

Receive the hospitality of a prominent Christian layman in North Africa who is apprehensive of the danger that an imminent change in government will bring to his family.

Keep in close touch with a candidate couple as they go through all the formalities and prayerfully wait month in and month out for a visa that will permit them to enter their chosen field in East Asia.

Attend the funeral of a pastor who has been murdered by a radical Muslim family member in Burkina Faso.

If you were to travel the world on missions fact-finding trips, experiences such as these would increasingly be your lot as we approach the end of the twentieth century.

Of course, discouragement, opposition, and persecution are not new to the missionary enterprise. In a very real sense, missions began with a persecution in Jerusalem that had the effect of catapulting ordinary believers throughout the regions of Judea and Samaria, where they shared their faith in the risen Lord (Acts 8:1–2). From that day to this, the Christian message has been proclaimed and the Christian mission has progressed in the face of opposition and even martyrdom. There is no need to repeat that story here, though it bears repetition and review. *Rather, the point to be emphasized and analyzed is that, despite the comfortable circumstances in which the majority of those who read this book presently find themselves, the sobering fact is that the twentieth century has been characterized by a terrible outcropping of opposition to the cause and people of Christ. Moreover, there are few signs of abatement on the horizon. Rather, there are many signs of an increased opposition directed especially to those involved in the spread of the Christian faith.*

An astute observer of the contemporary church and world scene, Donald G. Bloesch, writes:

> Today the foundations of civilization are being shaken as never before. . . . The old order is crumbling as the powers of darkness prepare to make their final stand. The shadow of persecution is falling upon the church, but. . . .[1]

It is appropriate that we complete that quotation, but not yet. All too often we fail to count the cost of discipleship by hurriedly recalling the victory already obtained by our Lord Christ. Or, to put it in Kierkegaardian terms, we seize upon the fact that a substitute sacrifice is already caught in the thicket before we even feel the anguish of an Abraham who has built the altar and raised the knife that would sacrifice his Isaac—yes, Isaac, the son through whom the promise that all the nations of the earth will be blessed in Abraham had to be fulfilled! It is best that we "get a feel" for what is really happening in the world and *then* claim the promise! Appreciation for God's promises grows in direct proportion to our awareness of the strength and strategy that characterize the opposition!

UNMASKING THE OPPOSITION

It is characteristic of the human memory that it tends to block out the unpleasant experiences of life and leave us with more of its happy side. This is good, lest we accumulate grievances to the point of breaking under the strain of present discouragements.

It is characteristic of contemporary missions that they emphasize our opportunities and victories while giving rather short shrift to opposition and defeats. To a certain extent perhaps this is appropriate, lest we lose sight of the fact that our Lord is in control and that he makes even the wrath of man to praise him.

But despite the fact that we often neglect to analyze carefully and systematically the mounting opposition to Christian mission world-wide, it is evident that if in any sense it ever was true that to engage in the Christian mission is to enjoy a picnic, it is true no longer. We are engaged in a battle, and the opposition assumes many forms.

The Advance of Totalitarianism

According to the *World Christian Encyclopedia*, the facts are that as we entered the decade of the 1980s seventy-four countries were politically free, eighty-one were partially free, and sixty-eight were not free. In seventy-nine countries where there were constitutional guarantees of religious freedom 2.2 billion people nevertheless lived under de facto restrictions on their religious freedom.[2]

Anticonversion Efforts

One of the most simple ways of differentiating biblical and unbiblical mission is to ascertain whether or not conversion is an essential part of it. Evangelicals insist on the necessity of conversion. But the world disdains the call to repentance and conversion. Thus anticonversion laws are not uncommon in our day, particularly in lands where Islam exercises significant power. In Malaysia, for example, a missionary may convert Hindus or Chinese, but if he tries to convert a Muslim, he faces the likelihood of deportation.

In other places, the law may be more subtle. In April of

1978 Israel's Knesset passed a law that made the offering of "material inducement" to change religions illegal and punishable by a five-year prison sentence.[3] Some report that this law applies only to a Jew's becoming a *Christian*. Moonies, Indian gurus, and even witches are said to be able to seek followers, but Christians are not.[4]

In Greece, charges of proselytism contrary to Greek law were brought against missionaries Don Stephens and Alan Williams and Greek national Costas Macris by Mrs. Katerina Douga. Mrs. Douga claimed that the three sowed seeds of proselytism in her son by saturating him with ideas contrary to doctrine of the Greek Orthodox Church (they encouraged him not to make the sign of the cross, pray to the icons, or believe in the perpetual virginity of the Mother of God and in Orthodox baptism). She also accused them of attempting to abduct him by offering to take him on the Anastasis mercy ship for fun and world travel. The three were convicted by a Greek court and sentenced to three and one-half years of imprisonment.

After leaders of the World Evangelical Fellowship and Youth With a Mission (the agency to which the missionaries belonged) succeeded in getting thousands of people the world over to write letters protesting such injustice, the case was heard by the Court of Appeals in Athens in May of 1986. The verdict of the lower court was reversed and the three were acquitted. About four years and great expenditures of time and money were required to secure this verdict.[5]

Conversionist mission runs the very real risk of being identified with all sorts of cults, some of which use unethical means to gain new converts. Opposition similar to that directed against the cults, therefore, has been directed at Evangelical organizations as well. In 1986 this kind of pressure caused the Inter-Varsity Christian Fellowship to bring a panel of experts together in 1985 in order to counter this kind of misunderstanding. The result was the formulation of a "Code of Ethics for the Christian Persuader."[6]

Closed and Partially Closed Doors

In his *Winds of Change in the Christian Mission*, J. Herbert Kane admonishes us not to think that all countries thought of as "closed" are really completely closed to the hearing of the gospel.[7] He also reminds us to concentrate on the large number of countries that are actually *open* to missionary endeavor.[8] This is excellent advice. However, closed and partially closed doors are very much a part of the current scene. To close our eyes to closed doors completely is to close our eyes to reality.

As we entered the 1980s, it was reported that "during the 20th century, it has become increasingly difficult for foreign missionary societies or personnel to enter or operate in a number of the non-Christian countries."[9] This statement was reenforced by the following statistics:

Countries closed to foreign missions——25
Countries partially closed to foreign missions——24
Countries restricting missionary entry——18
Total number of people in these 67 countries——3.1 billion[10]

As has been the case in the past, some countries closed today may be open tomorrow. But it is not likely that the overall situation will improve. In fact, a recent conference of Muslims meeting in Lahore, India, challenged Islamic nations to become free of all Christians by the year 2000.[11] In the light of the current Christian effort to reach Muslims and to evangelize the entire world, we can expect that increased openness on the part of some Muslim groups and individuals will be attended by increased opposition on the part of their Muslim governments.

Danger to Life Itself

The missionary enterprise has always been attended by danger. The nature of that danger is not always the same, however. In the nineteenth century the prevailing threat was that of disease. It was not at all unusual for missionaries to die of cholera or dysentery or typhoid or malaria—often before they had seen any fruit from their labors.

In the twentieth century the prevailing threat is that of violence. Whether from communism, fascism, nationalism, terrorism, or religious fanaticism, the opposition has been unrelenting. The facts that opposition may sometimes be directed against national Christians rather than the missionaries themselves, and that it may not be directed against missionaries because they are missionaries but because they are white or American or Western, does not really change the situation very much. The result is the same.

Under the caption "Missionaries Are in More Danger Now," *Missionary News Service* reports:

> "American missionaries are in more danger now than they were two or three years ago," Chester Quarles, vice-president of Contingency Preparation Consultants (CPC), told Missionary News Service. As Americans are targeted increasingly by terrorist groups, government and business spend millions of dollars to protect their people.
>
> "Governmental and business representatives drive around in armor-plated vehicles. Their chauffeurs are trained body guards with pistols. They are target hardened," said Quarles. Because missionaries often work in remote areas with relatively little protection, they may be perceived as a "soft" target.[12]

Accurate statistics are very hard to come by. A ranking expert on terrorism reports that he has no idea as to how many missionaries have been the victims of terrorist incidents in recent years because there has been little sharing of information among the different groups and denominations. But he indicates that the situation is more serious than is believed.[13] Evidently the widely reported attacks in such widely separated places as Lebanon, Uganda, Colombia, and the Philippines represent the tip of the iceberg.

Again, the identity of some twentieth-century missionary martyrs such as John and Betty Stam, the Auca martyrs, Paul Carlson, and Chet Bitterman are well known. Others are not. Missionary martyrdoms are nothing new and may not have increased greatly, but the fact that national Christians have been hunted and hounded and even killed in ever-larger numbers in recent years (and that the number is projected to increase in the future) is equally significant for missions. David Barrett's statistics on the number of crypto-Christians (secret believers) and Christian martyrs (of all confessions) are sobering. (See charts 10.1 and 10.2.)

The Encounter With Satan and Evil Spirits

In regard to the direct opposition of satanic forces, Timothy Warner draws attention to the experience of a missionary couple in Colombia. In spite of the fact that they were having a fruitful ministry, the husband wrote:

> We . . . faced the whole issue of the occult. . . . Practical knowledge in this area was just not a part of our

academic preparation! As we began to lead people to the Lord we discovered that *nearly nine out of ten had problems in this area,* for one reason or another. The Lord led a missionary into our lives who had the experience we didn't. We started taking our people to her, she'd pray, and God would free them (emphasis mine).[14]

Chart 10.1[15]

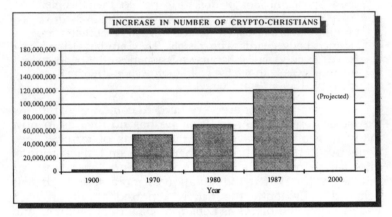

Chart 10.2

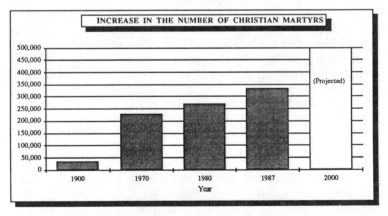

After over twenty years of service in Brazil, Mennonite Brethren missionary James Wiebe reported, "I've never met one family that didn't have at least some involvement in spiritism."[16]

There can be no question but that either direct satanic opposition in various forms is becoming increasingly prevalent or missionaries are simply becoming much more aware of it—or perhaps both are true. Cults and the occult, and Satanism and witchcraft, are not only surviving on the mission fields of the world, they are also thriving there and simultaneously invading the Western world! Missionary after missionary—and pastor after pastor—graduated from our schools and went out into our contemporary world prepared to engage in a truth encounter. And one after another has discovered that in ways only vaguely perceived previously, the *truth encounter* is attended by a *power encounter*.

Opposition From Resurgent Non-Christian Religions

A generation or two ago it was widely thought that the non-Christian religions could not long stand: they would eventually succumb either to secularism and technology or to the continuing advance of the Christian faith. Today that assessment seems to us to have been wishful thinking. I recall some personal experiences of the past thirty years that jolted my feelings in this regard.

First, there was the professor of Pali from the University of Ceylon who visited our philosophy class at the university and said, "Conversion is a dirty word. Hindus and Buddhists will no longer accept the claims of any religion to be the sole path of righteousness or happiness."

Second, there was the time that I first read the pledge of Josei Toda of Japan's Soka Gakkai (in Japanese): "We will first win Japan, then the Orient, then the world."

Third, there was the day when I walked to our Christian Center in Kyoto and first encountered the sign on a nearby building: "Buddhist Training Center for Missionaries to America."

Indeed, times have changed. *Church Around the World* reports that, on a per capita basis, three of the world's great religions—Islam, Hinduism, and Buddhism—are growing faster than Christianity.[17] The Ahmadiyya Movement (Islam) has opened missionary training centers around the world. Ramakrishna Mission (Hindu) centers can be found in many of our large urban centers. Look at the pages of major

Saturday newspapers that once were filled with church announcements and you will find that many of those announcements have been replaced with announcements from Vedanta societies, Zen Buddhism, and the New Age movement, among others. Radhakrishnan, Hindu philosopher and former president of India, writes, "After a long winter of some centuries, we are today in one of the creative periods of Hinduism."[18] Examine the exploits and inquire into the number of followers—whether in America, Europe, or Asia—of the likes of Mahara Ji, Muktananda, Sai Baba, and the Rajneesh (now in disfavor), and you become aware of the magnitude of this "creative period" when the "gods of the new age" blatantly challenge the true God and his risen Son!

THE RESPONSE OF CHRISTIAN MISSIONS

The response to increased opposition on the part of those engaged in the support, instruction, and practice of mission has been varied. Some 84 articles (8.9 percent) out of the 949 articles analyzed in the *International Review of Mission* featured material on the non-Christian religions, and almost half of these (33) focused on Islam. Although the major emphasis throughout the 949 articles had to do with injustice and social concern (157 articles or 16.5 percent of the 949), only 10 focused distinctly on governmental repression of Christians per se and no articles featured such items as closed doors and terrorism as they relate to missions (see Appendix 2).

The Evangelical Missions Quarterly has been even more muted on such subjects. Of the 604 articles examined, no more than 30 (5 percent) highlighted the non-Christian religions, and just over half (16) of those were concerned with Islam. The number of articles having to do with nationalism and repression and various types of difficulties occasioned by governments was somewhat larger (19 or 3.1 percent), but hardly commensurate with the impact of such problems (see Appendix 2).

Although 70 of 444 books reviewed in *Missiology* (15.8 percent) were concerned with injustice and social concerns, the number that majored on the kind of discrimination against Christians that is in view here was negligible. Fifty-eight books (13.1 percent) were concerned with non-Christian religions (about one-third of them with Islam), but encounter as such was not stressed in the majority of them (see Appendix 2).

One wonders if Western authors of mission-related materials are sufficiently aware of threats to Christian missions and to the Christian faith itself. It would seem that whether on the theological left or on the right, they do not give nearly enough attention to the implications of the growth of non-Christian religions and the relentless advance of totalitarianism *as these forces affect the future of Christianity and the Christian mission.* Do we suppose that the circumstance of freedom in which we write and strategize will always exist even to the degree that it does today? Do we think that such responses as those widely proposed in the Ecumenical movement, or that the (mainly) Evangelical responses indicated below, do not need to be augmented by still other strategic planning for tomorrow when freedom and liberty may be in shorter supply?

The churches and, especially, the missions and schools should give much more attention to developing coping and extending strategies to be employed under oppressive regimes. The advisability of disseminating information concerning these strategies and tactics also demands reflection lest countermeasures be encouraged—and an awareness of this may account for a muted voice on this subject. The propagation strategies of non-Christian organizations should be studied as well as their teaching and history. Much remains to be done, but we can be grateful that missions people today are becoming more aware of the nature of spiritual warfare and are responding in significant ways.

Intercessory Prayer

Whether or not more prayer for the missionary enterprise is actually forthcoming today as compared with previous times is an open question. It is certain, however, that more than ever before prods and aids to such prayer are in evidence. Inter-Varsity Fellowship's David Bryant and "concerts of prayer" have become almost synonymous. The U.S. Center disseminates information on unreached peoples as an aid to prayer. The fourth edition of Patrick Johnstone's *Operation World: A day-to-day guide to praying for the world* with its wealth of information on the state of the church and its missions has recently come off the press.[19] A *Global Prayer*

Digest is published regularly by the U.S. Center for World Mission. Wesley L. Duewel's new book *Touch the World Through Prayer*[20] is enjoying a wide reading. In addition to these there are missionary prayer letters, prayer days, conferences on prayer, area prayer groups in schools and churches, and much more.

Power Encounter

As we have noted, in October of 1986, Pentecostal Holiness leader Vinson Synan addressed 7,600 Charismatics in the Louisiana Superdome in New Orleans and said, "We've been in the upper room with our spiritual gifts. But we are supposed to go to the streets with our tongues and healings and prophecies."[21] Synan was expressing a feeling that is widespread in the Pentecostal stream.

But, though the emphases are different, the emphasis on the power dimension of the Christian faith is by no means confined to Pentecostals. Between the initial publication of C. Peter Wagner's *Look Out! the Pentecostals Are Coming* and its republishing in 1986 under the title *Spiritual Power and Church Growth*[22] a course on signs and wonders under the tutelage of Wagner and John Wimber that attracted national attention was introduced at Fuller Seminary's School of World Mission. Timothy Warner's power encounter course at Trinity's School of World Mission and Evangelism has subsequently attracted similar attention and considerable student interest.

The approaches have been decidedly different. The course at Fuller has tended to put greater stress on the more spectacular signs and wonders as a means of evangelism and attracting people to Christ. Trinity's approach has been characterized by a greater concern for the excesses of the signs and wonders phenomenon and more attention to the nature of the encounter with evil in its various manifestations. It emphasizes the fact that our fundamental opposition comes from satanic forces and that Christians need to know both Satan's strategies and Christ's power in combating them.

In any event, schools, missions, and missionary personnel are now becoming increasingly aware that we are engaged in a power encounter as well as a truth encounter and that in many parts of the world the former may even take precedence over the latter. If there is a concern on the part of Pentecostals that demonstrations of the power of the Spirit in Christian ministry come out of the Upper Room, there is a similar concern on the part of other Evangelicals that demonstrations of Divine power in Christian ministry come out of the closet. Thus today's missions are returning to one of the most important aspects of the missions of a much earlier day!

Counteracting Anti-Mission Laws and Biases

No end of tactics for circumventing laws directed against the free propagation and exercise of religion have been devised by those concerned for Christian mission. Some of the more bizarre, such as throwing bottles containing gospel messages into the ocean and smuggling Bibles, have occasioned some debate. Others—such as relocating Christian radio stations, deploying missionaries as legitimate students, and providing literacy and similar programs and services—are more conventional.

The current interest in nonprofessional, tentmaking missionary service mentioned in the previous chapter stems from various causes, but one of the most significant reasons for doing so is that nonprofessionals can enter places where it is difficult if not impossible for the professional missionary to find access. Tetsunao Yamamori calls for an army of a hundred thousand Christians trained in nonmission specialties who will become "God's New Envoys," bearing witness in the most spiritually needy—and physically dangerous—areas of the world. They will serve independently and will be self-supporting. In most cases these "new envoys" will be silent about their missionary vocation.[23] For those who desire to inquire into these and similar opportunities, such organizations as Inter-Christo and Tentmakers Incorporated stand ready to help. But ingenuity and independent inquiry are also encouraged.

Finally, as also mentioned in the previous chapter, one of the incentives for reaching foreign nationals in this country and for providing support to national evangelists abroad is that by so doing otherwise closed countries can be penetrated with Christian witness.

Providing "Safety Nets" for Missionary Personnel

There can be no airtight guarantees for the safety of missionaries any more than for other expatriate—especially

Western—personnel. In fact, insofar as statistics are accurate, it appears that business people are most often the targets of terrorists and assassins.

In any case, most missions are increasingly taking precautionary measures on behalf of their missionaries. Although very few, if any, are prepared to pay ransom monies to free missionary hostages, most, if not all, missions now set aside sufficient cash reserves to bring their personnel home if need be (often at the insistence of host governments). Missions have available the services of the newly formed Contingency Preparation Consultants, which provides training, crisis management, and recovery services to missionary personnel and organizations.

The policies of the various missions may be different in any given situation (various missions such as the Assemblies of God, the Southern Baptist Mission, and the Christian & Missionary Alliance allowed missionaries to stay in Beirut until the United States State Department strongly advised them to leave), but almost all insist that the ultimate factor apart from government insistence is whether or not the presence of missionary personnel endangers the witness and lives of national Christians.

"VICTORY WILL BE SECURED"

All of the above responses to contemporary challenges to missions need to be evaluated carefully. When the battle is at its height is not the time to begin to consider strategy. Much more prayerful strategizing for various possible scenarios of the future is needed.

At the same time, the power of the forces arrayed against us serve as a reminder that in the final analysis the battle is too great for us to fight in our own wisdom and strength. Our hope is in the Lord. What did he prophesy for our age? War, tribulation, hatred, lawlessness, and even false prophets showing great signs and wonders (Matt. 24:24)! But, in spite of it all, he also said that the gospel of the kingdom will be preached in all the world as a witness to all nations (v. 14).

It is imperative that we not forget that history is "his story" and that God sovereignly works out his purpose, even turning man's rebelliousness and Satan's opposition to his own divine purposes. Thus, although missionaries to Ethiopia were forced to "orphan" a fledgling Wallamo church early on in World War II, they subsequently returned to find a virile, missionizing church numbering as many as 15,000 souls. Thus also, although missionaries were expelled from China in 1949–50, leaving a relatively small church of approximately three million people, and although the 1966–67 Great Proletarian Revolution represented "history's most systematic attempt ever, by a single nation, to eradicate and destroy Christianity and all religion,"[24] estimates of the number of Christians in China today go as high as 50 million and even higher! Unwittingly the Chinese government considerably weakened one of the most formidable obstacles to conversion to Christ—ancestor worship and its attendant practices!

Biblical mission does not see God as being primarily or immediately involved in human revolution in such a way as to allow mission to become revolutionary involvement. But biblical mission sees God as active "mediately, through the church as it engages in Great Commission missions."[25] This New Testament understanding is radical indeed, but not in the usual sense of the word. It places the preaching of the gospel, which is foolishness to the world, at the heart of the missionary task. It makes the dynamic of the Holy Spirit to be the essential ingredient for an invasion of enemy territory. It makes intercessory prayer to be, in the words of David Wells, "the ultimate rebellion against the status quo."[26] And, when the King of the universe ultimately brings judgment on the nations, it makes the treatment of Christ's harassed, humble servants the basis of that judgment because as the world treats his emissaries, so it treats the King himself (Matt. 25:31–46)!

Now we are prepared to return to the prophetic and faithful words of Donald G. Bloesch at the beginning of this chapter:

> Today the foundations of civilization are being shaken as never before. . . . The old order is crumbling as the powers of darkness prepare to make their final stand. The shadow of persecution is falling on the church, but as Christians we have the assurance that through persecution and martyrdom *victory will be secured* (emphasis mine).[27]

In Christian missions today we are faced as never before with the necessity of drawing on the power of our God—Father, Son, and Holy Spirit. Ultimately, we have no other choice!

Part Two:

The Prophetic Background—
A Study of the Olivet Discourse

11

"WHAT WILL BE THE SIGN?"— MISSIONS AND THE END OF THE AGE

It is amazing, really. Reference after reference to the future of the Christian world mission contains but the barest mention of Bible prophecy. And yet all that we really know for sure about the future is that which is taught by the prophetic Word.

"That is precisely the problem," someone replies. "There are so many diverse interpretations concerning end-time events (the term *eschatology* may be used) that the only sure thing is that if you make reference to it, someone will invariably disagree with you."

Granted. In spite of a growing emphasis on the kingdom of God, there are varied understandings as to the nature of that kingdom in both its present and, especially, its future form. Some Christians (millennialists or chiliasts) believe that the Old Testament promises to Israel will be fulfilled in a thousand-year reign of Christ on earth. Other Christians (*a*millennialists) do not believe that the relevant Bible prophecies refer to a physical earthly reign at all. Some millennialists (*post*millennialists) believe that Christ will come at the end of the thousand-year reign. Others (*pre*millennialists) believe that he will come before the thousand-year reign. And premillennialists disagree as to whether he will come before, midway through, or after the Great Tribulation that precedes the thousand-year reign!

These differing understandings do affect the way in which Christians view the mission of the church, as Michael Pocock and others have attempted to show.[1] Amillennialists tend to think of the kingdom as Christ's present rulership of the world through his church. Postmillennialists tend to believe that the mission of the church is to work for the establishment of Christ's kingdom in the present order as a prelude to his coming.

Some premillennialists believe that Christians are to concentrate on a saving mission by proclaiming the gospel and winning people to Christ in anticipation of his coming to establish his kingdom. Others would also emphasize the need to extend God's kingdom in its present form in order to demonstrate the nature of God's character and rulership and to keep doors open for evangelism. Most premillennialists believe that world evangelization will precede Christ's coming to set up his kingdom, but some believe it will be accomplished by the church, while others believe that it will be accomplished by 144,000 Jewish witnesses who will be saved during the Tribulation.

Obviously, biblical prophecies concerning end-time events are not easy to interpret. The general perspective taken here is that Bible prophecy does call for a future for the Jewish people and that Christ will come to establish an earthly kingdom before the final wrap-up of history. But readers are encouraged to do three things whether or not they have adopted this basic premillennial view of the future.

First, they should remember that almost all of the teachings of Scripture are subject to various interpretations. Far from being a deterrent to studying Scripture, that fact should furnish an incentive to study Scripture more intently and diligently. There are many nuances of the Scripture text that cannot be dealt with here. I recognize that. But if those who read this book will look for areas of agreement rather than for occasions for dissent, then even general agreement will make this study of trends and issues an experience of positive value.

Second, they should be assured that our Lord and the Bible writers did not intend to confuse us. Their intention was to enlighten us! Unfortunately, all of us are tempted to interpret the Bible in ways that conform to the presuppositions and preferences with which we come to the Bible. Insofar as possible, we should allow the Bible to speak for itself.

Third, they should inquire as to their motives in studying prophecies having to do with the future. It may be that a unique factor is operating. *Sometimes our purpose in inquiring about the future is different from God's purpose in revealing the future!* If so, God and we are operating on different wavelengths. Personally, I believe that that is exactly what happens in many cases. Often our primary motive in looking at the prophetic Word is to satisfy our curiosity rather than to discover God's concerns for us and our times. That is a mistake—something like looking for a longwave radio program on the shortwave band. It happened to the first-century disciples. Just two days before the Crucifixion they were with the Lord at the temple site. Caught up with the beauty of the temple that King Herod's financial largesse and political savvy had made possible, they were unexpectedly apprized by Jesus of its impending destruction (Matt. 24:1-2). The curiosity of four of them (Peter, James, John, and Andrew—according to Mark 13:3) erupted into the inevitable question: "Tell us, when will these things be, and what will be the sign of Your coming and of the end of the age?" (Matt. 24:3).

Jesus' answer was all the more significant because in two days he would be crucified. His answer, then, was part of his final teaching. It comes to us in three complementary forms (cf. Matt. 24, Mark 13, Luke 21). And it appears that it can be meaningfully dealt with in relation to three assertions: (1) Our age has a *course* that it must run; (2) our age has its *kairoi* to be realized; and (3) our age has a *climax* toward which it is moving.

Let us look at these separately.

THE COURSE OF THIS AGE

The disciples' question focused on the end of the age (singular). Both Jesus and his disciples used the singular ("time" and "age") when speaking of the culmination of the present age and the events attending Christ's *parousia* or second coming. Accordingly, when Jesus gave the Great

Commission, he promised to be with his sent ones until "the end of the age" (Matt. 28:20).

The entire period between his two comings, however, is in view in such expressions as "the last days" (Acts 2:16–17; and 2 Peter 3:3), "the end of the ages" (1 Cor. 10:11; Heb. 9:26), and "the last hour" (1 John 2:18). Our age in its entirety constitutes the eschatological age, which looks back to the First Advent and ahead to the Second.

Although the disciples' question, therefore, focused on the end of the age, Jesus' answer focused on the entire age between his advents. Why? Because they needed to know that numerous events—the appearance of false Christs, wars and talk of wars, famines, earthquakes, persecution, apostasy, false prophets working deceptive signs and wonders, lawlessness, coldness of even believing hearts—are to occur and recur throughout the age and right up until its end (Matt. 24:5–12). In fact, as the end approaches, such events will reach a fever pitch in a Tribulation so great that if it were not cut short, no flesh would survive (Matt. 24:21–22). This being the case, it was important that the disciples not interpret the presence of such events as necessarily indicating that the age was coming to an end (Matt. 24:4). Rather, they were to see them as characteristic of this eschatological age in its entirety. *It is almost as though such events are to be considered "normal" in this world of fallen people.*

Three lessons stand out at this point.

First, these events are not to unsettle or surprise believers. Nor are we to view them as indicating that the end of the age must come immediately. They are not "signs" in that sense. But Mark says that they *are* birth pangs (Mark 13:8). Painful though they certainly are, they will give rise to a new age inaugurated by Christ himself. We are reminded of Paul's words to the effect that all of creation suffers the pains of childbirth and we ourselves groan within ourselves as we await the "redemption of the body" (Rom. 8:22–23).

Second, one happening is unlike all the others. All are negative except one, which is wholly positive. Moreover, the end of the age is somehow linked to this one event: "And this gospel of the kingdom," said Jesus, "shall be preached in the whole world for a witness to all the nations, and then the end shall come" (Matt. 24:14). "Kingdom" in Scripture (*malkuth* in the Old Testament, and *basileia* in the New Testament) has as its primary meaning the authority, sovereignty, and rulership of a king. For this reason, and also because the parallel verse in Mark's Gospel (13:10) simply says "the gospel," it is likely that our Lord was making reference to a widespread preaching of his message.

This missionary task will be carried out against the backdrop of a world condition that is anything but utopian— that will, in fact, become progressively worse as we approach the end of the age. *Ironically, history may be hastening toward a time when the only really good news will be that to which the world's peoples seem to be inscrutably deaf and about which a significant part of the church is inexplicably dumb!*

Third, the painful disasters of our age and the progress of the gospel are inextricably linked together. Not only do they occur simultaneously, but the persecution that believers often experience constitute an opportunity for testimony. As the New English Bible has it, "This will be your opportunity to testify" (Luke 21:13).

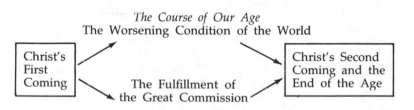

The Course of Our Age
The Worsening Condition of the World

Christ's First Coming

The Fulfillment of the Great Commission

Christ's Second Coming and the End of the Age

THE *KAIROI* OF OUR AGE

The Greek word *kairoi* is worth retaining here, not so much for the sake of alliteration as for the sake of clarity. It appears in the Lukan version of the Discourse (Luke 21:24). Were we to use the English word *times,* as many translations have it, we would not do the word justice because *kairoi* has reference, not to ongoing time, but to particular times of opportunity.

Jesus told his disciples that a siege of Jerusalem and the desolation of that city were impending (Luke 21:20–24). Vengeance, distress, and bloodshed were to be a part of the future. The Jewish people were to be led away captive into Gentile nations, and Jerusalem was to be trampled under feet by the Gentiles until the *"kairoi* of the Gentiles" is fulfilled.

Once again, we can better understand all of this in retrospect than the disciples could have understood it in prospect if for no other reason than the fact that this prophecy must have conveyed frightening implications to them as they heard it. And there is good reason why they would have been frightened. About forty years later, in A.D. 70, Titus and his Roman legionnaires entered Jerusalem after a devastating siege. Despite Titus' order to spare the temple, it was ransacked and set to the torch by his rapacious troops—an event that answers to the prophecy of an "abomination of the holy place" in Matthew 24:15 but does not exhaust that prophecy. Many Jews were taken captive to Rome, where they were forced to labor on the mammoth colosseum and other projects. In fact, a relief of the triumphal return of Titus leading his troops and their Jewish captives is still observable on the famous Arch of Titus erected in his honor.

(It is important to note that, as is true of many biblical prophecies, the prophecies of our Lord on Olivet had a more immediate fulfillment in the past and will have a more distant fulfillment in the future. Or, in another way of looking at it, the more immediate fulfillment itself was a precursor of another fulfillment in the more distant future.)

Jerusalem has indeed been trampled under the feet of Gentiles—the indignity perpetrated by the Romans in the first century subsequently having been aggravated by the Muslim invaders of the seventh century and a succession of others so that it changed hands some fourteen times in the intervening thirteen centuries. During this entire age and up until a few years ago, Jerusalem has been under Gentile rule, and the Jewish people have remained scattered among the nations in accordance with the prophecy of our Lord.

How then are we to understand the *"kairoi* of the Gentiles"? As we have seen, the phrase certainly has political implications. But in the light of such passages as Romans 11:11 ("by their transgression salvation is come to the Gentiles"), Romans 11:25 ("a partial hardening has happened to Israel until the fulness of the Gentiles has come in") and kindred passages, it is hard to conceive that the opportunity to hear and believe the gospel that is to be preached in all the world is not also in view. Of course, that opportunity is extended to Jew as well as to Gentile. But the point is that as far as salvation is concerned, the distinction has been erased. Gentile and Jew come into God's family on the basis of repentance and faith in Christ.

Once again we are brought to the missionary nature of the age in which we live. In this case, however, we see missions against the backdrop of Jewish persecution and dispersion and Gentile domination over Jerusalem. For almost two thousand years this homeless people and their conquered homeland have cast a dark shadow over the earth. But at the same time, the light of the glorious gospel of Christ has shined into even the dark corners of our world, and millions upon millions have come into the divine family. *This gathering will continue until the last believing soul that is to come into God's family has been reborn—until the "kairoi of the Gentiles" is fulfilled.*

Could it be that the recent regathering of Jews in a nation of their own and the establishment of Jewish rule in Jerusalem once again signals the end of this special opportunity for world-wide missionary outreach? The question is worth pondering! A former member of the WCC Committee on the Churches and the Jewish People, R. L. Lindsey, makes a charge of insensitivity against those of us who preach about the Jews as a "subject of God's future favour" and who see the regathering of Israel as a sign of God's working in the world. He thinks that we "almost invariably get more interested in the Jewish people as "signs of the time" and as "the proof that Jesus is coming soon," than we do in Jews as real, flesh-and-blood people."[2] To the extent that this is true, repentance is in order. But we wonder if Lindsey has taken into account the various Jewish missions such as the American Messianic Fellowship and Jews for Jesus, and the tens of thousands of Christians who support them—to say nothing of the many Evangelical premillennial scholars who bear witness to Christ while engaging in sensitive dialogue with Jewish rabbis. Seeing God's working among the Jewish people as prophetically significant and seeing them as persons for whom Christ died are not incompatible responses at all! They are complementary!

THE CLIMAX OF OUR AGE

Finally we come to that magnificent and crowning event, that eschatological denouement toward which all of history has been moving.

But immediately after the tribulation of those days THE SUN
WILL BE DARKENED, AND THE MOON WILL NOT GIVE ITS LIGHT, AND THE
STARS WILL FALL from the sky, and the powers of the heavens
will be shaken, and then the sign of the Son of Man will
appear in the sky, and then all the tribes of the earth will
mourn, and they will see the SON OF MAN COMING ON THE
CLOUDS OF THE SKY with power and great glory. And He will
send forth His angels with A GREAT TRUMPET and THEY WILL
GATHER TOGETHER His elect from the four winds, from one
end of the sky to the other (Matt. 24:29–31).

The Kairoi of Our Age

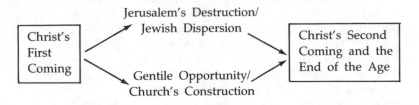

Only Matthew mentions that the disciples had asked the
question, "What will be the sign of Your coming, and of the
end of the age? (Matt. 24:3), and his account contains Jesus'
most direct answer: "And the sign of the Son of Man will
appear in the sky" (24:30). Luke puts it, "And there will be
signs in sun and moon and stars" (Luke 21:25). The other
predicted events are not specifically called "signs."

Exactly what are these celestial "signs"? Do they refer to
the visible aspects of the appearance of the Lord? Do they
refer to the changes in the heavenly bodies as predicted in
the Book of Revelation? Whether we may answer yes to one
or both of these questions, only the appearance of these
celestial events is specifically called a "sign," and neither
their appearance nor the litany of events considered previously would seem to function as the kind of "precursor" or
"indicator" of the end of the age, which the disciples sought
and which twentieth-century commentators so often talk
about.

If it is only these celestial events that function as "signs"
of his coming and the end of the age, what is the significance
of the false Christs, wars, earthquakes, and so on (Matt.

24:5ff.); the analogy of the fig tree (vv. 32–35); and the reference to the days of Noah (vv. 36–42)? It would seem that all of these prophecies and analogies were designed to motivate believers to be ready for the Second Coming or the parousia, but not by virtue of providing us with a Bible horoscope that enables us to set dates. The Lord distinctly said that "of that day and hour no one knows, not even the angels of heaven, nor the Son, but the Father alone" (v. 36). Rather, these predictions were designed to stimulate us to "be on the alert" precisely because we *do not know* on which day our Lord is coming (v. 42).

The difference is that between a "prophetic countdown" and a "prophetic alert." This distinction points up the contrast between Christ's concern and the disciples' (and often our) curiosity.

Let me explain. Believers are indeed to be alive to the significance of the happenings predicted for our age in the Olivet Discourse, and especially so as these predicted events begin to accumulate and accelerate. But in and of themselves these events do not so much constitute signs that enable us to start a "prophetic countdown" to the parousia as they constitute an "alert" that reminds us that God is in control, that his promises are sure, and that the parousia is impending. It is less like the launching of a satellite and more like an athletic contest in which only the umpire knows exactly when the final whistle will be blown. We witness, work, and worship always on the very brink of the climax of our age— the coming of Christ to inaugurate those great events that will eventuate in the kingdoms of this world giving way to the "kingdom of our Lord, and of His Christ" (Rev. 11:15)! If we put aside our curiosity as to the exact order and timing of these events and concentrate rather on Christ's purpose in predicting them, their importance becomes crystal clear. History is his story. He is not caught by surprise at the cataclysmic occurrences breaking around our heads. Nor should we be surprised. Rather, they serve to remind us that he is in control and that he is coming!

That we should forget for even one day that his coming draws ever nearer is unthinkable when one considers the signals of divine foreknowledge and faithfulness that are all around us. To forget why we are here—even for one day— is deplorable because it is patently clear that the confidence with which we face Christ, the quality of our own future existence, and the eternal condition of millions of others depend in large measure on our remembering that the parousia with all it entails will actually occur. And precisely that is the lesson that our Lord underscores in the parables and metaphors with which he concludes his discourse and to which we turn in the next chapter.

The Climax of Our Age

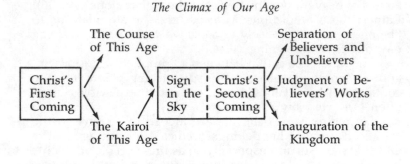

12

"WHAT SORT OF PEOPLE?"— WORLD CHRISTIANS AND THE END OF THE AGE

Motivated by curiosity, the disciples asked two questions that day on the Mount of Olives: "When will these things be?" and "What will be the sign of Your coming and the end of the age?" But the most pertinent question went unasked until Peter asked it years later when writing to believing Jews dispersed throughout the Mediterranean world. It is found in 2 Peter 3. Let's look at it briefly before returning to the Olivet Discourse.

Peter says that in this eschatological age ("the last days") many are going to call the promise of Christ's return into question and insist that history is nothing more or less than meaningless repetition (2 Peter 3:3–4). Nothing really changes. History is going nowhere. Peter counters this. He says that the world was once destroyed by water. In the end it will be destroyed by fire.

There is a sense in which modern science corroborates this. Not the judgment aspect per se, of course, but the idea that everything really is changing. In addition to older understandings of entropy (the world "running down"), scientists now tell us that the earth's magnetic field is being reduced and even the speed of light is slowing down. Nature is not the unchanging, stable entity it has often been assumed to be. We are heading for a "showdown," and this fact has significance not just for the distant future but also for the immediate future.

Still, from the perspective of the twentieth century as well as from that of the first, the end does seem to be a long time coming. God has good reason to send his Son and mete out his judgment without any delay whatsoever. Why does he put it off? Peter has the answer for that. *There is a consideration that takes precedence over the call for immediate judgment. It has to do with the claims of God's love. God is patient and desirous that none perish but that all come to repentance (2 Peter 3:9). The Great Commission must be fulfilled. The gospel must be preached among all the world's peoples.*

In the light of all of this, the apostle asks that all-important question that neither he nor his fellow disciples thought to ask on the mountain. It is this: "What sort of people ought you [we] to be in holy conduct and godliness, looking for and hastening the coming of the day of God?" (2 Peter 3:11–12). That, after all, is the paramount question. And the more one thinks about it, the more one is convinced that it was the question that Jesus answered most clearly in his Olivet Discourse even though the disciples failed to ask it! In fact, it seems that Jesus never did really satisfy their curiosity as to times and signs, because at Christ's ascension they were still inquiring as to when he would set up his kingdom: "Lord is it at this time You are restoring the kingdom to Israel?" (Acts 1:6). So Jesus answered very forthrightly, "It is not for you to know times or epochs . . . but you shall receive power when the Holy Spirit has come upon you; and you shall *be* My witnesses both in Jerusalem, and in all Judea and Samaria, and even to the remotest part of the earth" (vv. 7–8 [emphasis mine]).

The paramount question for all of us Christians living in this "age of the *eschaton*" is, "What sort of people ought we to *be*?" Students do not always know enough to ask the right questions, but wise teachers will find ways to answer the right questions whether they are asked or not. That is what Jesus did just before his ascension. And that is what he had done previously on Olivet. On that occasion he did it by giving a short series of analogies and parables that told the disciples—and tells us—what followers of Christ should be like and what they should be doing in this present age. In a word, we should be, not *worldly* Christians, but *world*

Christians who reflect our Lord's interest in the whole world and all of its peoples.

Let's look at those analogies, then, and attempt to ascertain their meaning and implications. We do so particularly with the mission of the church in view because that is our present concern and it was obviously the concern of our Lord, as the above paragraphs make abundantly clear.

THE SURPRISED HOUSEHOLDER (MATT. 24:43–44)

"But be sure of this," Jesus said, "that if the head of the house had known at what time of the night the thief was coming, he would have been on the alert and would not have allowed his house to be broken into." But the fact is that the householder did not know the exact time when the break-in would occur; he was not on the alert, and his goods were stolen.

The lesson? In his infinite wisdom God the Father knows when Christ's coming and the end of the age will occur, but no one else does. If believers knew the exact time, all but that tiny minority living just prior to his coming would lose out on one of the greatest incentives we have to holy living and biblical mission! As it is, no one knows, so all should be on the alert. To be caught unaware like the surprised householder is both lamentable and unnecessary. In missions, then, as in every other endeavor, we carry out world witness, knowing that he *will come* and he *may come soon*, but not knowing *when he will come*.

THE EVIL STEWARD (MATT. 24:45–51)

Now imagine a situation in which a steward (NASB reads "slave") is put in charge of the affairs of a large estate while the owner goes on an extended trip. If the steward is faithful, he will conduct affairs in such a way that all will be in readiness for the owner's return. The temporary appointment may even become a permanent one. But if the steward is the kind of person who says to himself, "The owner won't be returning for a considerable time; so this is my chance to 'live it up' and do what I want," and then proceeds to hang out with the wrong crowd and returns home to beat up on his underlings, what then? The answer is obvious. He will be punished.

The lesson? We would most likely answer that the lesson is that faithful Christians will be rewarded and unfaithful ones will be punished at Christ's coming. In a sense, that is a correct interpretation. But there is more. Notice that the focus of the parable is on the evil steward and the reason for his attitude and action. He wrongly assumed that the owner would not return for a long time and that he would have plenty of time to straighten out his affairs and relationships before the day of reckoning. That was where he got off on the wrong foot. On the basis of that erroneous presupposition he pleased himself rather than his employer.

We make a great mistake if we delude ourselves into thinking that Christ's coming and the end of the age is far enough in the future so that we will always have opportunity to get our priorities straightened out and to do his bidding at a later date. There may not be time. For many there *will not be time.* We should be alert and active in the work of our King. We do not have forever. We can and should discuss such subjects as "the next decade in missions." But as we do so we should remember that we may not have another decade. We may not have another day. The gospel will be preached in all the world to all its peoples. But only God the Father knows exactly what is involved in that. And only he will know when it has been accomplished to the satisfaction of his requirements.

THE WISE AND THE FOOLISH VIRGINS
(MATT. 25:1–13)

Ten virgins were invited to be part of a wedding party. Little imagination is required to conjecture as to the importance of the wedding feast to these maidens. But five of them never made it to the table. Why? Because they neglected to take extra oil for their lamps. Without lighted lamps they could not be a part of the procession. So when the bridegroom was detained, they found it necessary to go off to the store to buy more oil. Imagine their chagrin when sometime later they found themselves outside the banquet hall looking in.

The lesson? Once again the spotlight is on a miscalculation. The five foolish young ladies made a glaring mistake that their companions did not make. They became so preoccupied with getting their hairdos and gowns in order that they neglected to provide extra oil in case the wedding procession did not start "on time." They probably reasoned that the bridegroom would come by at such and such a time so there was no cause for alarm. But they were wrong.

If the culture Jesus referred to in this parable was like most traditional cultures, the timing of such events was not nearly so precise as in many Western cultures today. In the East, weddings and the like begin when the notables show up! The five virgins really were foolish to think that they could set a time by which the bridegroom had to appear. They made just the opposite mistake as the one made by the foolish steward. He assumed that his master would not be returning for a considerable time; these women assumed that in no time at all the bridegroom would appear. But for whatever reason, he did not come when they expected him. Their mistake was the opposite of the steward's but it had the same result.

Think about it. Those young attendants were really no more foolish than many Christians of the past and present who are so sure that Christ is coming at a certain time—or within a certain time period—that they neglect to prepare themselves adequately for whatever God may have in store for them. Think of all the dedicated young people who hurriedly get their support and equipment together and head for the mission field but do not take the time required to get the mental and spiritual equipment required for missionary service. They are sure that Jesus is coming soon and because so many people around the world are dying without him, they do not have time for solid preparation. And so they go half-prepared. And the months pass. And the years pass. Sooner or later they usually find that they have "run out of oil." Some return to school or enroll in various seminars and try to make up for past neglect. They return to "buy some oil." For many others it is simply too late. The opportunity to prepare themselves adequately for the challenges of missionary service has passed.

It is right to be looking for Christ's coming. *But it is wrong to make our decisions on the basis of our calculations as to the time of his coming.* As someone has said, we should act as though he were coming today, but we should plan as though he were not coming for a thousand years. There is a tension there. But, rightly understood, that is what Jesus was saying.

THE ENTRUSTED TALENTS (MATT. 25:14–30)

Next our Lord tells of a case where a man of means was about to go on a journey. He called his three servants (NASB: "slaves") and entrusted them with his finances in accordance with the ability and faithfulness they had demonstrated in the past. Accordingly, he gave five silver talents to the first servant, two to the second, and one to the third. Then he left. Immediately the first two servants put their talents to work. The third one, however, buried his in the ground for safekeeping.

After a long time the rich man returned and asked for an accounting. The two servants who had doubled their money by wise planning and hard work were commended and were promised even greater responsibilities. The third servant excused himself on the grounds that he knew his master to be a successful and exacting man. He therefore feared to take a risk. He was content to return the same talent that had been entrusted to him—unmarked and unused. But his carefully contrived confession was unavailing. He claimed to know his master, but he did not *really* know him. Otherwise at the very least he would have given the money to the bankers. For his ignorance and indolence he was reprimanded, divested of his lone talent, and severely judged.

The lesson? Let us not lose the fundamental lesson of this parable in a debate as to whether the talents represent abilities and skills, possessions and money, spiritual gifts, opportunities for service, or all of these. The fact is that those servants were entrusted with something valuable—something very valuable if we calculate the worth of silver talents at that time—and it was expected that they would use them to enhance the holdings of their master. Two did, and one did not. (For the first time in this series the "good guys" were in the majority!) They were dealt with accordingly. In fact, the servant who risked nothing and therefore gained nothing for his rich employer looked on remorsefully while his single talent was taken away and given to his most productive colleague. That may seem unfair to some. But we must understand that businessmen do not gain wealth by sitting on their money. Risk is always involved. The fearful servant proved that he understood neither the character of his employer nor the nature of his business.

We must remember that our Lord has a tremendous

investment in this business of missions. In the second Psalm it is said that the Gentile nations are "in an uproar," the peoples of the earth "devise a vain thing," and the rulers "take counsel against the Lord and against His Anointed." But God addresses his Son and says, "Ask of Me, and I will surely give the nations [or, Gentiles] as Thy inheritance, and the ends of the earth for Thy possession." The songwriter was correct: "Jesus shall reign where'er the sun does his successive journeys run." And his blood-bought saints will reign with him, each one having privileges and responsibilities in accordance with the way in which he or she put the entrusted talents to kingdom purposes. That is one side of the matter—the crown side of it.

There is another side as well—the cross side. Missions cost something. So let us prayerfully and wisely invest whatever he gives us in his mission on earth. In the light of the uncertainty of our times and from a human point of view, it is risky business. But to paraphrase missionary martyr Jim Elliot, "He is no fool who gives up what he cannot keep to gain what he cannot lose."

THE SHEEP AND THE GOATS (MATT. 25:31–46)

Finally, citizens of the Gentile nations to whom Christ has directed his witnesses are to be called into judgment at the end of the age. What happens is likened to the action of a keeper of animals who separates his sheep from the goats in order to deal with them appropriately. When Christ comes in his glory, he will gather the *ethnē* (as in the Great Commission, Gentiles but not excluding Jews), and as King, he will place the "sheep" on his right hand to become inheritors of the kingdom and the "goats" on his left to be relegated to a fiery judgment. When asked the basis on which this division is made, he responds that the former had received, fed, and clothed him and had visited him when he was in prison. The latter had refused or neglected to minister to him in his time of need. When asked exactly when he had been treated and mistreated in these ways, he responded that when his brothers (also called "little ones" or "humble ones") had been treated in these very different ways, it was as though they had done it to him.

The lesson? Some of us are convinced that few passages of Scripture have been subjected to more far-reaching misinterpretations than this one. Even many commentators who are crystal clear on the Reformation doctrine of justification by faith somehow succumb to an interpretation that implies a judgment on the basis of works when they come to this passage. It is easy to misconstrue these solemn words so as to make salvation dependent on deeds of mercy extended to the destitute and downtrodden of the world.

In fact, this passage has become a hallowed New Testament sanctuary for those who interpret mission horizontally—i.e., as consisting of social action designed to alleviate human suffering, ameliorate the social condition, and eradicate political injustice. Consider, for example, the following statement by T. Paul Verghese:

> The ultimate judgement . . . is not in terms of conscious acceptance of the Lordship of Christ and membership in the believing community. It is rather in terms of one's active compassion for the poor and needy (see the parable of the judgement of the nations in Mt. 25:31–46).[1]

Now all of these are commendable endeavors and particularly so in the light of the crying needs of our world and the biblical injunction to do good to all men and especially to those of the household of faith (Gal. 6:10). But the missiological question does not have to do with whether or not they constitute worthy endeavors. Of course they do. The missiological question has to do with whether or not they constitute the primary missionary task. And the exegetical question has to do with whether or not our Lord's words will sustain such an interpretation.

This passage parallels an earlier passage in Matthew where Jesus sent out his disciples to minister to the "lost sheep of the house of Israel" (Matt. 10:6). At that time Jesus had been engaged in teaching, preaching, and healing. Looking on the multitudes, he saw them as scattered, shepherdless sheep. Then, changing the metaphor, he said, "The harvest is plentiful, but the workers are few. Therefore beseech the Lord of the harvest to send out workers into His harvest" (Matt. 9:37–38). All of that constitutes the background of his commissioning the disciples to go to the people of Israel (not to Gentiles or Samaritans) and to minister by preaching the kingdom message, exorcising evil spirits, and healing the sick. He predicted difficulties along the way. He said that some would not receive them and would be dealt with accordingly. But he promised salvation to those who would confess him. And he concluded by saying, "He who receives you receives Me, and he who receives Me receives Him who sent Me. . . . And whoever in the name of a disciple gives to one of these little ones [or, "humble folk"—see margin] even a cup of cold water to drink, truly I say to you he shall not lose his reward" (Matt. 10:40 42).

This important incident in the mission of Christ's first coming should not be overlooked when interpreting the Matthew 25 passage, which has to do with his second coming. Once again, our Lord says that the way the people of the nations treat certain "brothers of Mine" (25:40) and "the least of them" (v. 45) is the way in which they treat him. Who are these representatives? George Peters says that the reference is to Christians.[2] Donald Grey Barnhouse says it refers to Jews.[3] Stanley Toussaint concludes that this is a way of designating "the godly remnant of Israel that will proclaim the gospel of the kingdom unto every nation of the world."[4] It does seem that the parallel with Matthew 10 is so obvious that the representatives spoken of here are those who will eventually fulfill the second, or Great, Commission. If one is not committed to an eschatology that necessarily insists that it will be the godly remnant of Israel who will fulfill the Great Commission and preach the gospel to the whole world during the Tribulation period, then it would seem that whoever is fulfilling that commission in the end time may well be in view.

By nature we as Christian workers will not welcome the prospect of hunger, thirst, nakedness, or imprisonment any more than those early disciples did, but it seems that increasingly as we approach the end of the age the Christian mission will often be carried out in the midst of dangerous and difficult circumstances. Although some of Christ's representatives will be well received, hunger, sickness, and even imprisonment will be the lot of others. In the light of the first part of the Olivet Discourse on the one hand and the plight of Christian workers in broad areas of the world today on the other, this should not surprise us even though the legacy of Western colonialism still shields us from seriously considering the prospect. The disciple, however, is not above his Master. The all-important thing is that the Commission be fulfilled and that Christ be as well represented at the end of the age as he was at its beginning. As inscrutable as it may seem, the treatment the world accords to Christ's true representatives it really accords to Christ. And it will be judged accordingly. Such is the station in life of those who are accorded ambassadorial rank, whether in the realm of politics or in the realm of Christ's kingdom.

It is debatable that any serious discussion of the Christian mission should proceed without a consideration of relevant passages of the prophetic Word. One of the most important of these passages, the Olivet Discourse, introduces a sobering realism to our thinking about world mission as it moves toward its inevitable finale. In most general terms, the dire events predicted by our Lord as characteristic of our age do indeed break around us and remind us of both his omniscience and his omnipotence. Simultaneously, however, the gospel is being preached to an ever-increasing number of the world's peoples. Already our generation is the first in all of history to see a truly universal religion in the sense that its representatives are to be found in almost every nation on earth. And that religion is Christianity. The church indeed is growing. But the unbelieving world grows still faster, and with it grows a totalitarian godlessness that sets itself against Christ and his mission.

"But take courage," our Lord reminds us; "I have overcome the world" (John 16:33).

A TESTIMONY

It is appropriate that I close this book with the testimony of Tal Brooke, one of the few Westerners to hold a privileged position in the very inner circle of one of India's leading gurus (Sai Baba). He speaks out of that kind of experience plus a thorough knowledge of classical Hinduism, Buddhism, and Taoism.

In powerful language and with compelling intimacy Tal Brooke tells of his taste of *nirvana* in the wilds of the Virginia countryside, of his enchantment with the magnetic personality and mighty wonders performed by Sai Baba, and of his bewilderment at the incongruous mixture of good and evil that lay at the door of the gateway to superconsciousness. Finally, he tells of the miracle that occurred when he looked once again to Jesus Christ and his Word:

I will never forget my thoughts at that time. I had discovered an absolutely Satanic thing operating behind Sai Baba's veneer. Now I was desperate. I crouched on a massive boulder on a hillside overlooking Baba's main ashram in Puttaparthi. My love affair with Vedanta was ending. I was dissolving inside, dying inside. I was a needle rolling on a thread. Soon after that, I would confront Baba publicly. In my perplexity, I was willing to look anywhere for an answer. There was one source of revelation I had avoided.

In my desperation, I laid a Bible on a hillside rock—a book I had long ago "transcended." Now in an act of faith, I threw open the pages. You could call it a kind of miracle at the time. What I read answered a need so deep I cannot explain it. . . .

Imagine what I felt when the Bible fell open to Matthew 24:23–24 (New International Version). It was Christ himself talking about a future age in our world. And suddenly a new perspective took shape for me:

"At that time if anyone says to you, 'Look, here is the Christ,' or 'There he is!' do not believe it. For false Christs and false prophets will appear and perform great signs and miracles to deceive even the elect—if that were possible. See I have told you ahead of time."

I looked down at Baba's green prayer hall below and thought,

That's it, that's what Sai Baba is, a miracle-working antichrist.[5]

APPENDIX 1
IDENTIFYING TRENDS AND ISSUES
IN CHRISTIAN MISSIONS TODAY

Since in the normal order of things issues grow out of trends, and not vice versa, it is important that we identify trends. But how can they best be identified? The usual way is to ask the experts. When *Christianity Today* decided to keep watch over current trends in the Christian church, the editors appointed various Christian scholars to the *Christianity Today* Institute and published their findings in a special issue of that magazine. The focus of this study was North America, however.[1]

When Howard Snyder decided to write a book on church trends, he sent questionnaires to fifty "knowledgeable people," who were asked to rank some thirty possible trends. A follow-up survey included a few additional people and was returned by thirty-eight respondents. The result was a helpful book emphasizing the fourteen highest ranking trends in the church world-wide, but with some "adjustments" due to the author's concerns.[2]

When William Knipe and Donald MacInnis proposed that the missions needed to be informed concerning trends in order to plan for future mission, one of their initial moves was to call together a panel of experts, each of whom contributed a paper on trends as he or she understood them. Between them, the twenty-two scholars enumerated a rather bewildering number of mission trends that are extremely difficult to categorize and collate, but when reduced to some twenty-six trends (by my count), the two or three highest ranking trends were mentioned by only nine or ten of the scholars.[3]

One of the primary factors triggering the current interest in trends has been the publication of John Naisbitt's *Megatrends*.[4] Interestingly, Naisbitt's method of identifying trends was quite different from that taken by many others. A fundamental axiom of Naisbitt's approach was that "trends are generated from the bottom up, fads from the top down."[5] Accordingly, he identified major trends on the basis of content analyses of more than two million locally written articles about local events in the cities and towns of America over a twelve-year period.

THE METHOD OF CONTENT ANALYSIS

The method of content analysis requires at least a brief explanation. Although some consideration had been given to this method of analysis earlier, the technique was elaborated in connection with the establishment of the Experimental Division for the Study of Wartime Communication at the Library of Congress during World War II in order to procure information on the situation in opposing nations. By analyzing the content of local newspapers in Germany and Japan, American intelligence learned about such things as factory openings and closings, military and civilian casualties, the availability of food and commodities, and so forth. Then, by comparing this information over broad areas and over a period of time, it was possible to piece together the larger picture, which, of course, the central governments of those nations would not divulge.

Since the war, communication theorists have fine-tuned the content-analysis approach to the point where it has become an important method of monitoring behavior, events, and opinions. Technically, it is called "quantitative semantics." (The more usual semantic method is qualitative—testing the flow of words in a single quotation for meaning and truth.) Content analysis or quantitative semantics analyzes the flow of words in a series of situations or contexts and measures them statistically. In simple terms, this is done by (1) establishing the categories, themes, or ideas to be studied; (2) determining the samples to be analyzed; (3) pretesting to check the coverage of the categories and the validity of the samples; (4) adjusting the study plan on the basis of pretests; (5) carrying through with the quantitative analysis; and (6) gathering and interpreting the results.

The method is especially helpful in identifying trends with a significant degree of objectivity and precision. I was introduced to it in the late 1950s by my mentor, Professor W. S. Howell of the University of Minnesota. He used it in heading up a team that made a comparative study of *Radio Moscow* and *Voice of America* broadcasts. Under his tutelage I used this method with good results in a doctoral study of the propagation methods of the rapidly growing Buddhist lay organization Soka Gakkai.[6] However, especially when used in connection with something as broad and variegated as the Christian mission, content analysis as carried out by Howell and Naisbitt becomes extremely costly in terms of manpower and money.

For that reason I have resorted to a modified form of content analysis in connection with this study. In an attempt to establish trends as objectively as possible within necessary limitations, I have done a *thematic* content analysis of two major mission periodicals and a series of book reviews. This was done by following the steps outlined above, *but only with respect to the major themes or emphases of the literature being analyzed.* This method does not necessarily tell us what is actually being thought and done by field missionaries. In a sense it monitors only the understandings of the experts who write books and articles relating to missions. But insofar as editors and writers tend to respond to missionary concerns and interests, it necessarily reflects field missionary thinking and activity, not theory alone. It does not yield information as to the positions taken on the various questions and issues raised in the literature, but it does inform us as to the subject matter of missiological thinking—topics, proposals, emphases, trends, predictions, and issues—as that thinking unfolds over a period of time. Therefore, when it comes to identifying trends and issues, it helps us to avoid such pitfalls as placing too much weight on the opinions of a limited number of experts, concentrating on the opinions and concerns that converge at one point in time, and giving preference to one's personal opinions.

THE OVERALL APPROACH TAKEN IN THIS STUDY

It would be well at this point to indicate the approach that has been taken in this book. This approach has three primary facets: interpreting prophecy, identifying trends, and examining issues. Let us look at these in some detail.

Each of the ten chapters in part 1 focuses on a major trend in missions today. Currently, the mission literature on trends is especially voluminous and variegated. As we would expect, all of it reflects the particular perspective of the authors. To a certain extent this is true even of the statistically oriented trend literature. I cannot claim immunity from personal biases, but, while acknowledging them, I have attempted to compensate by building on certain objective data.

First, a thematic content analysis of 949 major articles and editorials appearing in the *International Review of Mission (IRM)* over a period of twenty-two years (determined by the publication of the first issue of the *Evangelical Missions Quarterly (EMQ)* in 1964—see below). The *IRM* is published quarterly by the Commission on World Mission and Evangelism (CWME) of the World Council of Churches (WCC). As such, it is representative of the conciliar view of mission. (See Appendix 2.)

Second, a thematic content analysis of 604 major articles and editorials appearing in the *Evangelical Missions Quarterly* over the same twenty-two year period from 1965 to 1986 (1965 was the first year in which four issues appeared). The *EMQ* is a publication of the Evangelical Missions Information Service (EMIS). EMIS is sponsored jointly by the Interdenominational Foreign Mission Association (IFMA) and the Evangelical Foreign Missions Association (EFMA), which is the missionary arm of the National Association of Evangelicals (NAE). As such, the *EMQ* is undoubtedly as representative of the thinking of Evangelicals in mission as any publication available to us. (See Appendix 2.)

Third, a thematic content analysis of 444 book reviews appearing in *Missiology, an International Review* (hereafter referred to as *Missiology*) from 1973 (when the journal first appeared) through 1986 in order to ascertain the major directions taken by missiology as a discipline over the last fifteen years. *Missiology* is published quarterly by the American Society of Missiology (ASM), a professional association of professors of missions and closely related disciplines and including representatives of the major streams of the Christian church. (See Appendix 3.)

Fourth, data available in the standard reference works on missions and world Christianity: especially the *World Christian Encyclopedia*,[7] recent editions of *Mission Handbook: North American Protestant Missions Overseas* including the recently published thirteenth edition,[8] *UK Christian Handbook, 1985/86 Edition*,[9] and *Operation World*.[10]

Fifth, an analysis of a variety of publications focusing on trends and issues beginning with *Proceedings of the Inter-Church Consultation on Future Trends in Christian World Mission*.[11] *Foresight: 10 Major Trends that Will Dramatically Affect the Future of Christians and the Church*,[12] and the *Mission Trends* series,[13] but also including such works as *The Christian World Mission: Today and Tomorrow*,[14] *The Last Age of Missions*,[15] *The Third Force in Missions*,[16] *Crucial Issues in Missions Tomorrow*,[17] *The Crest of the Wave*,[18] *Issues in Missiology: An Introduction*,[19] *The Future of the Christian World Mission*,[20] *What Next in Mission?*[21] *Evangelical Missions Tomorrow*,[22] and others.

Next, each of the ten chapters in part 1 also highlights issues that grow out of contemporary trends. What are the major issues facing the Christian mission today? What will be the shape of the future for missions? How will our choices today affect that future? Are we on the right track? What are the pitfalls just ahead? What is the potential? These and similar questions should be considered in every church, in every school, and in every mission organization—by every missionary, by every candidate, by every mission professor, and by every mission leader. That is why a consideration of them constitutes such an important part of this book.

I entertain the hope that, as fraught with dangers as an analysis of so encompassing an enterprise as the world mission is, giving serious attention to the main lines of prophecy for this age, the directions taken by missions in recent times, and the major themes of the recent representative literature will help us focus on the basic issues confronting all true friends of missions today. Let us do so to the end that we may make the right choices today for missions tomorrow.

Finally, part 2 is concerned with the eschatological context that helps us understand the significance of contemporary trends and issues. Shortly before our Lord gave the commission to disciple the nations, he prophesied that all nations would receive a gospel witness. But he set that prophecy in the context of a certain picture of the course of this age and, in particular, its consummation. I refer, as you may recognize, to the Olivet Discourse. There are, of course, numerous other passages of Scripture that speak of this age and its consummation, but to attempt to deal with all of them would take us well beyond the limitations of this work. On the other hand, not to attempt to interpret and relate at least this much of the prophetic Word would be indefensible. The trends and issues we are about to consider assume their real significance when set in the context of prophecy.

APPENDIX 2

Note: The material on the following pages must be understood in the light of the discussion on my thematic-content-analysis approach as discussed in Appendix 1. Totals and percentages are comparable within the framework and objectives of this study only. They are not to be compared with data obtained by other types of quantitative analysis.

Thematic Content Analysis of 949 Articles Appearing in the *International Review of Mission* and 604 Articles Appearing in the *Evangelical Missions Quarterly* During the Period 1965 to 1986

THEMATIC FOCUS	NUMBER OF ARTICLES IN THE IRM						NUMBER OF ARTICLES IN THE EMQ					
	1966 to 1970	1971 to 1975	1976 to 1980	1981 to 1985	Total incl. 1964 & 1986	Percent of 949	1966 to 1970	1971 to 1975	1976 to 1980	1981 to 1985	Total incl. 1965 & 1986	Percent of 604
I. Geographic												
Africa	19	27	7	7	71	7.5%	3	5	4	5	21	3.5%
Asia (incl. Far East, South East, India)	20	19	13	32	94	9.9%	6	10	4	5	27	4.5%
Europe	10	15	16	7	50	5.2%	1	7	3	0	11	1.8%

Latin America (incl. Central and South America, and Carribean)	8	26	13	16	67	7.1%	9	9	2	2	25	4.1%
Middle East	4	0	0	0	5	.1%	0	1	0	2	3	.5%
North America (incl. minorities)	7	11	3	14	36	3.8%	0	0	0	0	0	
Oceania, Australia and New Zealand	6	1	7	2	19	2.0%	0	0	0	0	0	
TOTAL	74	99	59	78	342	35.6%	19	32	13	14	87	14.4
II. Religions												
Animism	1	3	0	0	6	.6%	0	1	0	1	2	.3%
Buddhism	1	1	1	1	4	.4%	3	0	0	0	3	.5%
Confucianism	0	0	0	0	0		0	0	0	0	0	
General	1	2	0	15	18	1.9%	0	0	0	1	1	.2%
Hinduism	0	1	0	3	4	.4%	0	0	0	2	2	.3%
Islam	8	5	11	6	33	3.4%	0	2	4	9	16	2.6%
Judaism	0	0	0	1	1	.1%	0	0	0	0	0	
New religions/cults	0	0	9	1	10	1.1%	0	0	0	2	2	.3%
Shintoism	0	0	0	0	0		0	0	0	0	0	
Syncretism	2	4	2	0	8	.8%	1	0	0	1	1	.2%
Taoism	0	0	0	0	0		0	0	0	0	0	
Whichcraft/occult	0	0	0	0	0		0	0	0	0	0	
TOTAL	13	16	23	27	84	8.7%	4	3	4	16	27	4.4

THEMATIC FOCUS	NUMBER OF ARTICLES IN THE IRM						NUMBER OF ARTICLES IN THE EMQ					
	1966 to 1970	1971 to 1975	1976 to 1980	1981 to 1985	Total incl. 1964 & 1986	Percent of 949	1966 to 1970	1971 to 1975	1976 to 1980	1981 to 1985	Total incl. 1964 & 1986	Percent of 604
III. Strategy												
Bible translation and distribution	0	1	0	3	4	.4%	3	0	0	0	3	.5%
Church planting and growth	10	2	0	2	17	1.9%	4	9	12	14	42	7.0%
Communication, contextualization	1	11	2	8	24	2.5%	4	7	12	11	37	6.1%
Development	10	7	1	6	25	2.7%	0	0	4	0	4	.7%
Dialogue	7	5	8	5	24	2.5%	2	1	0	0	3	.5%
Discipleship	1	1	0	0	2	.2%	0	0	3	1	4	.7%
Evangelism/witness	3	30	28	19	86	9.1%	4	10	14	14	42	7.0%
General strategy	3	0	1	2	6	.6%	8	7	12	12	40	6.6%
Justice, liberation	14	41	45	48	157	16.5%	1	4	0	0	6	1.0%
Media incl. literature	2	5	1	1	9	.9%	1	1	5	3	11	1.8%
Non-Theological education	0	0	0	0	0		0	1	2	0	3	.5%

Planning, research	0	0	0	0	0		0	2	0	0	2	.3%
Relief, incl. medical	10	4	0	2	18	1.9%	2	1	0	4	8	1.3%
Theological education	6	5	4	11	26	2.7%	4	13	3	4	26	4.3%
Urban/industrial mission	10	3	5	3	27	2.8%	2	0	0	5	7	1.2%
TOTAL	77	115	95	110	425	44.7%	35	56	57	68	238	39.5%
IV. Ecclesiastical Orientation												
Orthodox	1	4	3	10	21	2.2%	0	0	0	0	0	
Protestant, incl. 3 categories below	9	11	7	9	49	5.2%	16	10	8	7	43	7.1%
Conciliar, Ecumenicalm	(4)	(6)	(2)	(6)	(18)	(1.9%)	(3)	(4)	(2)	(0)	(9)	(1.4%)
Evangelical/Fundamental	(2)	(4)	(1)	(0)	(7)	(1.2%)	(9)	(5)	(6)	(7)	(29)	(4.8%)
Pentecostal/Charismatic	(1)	(1)	(2)	(0)	(17)	(1.8%)	(1)	(1)	(0)	(0)	(2)	(.3%)
Roman Catholic	13	2	5	1	22	2.3%	0	0	0	0	0	
Third World Christians and churches	6	8	14	21	51	5.4%	5	15	9	13	47	7.8%
Third World missions	0	0	0	0	0		0	1	1	2	5	.9%
TOTAL	29	25	29	41	143	15.1%	21	26	18	22	95	15.8%

THEMATIC FOCUS	NUMBER OF ARTICLES IN THE *IRM*						NUMBER OF ARTICLES IN THE *EMQ*					
	1966 to 1970	1971 to 1975	1976 to 1980	1981 to 1985	Total incl. 1964 & 1986	Percent of 949	1966 to 1970	1971 to 1975	1976 to 1980	1981 to 1985	Total incl. 1964 & 1986	Per-cent of 604
V. Theory and Theology of Mission												
Contribution the social sciences	3	5	0	5	14	1.5%	2	10	4	18	38	6.3%
History of missions	16	1	2	10	34	3.6%	2	0	4	2	8	1.3%
Introduction to missions and missiology	2	6	3	2	14	1.5%	0	1	1	2	4	.7%
Missionary and related biog.	5	5	0	4	17	1.8%	2	0	0	0	2	.3%
Missions bibliography, statistics	1	1	2	4	9	1.0%	0	1	1	4	7	1.2%
Theology *and* missions	17	22	24	20	90	9.5%	2	10	5	5	26	4.3%
Theology *of* missions	3	9	20	12	55	5.8%	8	3	3	5	19	3.0%
Women and mission	0	1	1	11	13	1.4%	0	0	4	2	10	1.8%
TOTAL	47	50	52	68	246	26.1%	16	25	22	38	114	18.9%

VI. Unity and Cooperation, incl. conferences

					%						%
Conferences and Consultations, incl. 3 categories below	5	21	23	31	84	8.9%	2	21	6	5	35	5.8%
International Regional	(2)	(5)	(1)	(1)	(10)	(1.1%)	(0)	(13)	(4)	(0)	(17)	(2.8%)
International Worldwide	(1)	(13)	(20)	(26)	(63)	(6.6%)	(0)	(3)	(0)	(0)	(3)	(.5%)
National (Within a country)	(2)	(3)	(2)	(4)	(11)	(1.2%)	(2)	(5)	(2)	(5)	(15)	(2.5%)
Support structures, missions agencies	8	0	0	4	12	1.3%	6	11	4	8	30	5.0%
Unity, ecumenicity, interdependence	12	19	17	25	79	8.3%	6	1	1	6	16	2.6%
TOTAL	25	40	40	60	175	18.5%	14	33	11	19	81	13.4%

VII. Governmental, political Relationships

					%						%
Closed, opened doors	0	0	0	0	0		0	2	0	0	2	.3%
Nationalism	3	0	0	0	3	.3%	1	1	0	0	2	.3%
Peace, non-violence	0	0	3	7	10	1.1%	0	0	0	0	0	
Relation between government and mission	0	2	2	0	4	.4%	0	0	2	1	3	.5%
Repression	1	1	3	5	10	1.1%	0	1	1	1	3	.5%
Requirements	0	0	0	0	0		1	0	0	0	2	.3%
Terrorism, revolution	3	0	0	0	3	.4%	0	1	2	0	6	2.6%
TOTAL	7	3	8	12	30	3.3%	2	5	5	2	18	4.5%

APPENDIX 3

Note: In addition to the caution expressed in the note in Appendix 2, it is important to remember that this analysis has to do with the book reviews appearing in *Missiology, an International Review*, and not with the books themselves. Only to the degree that the reviewers correctly and completely reflect the materials of the book(s) under review are the totals and percentages given here representative.

A Thematic Content Analysis of 444 Book Review Appearing in Missiology, An International Review *During the Period 1973–1986.*

Thematic Focus	Number of Books	Percentage of Total
GEOGRAPHY		
Africa	61	13.8%
Asia (incl. Far East, South East, India)	77	17.3%
Europe	6	1.4%
Latin American (incl. Central and South America, an Carribean)	36	8.1%
Middle East	4	.9%
North America (incl. minorities)	22	5.0%
Oceania, Australia, New Zealand	21	4.7%
TOTAL	227	51.2%
RELIGIONS		
Animism	10	2.3%
Buddhism	7	1.6%
Confucianism	2	.5%
General	14	3.2%
Hinduism	2	.5%
Islam	17	3.8%
Lesser religions	0	
New religions/cults	4 .9%	
Shintoism	1	.2%
Taoism	1	.2%
Witchcraft/occult	0	
TOTAL	58	13.2%

Thematic Focus	Number of Books	Percentage of Total
STRATEGY		
Bible translation and distribution	6	1.4%
Church planting/growth	21	4.7%
Communication, contextualization	19	4.3%
Development	0	
Dialogue	6	1.4%
Discipleship	0	
Evangelism/witness	6	1.4%
General strategy	3	
Justice, liberation	70	15.8%
Media (incl. literature)	3	
Non-theological education	0	
Planning, research	0	
Relief	6	1.4%
Theological education	4	1.0%
Urban/industrial mission	6	1.4%
TOTAL	150	32.8%
ECCLESIASTICAL ORIENTATION		
Orthodox	2	
Protestant	34	7.7%
Conciliar, Ecumenical	(21)	4.7%
Evangelical	(8)	1.8%
Fundamentalist	(0)	
Pentecostal/Charismatic	(5)	1.1%
Roman Catholic	17	3.8%
Third World Churches and Christians	28	6.3%
Third World Missions	3	.7%
TOTAL	84	18.9%
THEORY AND THEOLOGY OF MISSION		
Contribution of the social sciences	79	17.8%
History of mission	47	10.6%
Introduction to missions and missiology	18	4.1%
Missionary biography	26	5.9%
Missions bibliography, statistics	17	3.8%
Theology *and* mission	60	13.5%
Theology *of* mission	29	6.5%
Women in mission	7	1.6%
TOTAL	283	63.8%

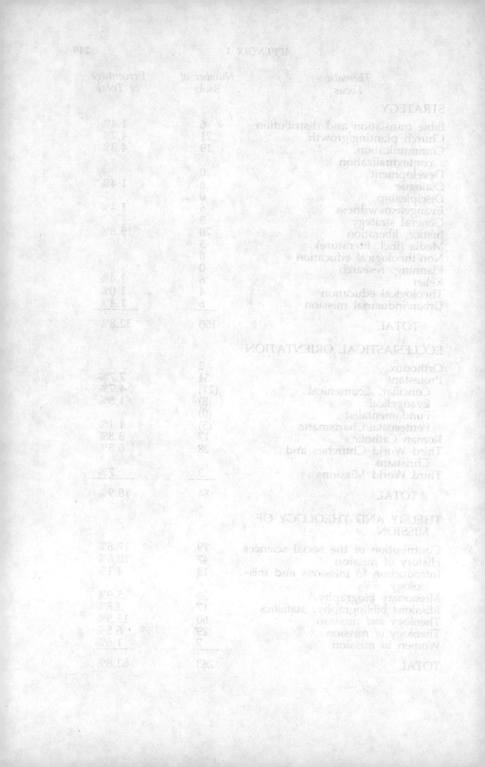

NOTES

PREFACE

[1] H. P. Van Dusen, *They Found the Church There* (London: SCM, 1945), 94.
[2] Jean-François Revel, *How Democracies Perish* (New York: Doubleday, 1984).
[3] John Naisbitt, *Megatrends: Ten New Directions Transforming Our Lives* (New York: Warner, 1984), xxi.
[4] Harold L. Bussell, *Unholy Devotion: Why Cults Lure Christians* (Grand Rapids: Zondervan, 1983).
[5] Kenneth S. Kantzer, "Orwell's Fatal Error," *Christianity Today* (January 13, 1984), 10–12.
[6] Stephen Charles Neill, *Creative Tension: The Duff Lectures, 1958* (London: Edinburgh House, 1959).
[7] Gerald H. Anderson and Thomas F. Stransky, eds., *Mission Trends, No. 3: Third World Theologies* (New York: Paulist, 1976).
[8] Ralph D. Winter, *The Twenty-Five Unbelievable Years, 1945–1969.* (South Pasadena: William Carey, 1970).
[9] John Naisbitt, *Megatrends. Ten New Directions Transforming Our Lives* (New York: Warner, 1984), xviii.

CHAPTER 1

[1] John Naisbitt, *Megatrends: Ten New Directions Transforming Our Lives* (New York: Warner, 1984), xxiii.
[2] "Praised, Decried and Joined, Associations Are Multiplying," *Insight* (May 26, 1986), 46.
[3] Johannes Aagaard, "Mission After Uppsala 1968" in Gerald H. Anderson and Thomas F. Stransky, eds. *Mission Trends No. 1: Crucial Issues in Mission Today* (New York: Paulist, and Grand Rapids: Eerdmans, 1974), 17.
[4] David B. Barrett, "Annual Global Statistical Table on Mission," *International Bulletin of Missionary Research* 11:1 (1987): 25.
[5] Samuel Wilson and John Siewert, eds., *Mission Handbook: North American Protestant Ministries Overseas*, 13th ed. (Monrovia, Calif.: MARC, 1986), 593–94.
[6] Patrick Johnstone, *Operation World: A Day-To-Day Guide to Praying for the World*, 4th ed. (Bromiley, Kent, England: STL, 1986), 34.
[7] Wilson and Siewert, *Mission Handbook*, 593.
[8] Ibid., 617.
[9] Ibid.
[10] Ibid., 578.
[11] Ibid., 564.
[12] Ibid.
[13] Ibid.
[14] Ibid., 573.
[15] Ibid., 565–66.
[16] Jose Marins, "Basic Ecclesial Communities in Latin America," *International Review of Missions* 68:271 (July 1979): 235.

[17] Ralph D. Winter, "The True Structure of God's Redemptive Mission," in Ralph D. Winter and Steven C. Hawthorne, eds., *Perspectives on the World Christ Movement: A Reader* (Pasadena: William Carey, 1981), 178–90.

[18] C. Peter Wagner, *On the Crest of the Wave: Becoming a World Christian* (Ventura, Calif., Gospel Light, Regal, 1983), 74–75.

[19] Wilson and Siewert, *Mission Handbook*, 563.

[20] Michael C. Griffith, *You and God's Work Overseas* (Chicago: InterVarsity, 1967), 20–21.

CHAPTER 2

[1] The foregoing is based on David B. Barrett, *Evangelize! A Historical Survey of the Concept: Global Evangelization Movement.* The A.D. 2000 series (Birmingham, Ala.: New Hope, 1987), 25–27, and on a personal discussion with Ralph D. Winter.

[2] Harold Lindsell, ed., *The Church's Worldwide Mission* (Waco: Word, 1966), 237.

[3] C. Peter Wagner and Edward R. Dayton, eds., *Unreached Peoples '81* (Elgin, Ill.: David C. Cook, 1981), 23.

[4] Ibid., 19.

[5] David B. Barrett, ed., *World Christian Encyclopedia: A Comparative Study of Churches and Religions in the Modern World AD 1900–2000* (Oxford: Oxford University Press, 1982).

[6] Ralph D. Winter, "What Is World Evangelization and Is It Possible to Achieve?" *Mission Frontiers* 9:7 (July 1987): 5.

[7] Samuel Wilson and John Siewert, eds., *Mission Handbook: North American Protestant Ministries Overseas*, 13th ed. (Monrovia, Calif.: MARC, 1986), 617.

[8] Samuel Wilson and John Siewert, eds. *Mission Handbook: North American Protestant Ministries Overseas*, 13th ed. (Monrovia, Calif.: MARC), 617.

[9] *Lausanne Communique* (August 1986), 2.

[10] Wesley L. Duewel, *Touch the World Through Prayer* (Grand Rapids: Francis Asbury, Zondervan, 1986).

[11] Lawrence E. Keyes, *The Last Age of Missions: A Study of Third World Missionary Societies* (Pasadena, Calif.: William Carey, 1983).

[12] Ralph D. Winter, "The Long Look: Eras of Mission History, in Ralph D. Winter and Stephen C. Hawthorne, eds., *Perspectives on the World Christian Mission: A Reader* (Pasadena: William Carey, 1981), 167–77.

[13] David B. Barrett, "Annual Statistical Table on Global Mission: 1987," *International Bulletin of Missionary Research* 11:1 (1987): 24–25.

[14] Ibid.

[15] Percentages of increase are based on Barrett, "Annual Statistical Table," 24–25. *The Church Around the World* (April 1986) indicates that over the past fifty years Islam has grown almost eleven times as fast as Christianity on a per capita basis and that both Hinduism and Buddhism have grown at a lesser rate than Islam but faster than Christianity. These figures have been challenged, however.

[16] Barrett, "Annual Statistical Table," 24–25.

[17] *Mission Frontiers* 8 (November–December 1986): 11.

[18] *Missionary New Service* 34 (January 2, 1987).

[19] John Naisbitt, *Re-inventing the Corporation: Transforming Your Job and Your Company for the New Information Society* (New York: Warner, 1985).

CHAPTER 3

[1] Samuel Wilson and John Siewert, eds., *Mission Handbook: North America Protestant Ministries Overseas*, 13th ed. (Monrovia, Calif.: MARC, 1986), 616.

[2] Efiong S. Utuk, "From Wheaton to Lausanne: The Road to Modification of Contemporary Evangelical Mission Theology," *Missiology: An International Review* 14 (April 1986): 205–20.

[3] Johannes Aagaard, "Trends in Missiological Thinking During the Sixties," *International Review of Mission* 62:283 (January 1973): 12.

[4] Johannes Christian Hoekendijk, *The Church Inside Out*, ed. L. A. Hoedemaker and Peter Tijmes, trans. Isaac C. Rotenberg (Philadelphia: Westminster, 1966).

[5] George Johnston, "Should the Church Still Talk About Salvation?" *International Review of Mission* 61:278 (January 1972): 59.

[6] Masao Takenaka, "Salvation: A Japanese Discussion," in *International Review of Mission* 61:278 (January 1972): 85.

[7] Gustavo Gutierrez, *A Theology of Liberation: History, Politics, and Salvation*, ed. and trans. Sister Caridad Inda and John Eagleson (Maryknoll, N.Y.: Orbis, 1973).

[8] C. Peter Wagner, *On the Crest of the Wave: Becoming a World Christian* (Ventura, Calif.: Gospel Light, Regal Books, 1983), 150.

[9] Howard R. Snyder with Daniel V. Runyon, *Foresight: 10 Major Trends That Will Drastically Affect the Future of Christians and the Church* (Nashville: Nelson, 1986).

[10] Waldron Scott, *Serving Our Generation: Evangelical Strategies for the Eighties* (Colorado Springs: World Evangelical Fellowship, 1980).

[11] Harvie M. Conn, *Evangelism: Doing Justice and Preaching Grace* (Grand Rapids: Zondervan, Academie, 1982).

[12] Miriam Adeney, *God's Foreign Policy* (Grand Rapids: Eerdmans, 1984).

[13] *USA Today* (May 9, 1986), 9A.

[14] David B. Barrett, *World Class Cities and World Evangelization* (Birmingham, Ala.: New Hope, 1986).

[15] *Insight* (June 12, 1986), 32.

[16] Alvin Toffler, *Future Shock* (New York: Random, 1970).

[17] John Naisbitt, *Megatrends: Ten New Directions Transforming Our Lives* (New York: Warner, 1984).

[18] John Naisbitt, *Re-inventing the Corporation: Transforming Your Job and Your Company for the New Information Society* (New York: Warner, 1985).

[19] Utuk, "From Wheaton to Lausanne": 205–20.

[20] John R. W. Stott, *Christian Mission in the Modern World: What the Church Should Be Doing Now* (Downers Grove: InterVarsity, 1975); idem, "The Significance of Lausanne," *International Review of Mission* 64:299 (July 1975): 291.

[21] Snyder with Runyon, *Foresight*, 68–69.

[22] Ibid., 178.

[23] Paul A. Pomerville, *The Third Force in Missions: A Pentecostal Contribution to Contemporary Mission Theology* (Peabody, Mass.: Hendrickson, 1985).

[24] Bruce Buursma, "Congressman's Plea to Church Is One from the Heartland," *Chicago Tribune* (June 17, 1986): sec. 1, p. 9.

[25] Snyder with Runyon, *Foresight*, 112–21.

[26] Edward R. Dayton, ed., *Mission Handbook: North American Protestant Ministries Overseas*, 10th ed. (Monrovia, Calif.: MARC, 1973), 48–65.

[27] Cf. Dayton, ed., *Mission Handbook*, 11th ed. (Monrovia, Calif.: MARC, 1976), 22; Wilson and Siewert, eds., *Mission Handbook*, 13th ed., 616.

[28] Naisbitt, *Re-inventing the Corporation*, 37.

[29] Wilson and Siewert, eds., *Mission Handbook*, 13th ed., 562.

[30] Naisbitt, *Re-inventing the Corporation*, 37.

[31] J. I. Packer, *Evangelism and the Sovereignty of God* (Downers Grove: InterVarsity, 1961), 41.

[32] Snyder with Runyon, *Foresight*, 116–17.

[33] John R. W. Stott, *Christian Mission in the Modern World*, 30.

[34] Gene Antonio, *The AIDS Coverup? The Real and Alarming Facts About AIDS* (San Francisco: Ignatius, 1987), 241.

CHAPTER 4

[1] David B. Barrett, ed., *World Christian Encyclopedia: A Comparative Study of Churches and Religions in the Modern World AD 1900–2000* (Oxford: Oxford University Press, 1982), 17.

[2] Visser't Hooft, ed., *The New Delhi Report* (New York: Association, 1962), 152.

[3] W. J. Hollenweger, "After Twenty Years' Research on Pentecostalism," *International Review of Mission* 75:297 (January 1986): 12.

[4] Efiong S. Utuk, "From Wheaton to Lausanne: The Road to Modification of Contemporary Evangelical Mission Theology," *Missiology: An International Review* 14:2 (April 1986): 218.

[5] Hollenweger, "After Twenty Years' Research," 8–9.

[6] Patrick J. Buchanan quoted in "Missionaries with a Leftist Mission," *Insight* (May 19, 1986), 54–56.

[7] David M. Howard, *The Dream That Would Not Die: The Birth and Growth of the World Evangelical Fellowship 1846–1986* (Exeter: Paternoster, 1986).

[8] Howard R. Snyder with Daniel V. Runyon, *Foresight: 10 Major Trends That Will Drastically Affect the Future of Christians and the Church* (Nashville: Nelson, 1986), 68–69.

[9] John Coventry Smith, *From Colonialism to World Community: The Church's Pilgrimage* (Philadelphia: Geneva, 1983).

[10] R. Pierce Beaver, "Mission Past and Present: A Brief Historical Survey and a Delineation of Some Current Issues," in Joel Underwood, ed., *In Search of Mission: An Inter-confessional and Inter-cultural Quest. A Special Issue Prepared by the Idoc Future of the Missionary Enterprise Project*," Dossier No. 9 (New York: Idoc/North America, 1974), 8.

[11] Samuel Wilson and John Siewert, eds., *Mission Handbook: North American Protestant Ministries Overseas*, 13th ed. (Monrovia, Calif.: MARC, 1986), 564.

[12] Beaver, "Mission Past and Present," 9.

[13] *Missionary News Service* (June 15, 1986).

[14] Kenneth Kantzer, "Do You Believe in Hell?" *Christianity Today* (February 21, 1986), 12.

[15] Klass Runia, "The Unity of the Church According to the New Testament," *Reformed Theological Review* 22 (October 1983): 83–84.

CHAPTER 5

[1] Henry P. Van Dusen, "The Third Force in Christendom," *Life*, June 9, 1958, p. 113, as quoted in Paul A. Pomerville, *The Third Force in Missions: A*

Pentecostal Contribution to Contemporary Mission Theology (Peabody, Mass.: Hendrickson, 1985), 20.

2 David B. Barrett, ed., *World Christian Encyclopedia: A Comparative Study of Churches and Religions in the Modern World AD 1900–2000* (Oxford: Oxford University Press, 1982), 838.

3 Ibid.

4 Ibid., 69.

5 John N. Vaughn, *The World's Twenty Largest Churches* (Grand Rapids: Baker, 1984).

6 This number is larger than the total reported by the 13th edition of *Mission Handbook: North American Protestant Ministries Overseas* but it is the figure reported to me in separate conversations with four or five leaders of the organization.

7 In addition to Van Dusen's article mentioned previously, see Lesslie Newbigin, *The Household of God* (New York: Friendship, 1954).

8 Vinson Synan, *The Holiness-Pentecostal Movement in the United States* (Grand Rapids: Eerdmans, 1971), 223.

9 W. J. Hollenweger, *The Pentecostals: The Charismatic Movement in the Churches*, trans. R. A. Wilson, rev. by author, 1st U.S. ed. (Minneapolis: Augsburg, 1972).

10 C. Peter Wagner, *Look Out! The Pentecostals Are Coming* (Carol Stream: Creation, 1973).

11 Gary B. McGee, *This Gospel Shall Be Preached: A History and Theology of Assembly of God Foreign Missions to 1959* (Springfield, Mo.: Gospel, 1986); L. Grant McLung, Jr., ed., *Azusa Street and Beyond: Pentecostal Missions and Church Growth in the Twentieth Century* (South Plainfield, N.J.: Bridge, 1986); C. Peter Wagner, *Spiritual Power and Church Growth: Lessons From the Amazing Growth of Pentecostal Churches in Latin America* (Altamonte Springs, Fla.: Strang Communications, 1986).

12 Martin E. Marty, "Pentecostalism in the Context of American Piety and Practice," in *Aspects of Pentecostal-Charismatic Origins*, ed. Vinson Synan (Plainfield: Logos International, 1975), 196, quoted in Pomerville, *Third Force in Missions*.

13 Roland Allen, *The Spontaneous Expansion of the Church; and the Causes Which Hinder It* (Grand Rapids: Eerdmans, 1962).

14 Harry R. Boer, *Pentecost and Missions* (Grand Rapids: Eerdmans, 1961).

15 Walter J. Hollenweger, "After Twenty Years' Research on Pentecostalism" *International Review of Missions* 75:297 (January 1986): 5.

16 William W. Menzies, *Anointed to Serve: The Story of the Assemblies of God* (Springfield, Mo.: Gospel, 1971), 86, quoted in Pomerville, *Third Force in Missions*, 56.

17 Ibid., 389, quoted in Pomerville, *Third Force in Missions*, 56.

18 "Signs and Wonders in New Orleans," *Christianity Today* (November 21, 1986), 26–27.

19 Pomerville, *Third Force in Missions*.

20 Ibid., 154–56.

21 Ibid., 156.

22 Ibid.

23 Melvin L. Hodges, "Creating Climate for Church Growth" in Donald A. McGavran, ed., *Church Growth and the Christian Mission* (New York: Harper & Row, 1965), 27–39.

24 B. G. M. Sundkler, *Bantu Prophets in South Africa* (London: Oxford University Press, 1961), 259–63.

25 G. C. Oosthuizen, *Post-Christianity in Africa: A Theological and Anthropological Study* (Grand Rapids: Eerdmans, 1968), 60–61.

26 Pomerville, *Third Force in Missions*, 30.

27 Philip M. Steyne, "The African Zionist Movement," 19–38, in David J. Hesselgrave, ed., *Dynamic Religious Movements: Case Studies of Rapidly Growing Religious Movements Around the World* (Grand Rapids: Baker, 1978), 21.

28 Ibid., 20.

29 Howard R. Snyder with Daniel V. Runyon, *Foresight: 10 Major Trends That Will Drastically Affect the Future of Christians and the Church* (Nashville: Nelson, 1986), 179.

30 Vinson Synan, *In the Latter Days: The Outpouring of the Holy Spirit in the Twentieth Century* (Ann Arbor: Servant, 1984), 7, quoted in Snyder with Runyon, *Foresight*, 33.

CHAPTER 6

1 J. Verkuyl, *Contemporary Missiology: An Introduction*, trans. and ed. Dale Cooper (Grand Rapids: Eerdmans, 1978), 6.

2 Ibid., 12.

3 Ibid., 9.

4 James Scherer, "The Future of Missiology as an Academic Discipline in Seminary Education," *Missiology: An International Review* 13:4 (October 1985): 446.

5 Verkuyl, *Contemporary Missiology*, 5.

6 *Missiology: An International Review* 14 (October 1986): inside back cover.

7 David B. Barrett, ed., *World Christian Encyclopedia: A Comparative Study of Churches and Religions in the Modern World AD 1900–2000* (Oxford: Oxford University Press, 1982), 834.

8 W. Holsten, "Gustav Warneck," in Stephen Neill, Gerald H. Anderson, and John Goodwin, eds., *Concise Dictionary of the Christian World Mission* (Nashville: Abingdon, 1971), 643.

9 Scherer, "Future of Missiology," 449.

10 Ibid., 452.

11 David B. Barrett, "Five Statistical Eras of Global Mission," *Missiology: An International Review* 12:1 (January 1984): 33.

12 David B. Barrett, "Annual Statistical Table on Global Mission: 1987," *International Bulletin of Missionary Research* 11:1 (January 1987): 25.

13 Cf. David J. Hesselgrave, *Communicating Christ Cross-Culturally* (Grand Rapids: Zondervan, 1978), 25–27.

14 Ed Rommen, David Hesselgrave, and John McIntosh, "American Missiology—Which Way?" *Trinity World Forum* 12 (Winter 1987): 1–3. (The sources identified in footnotes 15 through 20 are the sources noted in this article.)

15 D. Zoekler, "Mission und Wissenschaft," *Allgemeine Missionszeitschrift* 4 (1877): 4n.

16 G. Warneck, "Ein neues ethnologisches Unternehmen. Eine Bitte an die Missionare unter unseren Lesern," *Allgemeine Missionszeitschrift* 5 (1878): 477–81.

[17]H. W. Genseichen, "Christentum, Mission und Kultur. Ein Kapital aus Gustav Warneck's Missionsdenken nach 100 Jahren," *Evangelische Mission 1984* (Hamburg, 1984): 57–73.

[18]Verkuyl, *Contemporary Missiology,* 28.

[19]J. Richter, "Mission und Propaganda," *Neue Allgemeine Missionszeitschrift* 5 (1928): 257–60.

[20]McIntosh draws the conclusion from personal experience and the following references: Fridolin Ukur, *Tantang-Jawab Suku Dayak* (Challenge and Response of the Dayaks) (Jakarta: BPK Gunung Mulia, 1971); and Lothar Schreiner, *Adat und Evangelium* (Gutersloh: Gerd Mohn, 1972), 34–52.

[21]Rommen, Hesselgrave, and McIntosh, "American Missiology—Which Way?" 1–3.

[22]Harvie M. Conn, *Eternal Word and Changing Worlds: Theology, Anthropology, and Mission in Trialogue* (Grand Rapids: Zondervan, Academie, 1984).

[23]Charles H. Kraft, *Christianity in Culture: A Study in Dynamic Biblical Theologizing in Cross-Cultural Perspective* (Maryknoll, N.Y.: Orbis, 1979), 131–46, 392–94.

[24]Barrett, "Five Statistical Eras," 33.

CHAPTER 7

[1]Charles H. Kraft, *Christianity in Culture: A Study in Dynamic Biblical Theologizing in Cross-Cultural Perspective* (Maryknoll, N.Y.: Orbis, 1979), 287.

[2]Edward F. Hills, *The King James Version Defended* (Des Moines: Christian Research, 1956), 142–43.

[3]"The Second Declaration: Toward an Evangelical Theology for the Third World," in Bong Rin Ro and Ruth Eshenauer, eds., *The Bible and Theology in Asian Contexts* (Taichung, Taiwan: Asia Theological Association, 1984), 23.

[4]David J. Hesselgrave, "Contextualization and Revelational Epistemology," 691–738 in Earl D. Radmacher and Robert D. Preuss, eds., *Hermeneutics, Inerrancy, and the Bible* (Grand Rapids: Zondervan, Academie, 1984), 691–738.

[5]Shoki Coe, "Contextualizing Theology," in G. H. Anderson and T. F. Stransky, eds., *Mission Trends No. 3: Third World Theologies* (Grand Rapids: Eerdmans, and New York: Paulist, 1976), 21–22.

[6]Noted in Donald K. Swearer, *Dialogue: The Key to Understanding Other Religions* (Philadelphia: Westminster, 1977), 28.

[7]Ibid., 29.

[8]Stanley J. Samartha, "Dialogue Between Men of Living Faiths: The Ajaltoun Memorandum," in Stanley J. Samartha, ed., *Dialogue Between Men of Living Faiths* (Geneva: World Council of Churches, 1971), 114.

[9]John Hick, "The Outcome: Dialogue into Truth," In John Hick, ed., *Truth and Dialogue in World Religions: Conflicting Truth-Claims* (Philadelphia: Westminster, 1974), 155.

[10]John Hick and Hasan Askari, eds., *The Experience of Religious Diversity* (Brookfield, Vt.: Gower, 1985).

[11]Wilfred Cantwell Smith, *Towards a World Theology* (Philadelphia: Westminster, 1981).

[12]Bruce Nicholls, "Theological Education and Evangelization" in J. D. Douglas, ed. *Let the Earth Hear His Voice* (Minneapolis: World Wide Publications, 1975), 647.

[13] Willard Gordon Oxtoby, *The Meaning of Other Faiths*, 1st ed. (Philadelphia: Westminster, 1983), 101–2.

[14] From *Gospel in Context* 2:3 (July 1979).

CHAPTER 8

[1] Samuel Wilson and John Siewert, eds., *Mission Handbook: North American Protestant Ministries Overseas*, 13th ed. (Monrovia, Calif.: MARC, 1986), 613.

[2] David B. Barrett, "Statistical Table on Global Mission: 1987," *International Bulletin of Missionary Research* 11:1 (January 1987): 25.

[3] Wilson and Siewert, eds., *Mission Handbook*, 13th ed., 611–12.

[4] Ibid., 612.

[5] Ibid., 613.

[6] Ibid., 564.

[7] Phil Parshall, "How Spiritual Are Missionaries?" *Evangelical Missions Quarterly* 23 (January 1987): 10–16.

[8] K. P. Yohannan, *The Coming Revolution in World Missions* (Wheaton: Creation, 1986).

[9] K. P. Yohannan, "America Can't Win the World for Christ," *Christianity Today* (November 7, 1986), 15.

[10] Yohannan, *The Coming Revolution in World Missions*, 97.

[11] Institute of International Education news release (809 United Nations Plaza, NY 10017, October 21, 1986).

[12] J. Christy Wilson, Jr., *Today's Tentmakers: Self Support: An Alternative Model for Worldwide Witness* (Wheaton: Tyndale, 1979).

[13] Ibid., 609–10.

[14] J. Herbert Kane, *Wanted: World Christians* (Grand Rapids: Baker, 1986), 171.

[15] Howard J. Dayton, Jr., *Leadership Magazine* 2 (Spring 1981): 62.

CHAPTER 9

[1] John Naisbitt, *Megatrends: Ten New Directions Transforming Our Lives* (New York: Warner, 1984), 54.

[2] George D. Moffett III, "Study Says U.S. Capacity for International Leadership Has Fallen," *The Christian Science Monitor* (February 10, 1987), 7.

[3] Howard R. Snyder with Daniel V. Runyon, *Foresight: 10 Major Trends That Will Drastically Affect the Future of Christians and the Church* (Nashville: Nelson, 1986), 172–78.

[4] Patrick Johnstone, *Operation World: A Day-To-Day Guide to Praying for the World*, 4th ed. (Bromiley, Kent, England: STL, 1986), 32.

[5] See Vergil Gerber, ed., *Missions in Creative Tension: The Green Lake '71 Compendium* (Pasadena, Calif.: William Carey, 1971).

[6] W. Harold Fuller, *Mission-Church Dynamics: How to Change Bicultural Tensions into Dynamic Missionary Outreach* (Pasadena, Calif.: William Carey, 1980).

[7] Johnstone, *Operation World*, 33.

[8] Donald G. Bloesch, *Crumbling Foundations: Death and Rebirth in an Age of Upheaval* (Grand Rapids: Zondervan, Academie, 1984), 83–85.

[9] Johnstone, *Operation World*, 35.

[10] Ibid.

11 Lawrence E. Keyes, *The Last Age of Missions: A Study of Third World Mission Societies* (Pasadena: William Carey, 1983), 75–87.

12 "The Third World Reaches to the Ends of the Earth," *Christianity Today* (December 13, 1985): 63–64.

13 Larry D. Pate, "Asian Missions: Growth, Problems and Partnership," *Bridging Peoples* 5 (October 1986).

14 Ibid.

15 Marvin Mayers, "Training Missionaries for the 21st Century," *Evangelical Missions Quarterly* 22:3 (July 1986): 306–12.

16 Jorge Lara-Braud, "The Role of North Americans in the Future of the Missionary Enterprise," *International Bulletin of Missionary Research* 7:1 (January 1983): 2–3.

17 John N. Jonsson, "The Role of North Americans in the Future of the Missionary Enterprise: Reflections and a Response," *Review and Expositor* 81 (Spring 1984): 257.

CHAPTER 10

1 Donald G. Bloesch, *Crumbling Foundations: Death and Rebirth in an Age of Upheaval* (Grand Rapids: Zondervan, Academie, 1984), 122.

2 David B. Barrett, ed., *World Christian Encyclopedia: A Comparative Study of Churches and Religions in the Modern World AD 1900 2000* (Oxford: Oxford University Press, 1982), 5.

3 Richard Nyrop, ed., *Israel: A Country Study* (Washington, D.C.: America University Press, 1979), 105.

4 Zola Levitt, *The Underground Church in Jerusalem* (Nashville: Nelson, 1978), 17.

5 Robert Hill, "Proselytism Case Decided by Appeals Court in Greece," *Missionary News Service* 33 (June 15, 1986), 1.

6 "Cults, Evangelicals and the Ethics of Social Influence," *Cultic Studies Journal* 2:2 Special Issue (Fall/Winter 1985). This entire issue is given to various articles pertinent to the subject.

7 J. Herbert Kane, *Winds of Change in the Christian Mission* (Chicago: Moody, 1973), 159–60.

8 Ibid., 159.

9 Barrett, *World Christian Encyclopedia*, 17.

10 Ibid.

11 *Missionary News Service* 33 (February 1986).

12 *Missionary News Service* 33 (November 1, 1986).

13 The opinion of Chester L. Quarles, vice-president of Contingency Preparation Consultants as reported in "Terrorism: A Growing Problem for Missionaries," *Christianity Today* (November 21, 1986), 36.

14 Timothy Warner, "Power Encounter in Evangelism," *Trinity World Forum* 10 (Winter 1985): 1.

15 David B. Barrett, "Statistical Table on Global Mission: 1987," *International Bulletin of Missionary Research* 11:1 (January 1987): 25.

16 "The Land Where Spirits Thrive," *Christianity Today* (December 13, 1985): 48.

17 *Church Around the World*, April 1968.

18 Radhakrishnan, *The Hindu View of Life* (New York: Macmillan, 1927), 92.

19 Patrick Johnstone, *Operation World: A Day-to-Day Guide to Praying for the World*, 4th ed. (Bromiley, Kent, England: STL, 1986).

[20]"Signs and Wonders in New Orleans," *Christianity Today* (November 21, 1986): 27.

[21]Wesley L. Duewel, *Touch the World Through Prayer* (Grand Rapids: Zondervan, Francis Asbury, 1986).

[22]C. Peter Wagner, *Spiritual Power and Church Growth* (Altamonte Springs, Fla.: Strang Communications, 1986).

[23]Tsetsunao Yamamori, *God's New Envoys: A Bold Strategy for Penetrating "Closed Countries"* (Portland: Multnomah, 1987).

[24]Barrett, *World Christian Encyclopedia*, 5; Paul A. Pomerville, *The Third Force in Missions: A Pentecostal Contribution to Contemporary Mission Theology* (Peabody, Mass.: Hendrickson, 1985), 148.

[25]Pomerville, *Third Force in Missions*, p. 129.

[26]David E. Wells, "Prayer: Rebelling Against the Status Quo," in Ralph D. Winter and Steven C. Hawthorne, eds., *Perspectives on the World Christian Movement: A Reader* (Pasadena: William Carey, 1984), 123–26.

[25]Donald G. Bloesch, *Crumbling Foundations: Death and Rebirth in an Age of Upheaval* (Grand Rapids: Zondervan, Academie, 1984), 122.

CHAPTER 11

[1]Michael Pocock, "The Destiny of the World and the Work of Missions," *Intercultural Journal of Frontier Missions* 1:2 (1984): 216–34.

[2]R. L. Lindsey, "Salvation and the Jews," *International Review of Missions* 61:241 (January 1972): 24.

CHAPTER 12

[1]T. Paul Verghese, "Salvation: The Meanings of a Biblical Word," *International Review of Mission* 57:228 (October 1968): 416.

[2]George N. H. Peters, *The Theocratic Kingdom of Our Lord Jesus, the Christ, as Covenanted in the Old Testament, and Presented in the New Testament*, 3 vols. (New York: Funk and Wagnalls, 1884; reprint ed. Grand Rapids: Kregel, 1972), 2:376; noted in Stanley D. Toussaint, *Behold the King: A Study of Matthew* (Portland, Ore.: Multnomah, 1980), 291.

[3]Donald Grey Barnhouse, *Romans. Vol. I: Man's Ruin. God's Wrath* (Grand Rapids: Eerdmans, 1952), 2:38–39, noted in Toussaint, *Behold the King*, 291.

[4]Toussaint, *Behold the King*, 29.

[5]Tal Brook, *Riders of the Cosmic Circuit* (Batavia, Ill.: Lion, 1986), 171–72.

APPENDIX 1

[1]Christianity Today Institute, *Into the Next Century: Trends Facing the Church* (Carol Stream, Ill.: Christianity Today, 1986).

[2]Howard R. Snyder with Daniel V. Runyon, *Foresight: 10 Major Trends That Will Drastically Affect the Future of Christians and the Church* (Nashville: Nelson, 1986).

[3]"Proceedings of the Inter-Church Consultation on Future Trends in Christian World Mission" (Maryknoll, N.Y., February 15–17, 1985, Mimeographed.

[4]John Naisbitt, *Megatrends: Ten New Directions Transforming Our Lives* (New York: Warner, 1984).

[5]Ibid., xxiv.

⁶David J. Hesselgrave, "A Propagation Profile of the Soka Gakkai" (Ph.D. dissertation, University of Minnesota, 1965).

⁷David B. Barrett, ed., *World Christian Encyclopedia: A Comparative Study of Churches and Religions in the Modern World AD 1900–2000* (Oxford: Oxford University Press, 1982).

⁸Samuel Wilson and John Siewert, eds., *Mission Handbook: North America Protestant Ministries Overseas,* 13th ed. (Monrovia, Calif.: MARC, 1986).

⁹Peter Brierley, ed., *U.K. Christian Handbook 1985/86 Edition* (London: MARC Europe, 1984).

¹⁰Patrick Johnstone, *Operation World: A Day-to-Day Guide to Praying for the World,* 4th ed. (Bromiley, Kent: STL, 1986).

¹¹Proceedings of the Inter-Church Consultation on Future Trends."

¹²Snyder with Runyon, *Foresight.*

¹³Gerald H. Anderson and Thomas F. Stransky, eds., *Mission Trends, No. 1: Crucial Issues in Mission Today* (New York: Paulist, and Grand Rapids: Eerdmans, 1973); idem, *Mission Trends, No. 2: Evangelization* (New York: Paulist, and Grand Rapids: Eerdmans, 1975); idem, *Mission Trends, No. 3: Third World Theologies* (New York: Paulist, and Grand Rapids: Eerdmans, 1976); idem, *Mission Trends, No. 4: Liberation Theologies in North America and Europe* (New York: Paulist, and Grand Rapids: Eerdmans, 1979); and idem, *Mission Trends No. 5: Faith Meets Faith* (New York: Paulist, and Grand Rapids: Eerdmans, 1981).

¹⁴William J. Danker and Wi Jo Kang, eds., *The Future of the Christian World Mission: Studies in Honor of R. Pierce Beaver* (Grand Rapids: Eerdmans, 1971).

¹⁵Lawrence E. Keyes, *The Last Age of Mission: A Study of Third World Missionary Societies* (Pasadena, Calif.: William Carey, 1983).

¹⁶Paul A. Pomerville, *The Third Force in Missions: A Pentecostal Contribution to Contemporary Mission Theology* (Peabody, Mass.: Hendrickson, 1985).

¹⁷Donald A. McGavran, ed., *Crucial Issues in Missions Tomorrow,* Moody Church Growth Series (Chicago: Moody, 1972).

¹⁸C. Peter Wagner, *On the Crest of the Wave: Becoming a World Christian* (Ventura, Calif.: Gospel Light, Regal, 1983).

¹⁹Edward C. Pentecost, *Issues in Missiology* (Grand Rapids: Baker, 1982).

²⁰Danker and Kang, *The Future of the Christian World Mission.*

²¹Paul A. Hopkins, *What Next in Mission?* (Philadelphia: Westminster, 1977).

²²Wade T. Coggins and E. L. Frizen, Jr., eds., *Evangelical Missions Tomorrow* (Pasadena, Calif.: William Carey, 1977).

INDEX OF PERSONS

INDEX OF SUBJECTS

INDEX OF SCRIPTURE REFERENCES

272

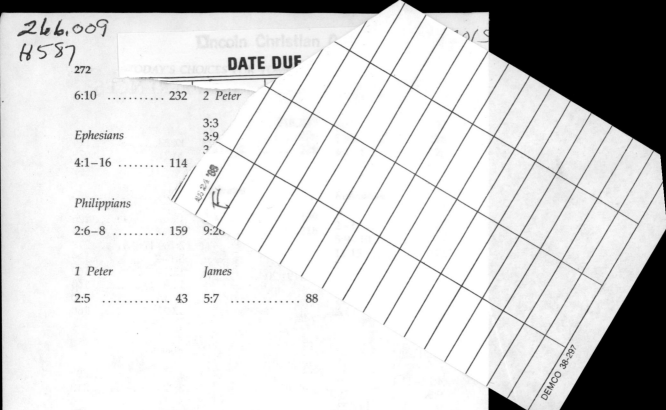